FOCUS ON DESTINY

12 KEYWORDS TO HELP YOU DISCOVER, DESIGN, DEVELOP AND DEPLOY YOUR GOD-GIVEN DESTINY ON EARTH

CLYDE S. SHARADY

A Note from the Publisher

The publisher wishes to acknowledge and thank Dr Douglas H. Johnson for his invaluable help and support for Africa World Books and its mission of preserving and promoting African cultural and literary traditions and history. Dr Johnson and fellow historians have been instrumental in ensuring that African people remain connected to their past and their identity. Africa World Books is proud to carry on this mission.

© Clyde S. Sharady, 2020

ISBN: 978-0-6489291-7-8

All rights reserved. No part of this publication may be reproduced, stored in a retrieval system, or transmitted, in any form, or by any means, electronic, mechanical, photocopying, recording or otherwise, without the prior permission of the publishers.
This book is sold subject to the conditions that it shall not, by way of trade or otherwise, be lent, re-sold, hired out or otherwise circulated without the publisher's prior consent in any form of binding or cover other than in which it is published and without a similar condition including the condition being imposed on the subsequent purchaser.
Design and typesetting: Africa World Books

Dedication

This book is dedicated with love and affection
to my beloved wife Regine Dienda Mbuyi,
and her gentle and caring spirit.
Thank you for supporting me and my Christian journey

and to my sons Joshua and Dennis
Whose very presence in my life
inspires me to focus on leaving a Christ-focus legacy
on this planet before rejoining eternity

and to all the ministers of God I have worked with over the years
Ps Peter Bondole, Ps Decal Nono, Ps Jean-Louis Wedi, Ps Willy Ntumba, Ps Geblock Nzuzi
your work has inspired me in more ways than one

and to my Creator, the Source of my life, the provider of all true visions and the sustainer of all dreams, The Almighty God and His only begotten son Jesus Christ.

"Your faith creates your fate"

Clyde Sharady

Divine is your Source

Devine is your source, divine is your destiny
Delight in Yahweh your Lord, He designed you for a purpose
Dig deep into your holy desires and you will discover a divine deposit
Design your life and create your future by developing and delivering your gifts to humanity.
Decide to dedicate your life for your God-given mission on earth
Dump the world and do not let yourself be diverted by its distractions
Deploy everything Heaven has entrusted you with to transform the world
Display excellence in everything you do and deliver it wrapped in love
Do the things that you must do, plan and do them with passion and commitment
Discipline your mind and live as a soldier of Christ, serving humanity in His name
Direct all your plans to God and doubt no more, you were destined for greatness
Discharge your divine destiny on earth and leave this world fully unloaded.
Die empty, do not take anything back to your grave.

"Destiny Living is the process through which you discover, design, develop and deliver your God-ordained destiny to your generation"

"People of the world are interested in success, people of God are interested in purpose and Destiny"

THE 12 KEY WORDS

Divine
Design
Desire
Discover
Decide
Do
Dominate
Discipline
Drive
Destination
Determination
Deployment

Introduction

THE BIBLE SAYS THAT "IN THE BEGINNING GOD CREATED THE heavens and the earth" (Genesis 1:1). This simple sentence is loaded with abundant divine wisdom. It has many secrets. "In the beginning" is about "time", "the heavens" is about "space" and "the earth" is about matter, physical matter. Together, these words, which form the very first sentence of the Bible, contain a powerful secret for the Christian faith. That secret is a formula to help all believers and disciples of Christ to accomplish their God-given destiny on earth. The formula is: T+S=M (Time + Space = Matter). This means that in the beginning God had a plan that He wanted to materialize in the physical world. He started by creating time (in the beginning) and then space (heavens) and lastly, He created matter (earth). Together these three things form what we call "reality". There is no 'reality" without time, space and matter. The practical meaning of this spiritual formula in the life of every Christian is a simple truth: if you create "time" and "space" in your life for God, then He will make your life "matter" and give you what "matters" to you, as a product of His hands. An even deeper meaning of this first verse of the Bible is that your God-given destiny on earth depends on how much "Time" and "Space" you dedicate to God in your life. If you create time and space for God in your life, He fills it with everything that matters for His destiny to manifest in your life.

8
Focus on Destiny

Through this book we are submitting that accomplishing our God-given destiny is what matters the most for all Christians, besides eternal salvation. Christianity is more than simply believing in Jesus, it is about living like Jesus, both in faith and in deeds. Believing is just the beginning, it is really part of an elementary process to build a relationship with God. We know from the Bible that Jesus came on earth for a mission and He dedicated His life for it. He accomplished it and then returned to eternity. In the same way, all Christians need to live like Jesus and live with a permanent focus on the accomplishment of their destiny here on earth. Anything else is accessory. Accomplishing your destiny means making your life matter, giving it substance in line with God's will and purpose for you. You can only do this if you give God the time and space He deserves in your life. You can tell whether you are focused on your destiny or not by asking yourself how much time you give to God and everything else that connects to His will for your life.

Giving time to God or being busy with "the things of God" is not just about attending church or taking care of other church-related activities. It is more about the amount of time and the level of focus you invest concerning the will of God in your life. It can be measured by looking how the will of God occupies your thoughts, feelings, aspirations and dreams and how these things are translated into your own life plans and daily actions, your behaviours and interactions with other human beings. Where are you with God today, as you read this book? Apart from believing in God, what are you planning or doing to impact your generation in the name of God? Do you actually know what your God-given destiny is? If so, where are you in your plans to accomplish it? If you are unclear about your destiny, what are you doing to find out about what God has pre-destined you for and how you can make it happen?

Introduction

The Gospel, the Church and You

The purpose of the Gospel is not just to reconnect humanity to God, but to reconnect every believer to his or her God-ordained destiny. These two things are the essence of Christianity. The first one is what is generally referred to as the "reconciliation" aspect of the gospel and the second one is what we propose to call in this book the "assignment" aspect of the gospel. The reconciliation aspect of the Gospel focuses on reconnecting us to God as our source, our Father and the creator of life and all things that exist. All human beings are born disconnected from God, not just because of the original sin, but simply by virtue of being rooted in physicality, as physical beings. God is primarily spiritual not physical. Through the message and the power of the gospel our reconnection to our Father is enabled, facilitated and strengthened. Once the reconnection or the reconciliation is achieved then the focus must dwell on God's purpose, God's plans and assignment for our lives. Jesus says:

> *"I am the vine and you are the branches. If you remain in me and I in you, you will bear much fruit; a part from me you can do nothing. If you do not remain in me, you are like a branch that is thrown away and withers; such branches are picked up, thrown into the fire and burned".*
>
> John 15:5-6

Through this passage we are reminded that the purpose of a vine tree's branch is not to be connected to the vine (tree), but to bear fruits. The connection to the tree is only necessary to enable fructification, which is the ultimate purpose or destiny of the vine tree. Additionally, we also see in Mark 11: 12-25 where

Focus on Destiny

Jesus curses a fruitless fig tree, because it had no fruits. When you put together these two passages, you get a picture that God doesn't give us life just for the sake of giving it. He gives us life because He has something He wants us to achieve with it, He has fruits that He wants to deliver to humanity. He is the tree and we are the branches. He can only produce fruits through us. If we fail to deliver that which He gave us life for, we fail to be useful to Him. If we fail our destiny mission, we become useless and just like Jesus cursed a fig tree because of its fruitlessness, He may deny us in heaven, even if we cry Lord! Lord! and do great things in His name. (Mathew 7:21).

It is important for all Christians to understand and focus on the "assignment" aspect of faith. Faith is useless unless it leads into action. Christianity is drifting into a religion rather than remaining a movement of transformation that it is meant to be. This is happening because believers focus more on "faith and grace" and neglect the other side of the gospel coin: "action and mission". Today, many preachers and teachers tend to talk more about the goodness of God, the love of Jesus, the mystery of the cross, the power and gifts of the spirit and many other things that make us feel good and special. However, in this book, we are inviting Christians to focus on the assignment role of the Gospel, and we are providing tools and keys to facilitate the production of "spiritual fruits" that our Lord Jesus expects us to deliver. We hope to be able to shed sufficient light on what Christians need to do to discover, design, create and successfully deploy their divine destiny on earth.

In a world that is increasingly schizophrenic and confused, today's Christian leadership has a lot of responsibility to ensure that believers are appropriately led, taught, equipped, trained, mentored and coached to be able to discharge their God-given destiny on earth. Christianity should not just be about waiting for eternal salvation that we hope to receive in the spiritual realm. A life that is truly transformed by the gospel of Jesus Christ must focus on impacting the world and expanding the kingdom of God on earth. The gospel of spiritual salvation and eternal life is important, but it is incomplete if not linked to the assignment and mission requirements of the Good News. This is why the focus of every Christian congregation should not be on filling pews with lots of excited people who want to shout "Jesus is Lord" every few seconds, but the focus must be on bringing people to Jesus and turning believers into disciples of Christ and agents for a divine transformation of the world. This requires serious work to equip believers appropriately and encourage them to focus on discharging their destiny, using whatever gifts that God invested in them. Jesus wants to see more people who are truly connected to Him and who are fully immersed in discharging their destiny on earth, rather than the crowds of excited believers who sing and shout every Sunday at church, but have no clue about what their destiny is.

The road to your destiny: where are you now?

God is our creator and we are His products. He manufactured us for His divine purpose. As such, God has a purpose for the life of every human being, and He has established our destiny in the "supernatural" realm. However, here on earth God cannot "remote control" us to accomplish the destiny He set for us. He can only help us with His divine guidance and through the Holy Spirit steer us towards the right direction and lead us to our destiny. He gave us freedom of choice and He expects us to make the right choices that connect with His will. What is clear in the Bible is that God has packaged, wired and programmed us in ways that we can accomplish our destiny with His help and directions, if we choose to listen to Him. If we do, we get life in abundance, and if we don't, we get condemnation and death. Everything in life is a matter of choice. But, as a loving Father, God whispers in our ears and says: *'choose life"*. (Deuteronomy 30: 19:20).

God has equipped us all with the necessary tools to discover, create, develop and accomplish our destiny on earth. He seats in the heavenly realm and has given us dominion over the physical world. He also gave us a free will to enable us to participate in His grand scheme of things. In the supernatural world where God operates, He is outside of time and space, and He has finished everything. But in the physical realm where we live and operate, every one of us must act, move and take steps to attract both the supernatural and the natural elements that we need to produce and materialise our destiny.

As conscious beings with our own will and the capacity for independent thoughts, God has given us human beings the choice to do His will and transform the natural world under His inspiration and guidance. Jesus is the perfect example of what God the father wants from every human being. The son came to the world to do the will of the Father. *"Here am I. Send me!"*, He said in Isaiah 6:8. He came down to earth for a mission. He was aware of His mission and from an early age He employed Himself assiduously to achieve it by obeying the Father. He consolidated and deployed all His resources (supernatural, intellectual, emotional and physical energy) to get the work done. He started to get busy with His destiny as a young boy by teaching scholars in the synagogues and He carried His mission all the way to the cross and under the earth.

Introduction

Most of us ask ourselves a lot of questions about our destiny in our quiet moments. Many such questions come from an understanding that God created us with a purpose and destiny, as it is written in many parts of the Bible. We know that God wants us to focus on our destiny, but not many of us actually fully understand what this entails.

Once I was preaching at my local church and I asked my audience if they could tell me what their destiny was. The answers I received were mostly general responses that could apply to all humans and almost no one was able to give me a clear answer about their very own destiny and God-given purpose on earth.

We all know that such questions are not easy to answer, because they are very profound. But it is the job of our church leaders to help believers grow spiritually and invest sufficient time diving deeply into a soul-searching investigation to find out clear answers about their destiny, with the help of the Holy Spirit. The nature of the world today requires our spiritual leaders to spend more time to teach, coach and mentor their congregants for purposeful living and destiny deployment.

Most Christian congregations have three types of people who fill their pews: believers who have no idea about their God-given destiny (1), believers who have some idea about their destiny, but are not actively engaged in discharging it (2) and believers who have developed into disciples of Christ and who are not just clear about their destiny, but they are busy with their mission to deliver it on earth (3). The majority of Christians are either part of the first group or the second one. Some church leaders such as the late Dr Myles Munroe, Pastor Rick Warren who wrote the book *Purpose Driven Life*, Bishop T. D Jakes and many other internationally renowned preachers have made a lot of contribution over recent years to teach people about the need to know and focus on their destiny. However, when you look closely, it appears that Christians have just increased their head knowledge and intellectual understanding about this topic, but that knowledge has not translated into effective life transforming habits and behaviours in their daily living. People may know that they have a God-given purpose on earth, but they are not quite sure about what that purpose is exactly and how to go about discharging it in line with God's expectations. Many people still do not receive adequate leadership on what we propose to call "Destiny Living" in this book and this is a big problem in the Christian family today.

What is destiny, anyways?

Most of us associate destiny with fate, which means things that have to happen in our lives and that are outside of our control. But in the Christian perspective, destiny is more about what God has pre-planned for us and what we make happen in life with His help, rather than what happens to us as part of some pre-determined events that we have to endure in life. In our Christian perspective, life is understood to be as a vehicle for the delivery of our divine mission here on earth. God gave us life before the foundation of time, and He elected us to do something special in the physical realm that no other person can do. Life is given to us to transport us from eternity into physicality and enable us to be deployed as a means to deliver the divine gift and the value that is deposited in us for the sake of God's Kingdom on earth. We come on earth to deliver the resources that God has placed in us so that His plans for humanity are accomplished, His love, care, wisdom are delivered, and His work is done. In this sense we are a gift and we have a gift. We are a gift to the world from God and we have a gift in us that we need to deliver.

All human beings are destined for something special that God wants them to accomplish, directly or indirectly, through their physical lifetime experience on planet earth. Therefore, the Bible speaks of pre-destination. God has set a destination for us before we even realise who we are and where we want to go with our lives. To put it simply, our destiny is simply God's purpose and plans embedded in our life. We are pre-destined to do special things and achieve a particular mission for God. Sometimes we may not like how circumstances unfold in our lives, but we must trust that whatever circumstances we may find ourselves in, whether good or bad, somehow all these things connect us to the bigger plan that God has for us. This is why the Bible says that:

"We know that all things work together for good to those who love God, to those who are called according to His purpose"

Romans 8:28

Are you busy with your divine PHD?

A good way to conceptualise our destiny as Christians is to refer to it as PHD (Purpose-driven and Heavenly-inspired Destiny). In our modern-day education system PhD (Doctor of Philosophy) is one of the highest levels of education one can achieve. Similarly, God has the highest level of education and achievement He expects from us in the spiritual realm. Christian PHD is about focusing on what God wants us to achieve before we leave earth and return to Him. To assist us for our PHD, He gave us a heavenly-inspired manual for it. A friend of mine refers to it as "Basic Instructions Before Leaving Earth" (BIBLE). God gave us faith and a reference manual just to ensure we are adequately resourced spiritually and materially. He gave us these things for the purpose of enabling us to revere Him or worship Him through songs and hymns. God gave us faith as a kind of spiritual "software" for a new consciousness needed for self-actualisation. Faith is a program designed to get us to transact with God, navigate with confidence through the meanders of life and get His work done here on earth. Faith also gives us spiritual salvation through God's grace and, when matured, it brings an awareness and understanding of our divine assignment on earth. When this happens, we develop into active distributors of God's love, grace and mercy on earth. There is only one assignment for our PHD, which is to use our gifts to operate as divine agents for the transformation of the world, with a focus on caring for His people.

Your PHD is centred on three things: vision, knowledge and leadership. Faith brings God's vision into our consciousness; knowledge facilitates the management of life and leadership brings direction towards God's destiny. There are three levels of leadership that we need to be aware of in relation to our PHD. The first one is the spiritual leadership from God, which is made possible only through faith. Faith is the medium through which God draws us to Him and enables us to heed His call. The next level of leadership we need is self-leadership (from within), which enables us to take our destiny in our own hands, armed with the knowledge of God's vision and His grace upon our lives. The third level of leadership is the lateral leadership, which we need to extend to our fellow human beings to impact the world with what we have received from God.

Every human being on earth has leadership potential and

every human being needs leadership in their own life. Most of us have developed into adulthood thanks to the leadership and care of our parents and many other people in the community who have contributed to our life journey and have helped us become responsible, independent and mature individuals. These people have given us their leadership lessons in different settings such as school, work, business, church, society or the political field. Without good leadership from others many of us could end up with wrecked lives. Because we have received leadership from others to become who we are, we are also expected to give back leadership to others. That leadership is not necessarily linked to leading crowds of people, but to show love and care, understanding and compassion to others in the name of our faith and our Lord. God expects us to help our generation with the leadership skills He placed within us. Those skills need to be used to enable the younger generation to discover and develop their true identity and accomplish their divine destiny on earth. We must not break the leadership chain that has contributed to us becoming who we are. Our PHD is one that we do not graduate from until when we leave planet earth. It is centred on an eternal vision of God, the knowledge of His Will and the leadership we are expected to provide to help expand God's Kingdom on earth.

God is not religious

A lot of us tend to relate to God on a religious basis, but God is actually not religious per se. Our Father is not really interested in religion, understood as a set of beliefs combined with tradition, rituals and laws linked to a divinity. God is primarily interested in reconnecting with us and leading us to achieve His destiny on earth. He wants us to grow, gain understanding and release everything He invested in us. Since Adam and Eve sinned, God has been focused on the restoration of humanity. He has been working with prophets, teachers, evangelists and ordinary individuals to lead humanity on the restoration path, back to His original plans. This is why most of us admire stories of leadership, liberation and freedom. In the Bible, we admire the leadership of regular people who accomplished extraordinary things with the leadership of God, such as Moses, Joshua, Nehemiah, David, Apostle Paul and many others.

The message of the Gospel is all about divine leadership. The Bible is actually a leadership book, rather than a religious book. Although many books of the Old Testament may appear to depict a more religious aspect of the relationship between God and humanity, this is because of the fall of man and the low level of spiritual awareness that resulted from it. But with the coming of Jesus, we see that religion is not what God wants to focus on. Jesus was always very critical of religious sects and He instead focused on discipleship, asking people to drop everything and follow Him as the leader.

When Jesus says in Matthew 6:33: *"Seek first the kingdom of God and everything else will be given to you"*, what He means through this passage is that we need to first let God lead our lives completely and then we will get everything we actually need from Him. If God is our personal leader, He will be the provider as well. He is the greatest provider and He will cover all our needs.

Kingdom is a type of government leadership over a populated territory. Our physical body is God's territory and God wants us to submit our whole "self" to His government (leadership) by following His instructions, obeying His laws, embracing His heavenly culture and connecting with His purpose on earth. When there is no good leadership in the society people perish because there is no one to help them discover their own true identity and focus on their destiny, as expected by God.

Christian leadership and Destiny Living

Many preachers tell us that Christianity is not a religion, it is a relationship with Jesus. While this is true, many times those who say this don't always go deep enough in explaining what type of relationship there is between Jesus and us believers or disciples. When this question is examined carefully in the Bible, it becomes clear that the essence of the relationship we have with God is all about three things: love, purpose and leadership. God loves us, He has a plan for us and wants to lead us to His destiny for us. His scriptures are meant to guide us in the journey of life like a map, so that we can successfully move from total oblivion or spiritual darkness into Destiny Living or purposeful existence. God's purpose for our lives is not for us to have a religious relationship with Him, but a leadership relationship that is geared towards reconnection, reconciliation, restoration and life assignment.

When you view the Bible as a leadership book, it brings a fundamental shift in your spirituality. In today's troubled world, Christian leadership is needed more than ever. In Western countries people are walking away from God en masse and they are embracing various ideologies, philosophies and other self-serving and flesh-loving lifestyles. The self-help industry is trying to help people fill the void left by the "death of god" announced by philosophers. However, when you look closely, you notice that most of the self-help material that has circulated in western societies for several decades is nothing more than recycled and repackaged biblical material. The gurus in this field simply pick stuff from the Bible, give it a new "sexy" name and link it to familiar concepts in today's life and they sell it under a different label. Many people are attracted to this because they are led to believe that they are given full control of their life and their destiny and they like that feeling.

Today's Christian leadership needs to adapt to modern societies. We need to develop a new bible-based toolkit and a new vocabulary for the repackaging of the biblical teachings into new attractive concepts that connect with this generation and that still delivers the gospel truth in its essence. We can communicate biblical truths in ways that connects with the imagery of 21st century life and that strike a chord with the aspirations and longings of current generations, without compromising the Gospel. Much of this is simply related to the language we need to use in communicating the gospel to today's generation, especially the youth. We don't have to teach the Gospel using only biblical language that was used more than 2000 years ago. We can and should use a new vocabulary to convey the same eternal truths that are revealed in the Bible. This is obviously a big challenge, but one that all Christian leaders must embrace.

The Bible is written with an imagery and vocabulary of village life in the Middle Ages where most people lived mostly off farming and fishing activities. Today, the world has evolved, people of this generation are confronted with many more challenges, they live in urban areas where the mentalities, the realities and expectations are very different from first century Israel. Today's "market of ideas", beliefs and lifestyles is a whole lot bigger and more competitive and complicated than ever

Introduction

before. Because of this we need "to package and re-package" the Gospel in new ways and use novel sales strategies for what is undoubtedly the most valuable spiritual message in the history of humankind. Although it is the spirit of God that touches people's hearts and changes their lives, but the language and vocabulary we use to teach and preach the gospel will go a long way towards accelerating the transformation of today's society. It is our duty to do our best in conveying the truth of the Gospel and then leave it to God to do the rest.

For example, a lot of our human communication these days is electronic. The devil is using new technologies that many people use, such as Facebook and other social media platforms to spread his sugar-coated venin widely. Because of this, the people of God also need to use the same technologies in creative and aggressive ways to spread the Gospel to the masses. Given that the devil is now officially "on steroid" (in case you haven't noticed) and taking advantage of the latter day's dominion given to him by the Lord, we must equally show our determination to promote the truth of the Gospel. We must use our energy and our creativity not just to defend our identity as people of God, but also to promote and help expand the Kingdom of God through the message of our Lord. Unlike previous generations, ours is the first one that is exposed to 24 hours intimate communication and entertainment through digital technologies where moving images and sound are craftly used to spread dubious ideas, ideologies, philosophies and all sorts of quirky lifestyles to the masses. These messages are enticing many to adopt spiritually self-destructive lifestyles that are packaged with the label of individual freedom and freedom of speech.

In the midst of all this, because our attention span is shrinking, our capacity for discernment is greatly compromised, leaving many of us defenceless and vulnerable to the devil's destructive philosophical viruses. The Christian leadership around the world needs to lift its game by offering more serious and nutritious teachings to build people up, rather than simply fire them up with dramatic evangelical excitement and other prophetic pronouncements that are delivered in quasi theatrical ways to impress the masses. While there may be a need for a "spectacular gospel delivery" to get people excited for Jesus, we must not lose focus on the need to develop believers into disciples by feeding them spiritual meat, not just milk. In the end, God is expecting Christians to show leadership and become agents of restoration of humanity. Christians are on earth to deliver their mission, not just to profess the greatness and goodness of God or play holiness every Sunday morning at church. It takes good leadership for people to realise this. We must get busy by deploying all the resources bestowed onto us by the Almighty God to help us accomplish His plans on earth, both individually and collectively, as a body of Christ.

The Christian community also needs to raise the right pedigree of disciples and leaders who are not just saved, but who are fully active in deploying their spiritual, intellectual and physical resources to do God's work and impact their generation. Destiny Living is what churches must focus on, in addition to winning souls for Christ. Christian congregations must frame their work and deliver it within the "Destiny Living Framework", where both the leaders and their flocks constantly and relentlessly work to achieve their God-given destiny on earth. Every preaching, every teaching, every prophecy, every activity and every work within Christian congregations need to be connected to how the people of God are climbing the "destiny ladder", how they are progressing towards their God-ordained destination.

Introduction

This book is written as an effort to draw and shape the Christian family's attention and focus for "Destiny Living" and "Destiny Leadership". We have selected 12 key concepts that we believe encapsulate the very essence of what we need to focus on in practical ways to deliver our PHD on earth. Jesus selected 12 disciples to help Him accomplish His mission on earth and spread the Gospel to every corner of the earth. Likewise, we believe that the twelve keywords that are presented in this book can help every Christian to know, understand, increase and utilise their spiritual, intellectual, and physical energy to meet God's expectations regarding the reason why they have been given the gift of life. We hold these keywords to be intangible keys that Christians need to have so that they can activate, process and produce their destiny on earth. God ordains destiny in heaven and man delivers it on earth. It is meant to be a partnership. If you fail to do your part in this divine deal, regardless of whether you are a practicing, church-going, tongue-speaking and God-fearing Christian, you run the very high risk of meeting Jesus in Heaven and being told: "I do not know you".

CHAPTER ONE

Keyword 1
Divine

> **KEY POINTS**
> - As a Christian, you are divine because you are a product of a divine creator
> - You have divine DNA, you belong to a divine family and you are a royalty
> - Your divine origin and identity give you a divine destiny with a divine provision
> - You are made to divinely impact and dominate your generation

LIFE IS A DIVINE EXPERIENCE MANIFESTED IN THE PHYSICAL REALITY. The first keyword that we all need to know as Christians is the word "divine". From a Christian perspective, everything in life starts with God. What we call reality and everything that is part of it, including both the physical and non-physical elements of the universe and the cosmos, all of them are products of a divine mind, divine will, power and purpose. Some scientists may be trying to convince us that human life is a product of serendipity (chance), but we know through the scriptures, by revelation and even through simple observation of the world that it is not possible for life to have come from nothing. It has never been demonstrated in any scientific experiment that something can come out of nothingness.

Science has no explanation regarding the origin of life. The best scientific explanation about the origin of life is that life on earth may have come from outer space (other planets) and it may have started from simple molecules that gradually developed into more complex forms of life. The theory of evolution attempts to explain how life developed on earth, but it does not explain the origin of life. There is no doubt that one day, as science develops and more knowledge is gained, especially on molecular biology, it will become more evident that life is a product of design. This shift is already starting to take place within the scientific community where more scientists agree that what is observable in molecular biology (at DNA level) is not just appearance of design, but it is evidence of design.

The presence of intelligent beings that we are, on the one hand, and the existence a highly ordered and mathematically precise universe, on the other, cannot be products of chance or serendipity. No scientist is yet to demonstrate in a lab or in any computer modelling how, in the absence of any intelligible laws or principles of nature, either pure chance or what some refer to as "natural selection" can create anything that is both tangible and intelligible and continue to perfect it in an orderly manner, whilst remaining unguided in the process. As a matter of fact, more scientific progress made possible through the development of computer science, molecular biology and nanotechnology over the last few decades is increasingly pointing to the existence of design or an intelligent source of life. The evidence is so clear that even some of the most radical atheists such as

Focus on Destiny

Richard Dawkins now agree that there are some elements of design in life. Not long ago, the suggestion that there was design at the molecular level of biological life was repeatedly and vehemently being refuted by the so-called evolutionists. But even after admitting the existence of design in nature, Dawkins still stubbornly refuses to connect "design" with the existence of God. However, it is only a matter of time before we see a shift within the scientific community and a clear admission of design and intelligence in the natural universe.

Not so long ago, science was telling us that the universe was never created and that it has always been there as an eternal thing. This view was held for several decades until evidence became overwhelming clear that the universe had a beginning, which they refer to as the Big Bang. Fortunately, or unfortunately, depending on where you are standing, science is never ashamed to change its mind. I like watching documentaries and I always rejoice when I hear the voice over on a documentary that goes like:

> "… until recently, scientists thought that… but now new evidence is emerging, suggesting that …".

I look forward to the day when I will hear:

> "… now mounting evidence shows that "natural selection" alone cannot explain the evolution of life and there is now overwhelming evidence supporting the view that life is a product of design".

I may be in my grave by then, but I will surely rejoice. If science is not ashamed to change its mind, Christianity should never

Divine

be ashamed to stay put, until science joins it on the top of the mountain where it has been waiting, enjoying a clear and awesome view of the greatness of God and His divine mind, power and purpose that have brought life and nature into reality.

Several years ago, an eminent Jewish professor called Gerald Schroeder published a very interesting video through which he eloquently and scientifically demonstrated the proof of the existence of God. He used a modelling developed by NASA that provides a condensed knowledge of what the scientific community holds to be the best explanation of how the universe was created and developed from the beginning of time to now. That modelling is represented in the diagram below.

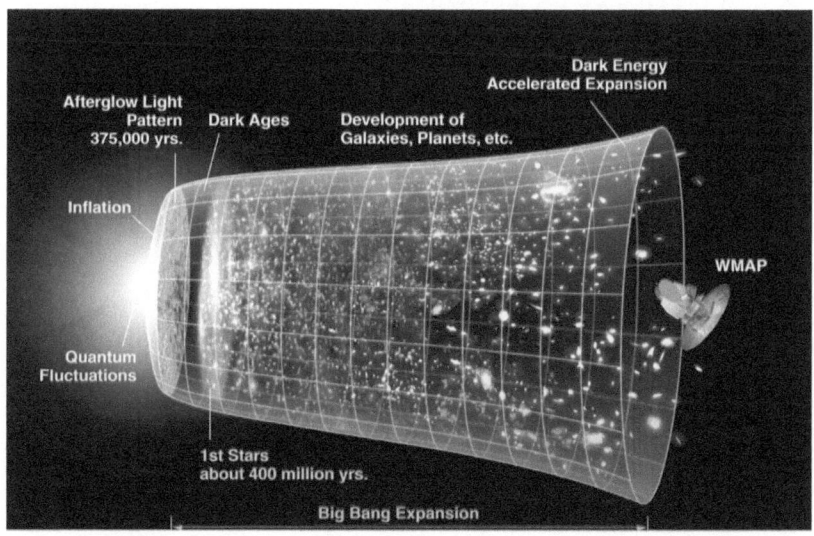

When you look at the diagram, it shows the development of the universe from quantum fluctuations, which contends that you can create something from nothing provided that you have the laws of nature in place. These laws are not physical in themselves, but they do act in the physical world. The quantum fluctuations are conceptualised as a set of forces that have the following characteristics:

1- They are not physical
2- They act on the physical
3- They created the physical from nothing
4- They predate the universe

The professor went on to show how these characteristics perfectly match the biblical definition or description of God. The Bible clearly describes the characteristics of God as a spirit (understood as non-physical intelligent force), and in the book of Genesis where creation is explained we learn that God predates time (1), stands outside of time (2), is not physical, but a force (3) and He created the universe (4).

In Genesis, God is referred to as Elohim, which in Hebrews means God as manifested in the universe. This clearly demonstrate how the best scientific explanation regarding the onset and evolution of the universe matches the description of what the Bible refers to as God almighty, Elohim. Many atheists will continue to argue God out of their mind and ego, but for us Christians, we can now rejoice that our belief in God is no longer just a matter of faith, which can't be proven scientifically, but it is also founded on the best scientific knowledge to date. This gives us confidence in a world that is increasingly becoming not just atheistic, but also ungodly and immoral. While some atheists are being converted, many others, including the agnostics will continue to use junk science to explain God away, but God will remain God until the end of time.

The Bible is clear, God created the world and everything that is in it. God said: "*Let us create man in our image*" (Gen 1; 26-28). This statement means two things. First, it shows the nature and purpose of God. The nature of God is that of a creator. He is the creator who brings things into existence by creating laws of nature and by enabling biology to emerge out of chemistry. God also embedded a sophisticated software program that connects these two things. Science has no explanation of how biology emerged out of chemistry. We know that in the beginning there was nothing but chemistry (gases and other chemical elements), how did biology emerge out of chemistry? No scientist can explain this. But the Bible tells us how God created man by using dirt (chemistry), mixing it with water and giving it a shape (engineering) and He breathed into it (spiritual engineering) to give it life. The beauty of creation is mind-blowing when you penetrate its depth. God is the greatest engineer of all time.

The second thing that comes of the Genesis 1: 26-28 is that that mankind has been created in the image of the creator, and as such, we are not just products of simple evolution of natural laws acting on the physical world, but we have been engineered/wired/coded/designed to reflect our creator's very nature. As a result of this, we are little "creators" by nature, just like our father. The one who created us wanted us to reproduce His character and His abilities, especially His "creating" and "loving" traits. You are a product of divine creation and naturally have divine traits in you.

The divine "I" in you

In order for life to make sense, we need to 'create" our own psycho-cognitive awareness so that we can realise that we actually exist and that existence is an element of a bigger ensemble that includes our surroundings and much more than we can see, touch feel, hear or even conceive, in general term. At every minute of our existence, our brain is creating our internal reality with the data it gets from both the external (physical) world and the internal system (the body). What we call reality is so immensely complex and vast that our brain literally has to edit billions of data and present it in digestible bits to our consciousness. When that editing is taking place, there is a mind-blowing mechanical and data manipulation process that is taking place inside of us, mostly at an unconscious level. The "construction" of reality in the human mind is so high-tech that only a divine creator could have made it possible. In a world without God, there is no reason for chemistry to turn into biology and there is no reason for biology to evolve into consciousness.

When we are busy creating reality, the "I" inside us is neither our brain, nor our mind. The mind is not the brain and our consciousness is not in the brain either. If the "I" can think of the mind, therefore the "I" is not the mind. The "I" in us is much more complex than what we can think. We can call it "consciousness" to simplify things, but what is consciousness? Philosophers and scientists who have been trying to seriously study and understand what consciousness is will tell you how difficult it is to even define it appropriately. The "I" in us is such a complex thing, because that is where humanity meets "divinity". It seats at the intersection of chemistry, biology and spirituality. The divine in us rests in the "I" and that "I" is All Mighty, hence why the most powerful statement in our life is "I AM". It is in the I AM (short for I All Mighty) that we project and deploy the divine from within into the outer world, the physical realm that stands outside of us. God told Moses that He was "the I Am that I Am". As His children we too share that nature, albeit it at a lower form.

Our ability to create our own reality, to be aware of our own self, our existence and our surroundings, to affect both the inside and the outside of us, that ability is the most powerful force we have and God has given it to us for a purpose so that we can create our future and our "earthly" destiny. Unlike plants that are not conscious beings or things (at least not at the same level as human beings), even if they can interact with their surroundings, God has equipped us with consciousness to create our own reality, which is experienced spiritually, psychologically, emotionally and physically. Through that reality within us we are then able to contribute in the creation of a "global reality" that connects with other human beings and the spiritual realm as well. God gave us the capacity to "create" in order for us to continue the creation work He left unfinished when He created the world. This is why of all created beings, mankind is the only one with a sufficiently elevated capacity to purposefully create things. No other animal comes even close to what man is capable of achieving in terms of creation capacity.

When God says *"The just shall live by faith"* (Romans 1:17), this means that we need to create our own psycho-cognitive-spiritual reality based on what we believe inside of us as illuminated by God's Word and revelation, rather than what we see in the physical reality. Life may be lived in the physical, but it is experienced in the non-physical dimension. It is "all in the mind" as the saying goes, although mind is actually bigger than just the brain.

Destiny is the total journey of the "I" inside of us as it traverses the compartments of time from eternity, into the present, past and future and back into eternity. That destiny is primarily an immaterial (spiritual) reality that needs to be translated into a material experience within the physical world. This is quite a profound insight, because it shows that we need to program ourselves internally or immaterially (spiritually) first and then we will see the external manifestation of that programming come to past in the physical. No wonder why God says that we need to believe first before we can see.

It is in the coding or programming of the "I" that we are able to birth the shape and character of our identity and be able to impact the physical world in ways that will make things materialise. In the story of creation, as recounted in the Bible, God speaks first and then things materialise. The speaking is the coding of reality, the structure of the "creation magic" (so to speak), which is necessary before the physical manifestation of things can occur. For us human beings, the believing, visualising, planning and working is the equivalent of God speaking, before things can manifest in the physical world. "Let there be light" is the coding for "light" to materialise. Hence, light came from sound and so did the rest of the natural world. The whole world came from the sound of the voice of God as He kept calling things into reality. Even in a scientific perspective, if the so called "Big Bang" started everything, then it is scientifically correct to assert that the physical world is a product of the sound that was emitted first before the whole thing "banged". If you observe any explosion, you will notice that the sound is heard first, before things can be observed to fly apart.

As you read this book, the very act of reading is a result of a very sophisticated information/data processing mechanism. This process allows your mind to conceive and make sense of things, to transcribe and interpret intangible things that we call ideas into tangible things such as letters and symbols and then reconstruct meaning from those. The combination of letters and symbols is done in specific sequences that allow other minds to capture the ideas conveyed by the author in the same ways he/she intended (more or less) and get meaning out of them. Just reflect on this for a minute and realise how brilliant it is to read and penetrate the deep mind of the author and connect with the energy in his brain, as you are doing at this very moment. The invention of writing is certainly one of the greatest human achievements of all time. No other animals communicate in writing. This shows how special the human family is and why God said that He created us in His image. It also explains why God encourages us to study the scriptures (His word in writing form).

Spiritually, things are not too different. In fact, the physical reality is modelled on the spiritual world. Some of the things we see in the IT (Information Technology) world is actually a reflection of the spiritual world. Your divine destiny comes from a divine engineer who has built (or coded) it for you in the spiritual realm and is expecting you to activate the downloading mechanism of that program inside your "I", i.e. inside of YOU and install it and use it so that both yourself and the world can benefit from it. That download process can only take place if there is a connection with the source. The connection is what we call "faith". There must also be a coded program enabling the downloading and that program is what we call "The Word of God". Furthermore, there must also be a user to kickstart and enable the installation. That user is what we call consciousness. In the end, things take place in the physical world after the download is completed and the program installed. Those things are what we call actions or deeds, which manifest in different ways.

All these things are only possible in the right environment that enables everything to work and fulfil their relevant functions. It is important for every Christian to understand the spiritual mechanics that God uses to sustain the physical world. That understanding helps us all to achieve our destiny. When a spiritual truth is understood clearly and deeply enough, it helps to strengthen the spirit, embolden the mind and activate the intangible "mechanics" that brings things into existence. Knowing that we are divine, and we have capacity to create reality is the beginning of wisdom, the right wisdom that we must have in order to accomplish our destiny. Besides the divine insight, we also need to understand the divine character that we have been given by our father and how that character affects our ability to do things and how it can be leveraged to help us achieve our destiny.

Mind your divine character

"Let us make man in our image" God said. (Gen 1:26). This is one of the most important verses in the bible. Without this, God would have remained God in His fullness, unknown by any human mind, because there is no mind to conceive of Him. God created us in His image, not a physical image, because He is not physical, but the image of His character. This gives us the attributes that resembles His identity, including the ability to be conscious (aware of ourselves), to conceive things (conceptualise reality), to express ourselves (to speak things into reality), to love (to project feelings towards something or someone), to create (to design and make things happen), to will (to express an intent), to decide (to shape one's will or mind firmly), to lead (to shape and guide energy), to nurture and care for creation.

It is important for every human being who is serious about discovering, designing, creating and deploying their destiny on earth to understand what "character" is and how it affects everything in our relationship with God and in our experience of reality. Character is what makes us unique as individuals and defines the very nature of our identity and consciousness. The dictionary defines character as "the mental and moral qualities distinctive to an individual". Character is formed in the deepest part of us. It is the outside manifestation of all that goes in the deepest part of our psyche, our personal culture, our self-identity and our spirit. We go to school to develop and refine our intellect and not necessarily our character. While school can help refine our character it often fails to do this because it is mostly preoccupied by our ability to understand, retain, manipulate and regurgitate information previously transmitted to us. Only some schools, mostly religious ones, understand the need to shape character as part of the general education process, but often they don't have enough time to do this effectively because of all the other requirements of the official (government) curriculum.

Attending Church regularly can help us refine our character, but not all churches achieve this goal. It is not the frequency of attendance that counts, it is the exposure to the right teaching, preaching and manifestation of God's spirit that can make a real difference in this regard. Character is about the morality, integrity, instinct and inclination of our personality and our identity. It has to do more with morality, but it is not divorced from the intellectual and mental framework of a person. It is the actual moral skeleton of the person, not what they pretend to be in the outside, but what shapes them from inside. At the core of it, we find the principles and integrity (or lack of) that defines a person. When someone has no integrity, boundaries and principles, he or she is said to lack character.

Focus on Destiny

The first consequence of the original sin in the garden of Eden is that humanity got disconnected from God and lost its divine character. The work of the Gospel and the very reason why Jesus came on earth was to reconnect us to God, to re-inject the divine character back into us, as sons and daughters of God. When one accepts Jesus, nothing changes in the body, but something changes in their character. Their eyes do not change, but their vision does, their voice doesn't change, but their speaking does, their feet don't change, but their path does. However, the change in their mind and in the spirit can only develop further and be established through a voluntary process of mental reprogramming or what the Bible calls the renewal of the mind.

The Bible tells us to renew our mind, because this is the process through which we build a new character that aligns with our true divine identity that was lost through sin. The old mind must be replaced with a new mind for the new identity we get in Christ. This change is initiated by God, but it requires a conscious programming and reprogramming effort from the person, that is framed in a much broader understanding of a new identity from God. The new identity always has a purpose bestowed onto it and a mission given to it to impact the world, to create a new reality, to exercise dominion based on the gifts of their character. This is why when we "Focus on Destiny", in practice it means we are developing a new understanding of our divine nature and refining our divine character for the purpose accomplishing our divine mission on earth. It is our character that will support and supervise the whole process through which our new and inspired spirit and mind and our anointed body are drawn to a new focus centred on accomplishing God's mission in our life.

You are an expression of God's will and purpose.

When God says "*Let us make man in our image*", that statement shows the will and purpose of God in creating mankind. Through this verse God is expressing His will to create. He does so in a plural form rather than as a singular expression. "Let us" rather than "Let me". There is a reason for this. God does nothing by chance. The plural nature of that expression is designed to demonstrate the wholeness of God (Father, Son and Holy spirit) being involved in the decision-making process to create humanity. It is meant to tell us that every bit of God was engaged in the process to create humanity. God could have said "Let man be" in the same way He said "Let there be light". He also could have said "Let me create man", but He said "Let us make man in our image". God was indeed very focused when He created mankind and that focus and seriousness in the beginning of the creation process of mankind is also present in the outcome. We are the most serious of all God's creation in the physical world and the closest to His very own nature. For this reason, our destiny is encoded as part of a divine expression. Our divine Father, in His capacity as the Creator (Father), in His divine expression through His Word (Son) and His infinite power (Holy Spirit) has contributed in the spiritual engineering and physical manifestation of mankind. God shaped us spiritually first, through His expression (non-material), before we were crafted by the work of His hand (material shape) and then infused with His breath (life force), to complete the creation process. These are all important elements that play a critical role in understanding our divine origin and our original character, on the one hand, as well as how these things do play out in determining our destiny in the physical world, on the other hand.

From divine design to divine destiny

The destiny of anything depends on three things: the purpose, design and the material used in putting it together. God's design, which will be discussed in detail in the second chapter, holds the key to our destiny. It has two components, including the "image" of the creature before it is created and then the "material" used to complete the expression of that image in real life. As an outcome of a divine expression, we need to understand that before the creation of humanity, God existed veiled in his deity with no human mind to conceive Him, no eyes to see Him and no ears to hear Him, as we highlighted earlier. At the time, He is the only being that is and there is nothing else, no one else, no time, no space and no matter. In that divine realm, God occupied the whole spectrum of reality and there is no "space" or dimension from which any "knowing" is possible outside of Him alone. God becomes knowable or conceivable only when He expresses himself in some way and the very act of "expressing" His desire results in "creation". Whatever God says comes into existence, therefore His Word, which is part of Him becomes the means through which we can know Him. God is only knowable through His word.

As things come into existence, following from His divine expression, we as creatures of His affirmation are the manifestation of His will, made possible through His divine power that engineers things and produces them instantaneously (time doesn't exist in His realm). That power, when seen from a human perspective, is miraculous, but God knows no miracle, all He knows is His expression. Because we are the best expression of God in the physical world, and given our nature and character, mankind as a race and Christians as an elected group of God's creation, we have the responsibility to reflect the best of everything we are and everything we have inherited from Him, to bring it into the physical world. We need to take what God invested in us in the spiritual and deliver it in the physical, as an expression of His nature in us. Our destiny is about enabling God to express Himself through us and impact the world through our breath, words and hands, in the same way He did when He created us. We must first proclaim the vision He has in us, then work with our hands (physical work) to shape things and breathe everything we have into that vision. When we breathe into our vision, it means we give our very life force into it, giving it all we have. Because we were designed and created by the divine, we get a divine destiny. We may have lost it with sin, but Christ has come to reconnect us to what is by God's design our natural heritage and fate.

God proudly owns you and wants you to do better as a product of His hands. When God says "let us make man in our image", in this statement the pronoun "our" conveys a sense of ownership and belonging combined. Not only God summoned every bit of Himself in declaring and exercising His power for creation, He also claimed ownership of that creation even before it was manifested. Ownership is very valuable when one has worked on the thing being owned. If you buy an established house, you won't feel the same for that house compared to a house that you have built with your own hands. The investment in the concept, ideas, work, creativity and energy you use in building the house will surely give you a sense of pride and more attachment and value for that house you build, especially when the final outcome is "divine". This is why God loves humanity more than any other created being or thing. He worked on man and declared ownership of him. God owns you and wants you to succeed, because everyone who owns something want to see it flourish in the best possible way.

Understanding our divine source, our divine nature and our divine character is the first step that leads us to focus on what we are here on earth for. We are not on earth just to earn a living, we are on earth to live a divine experience, grow physically and spiritually and produce fruits that impact on our generation and enable us to leave a divine legacy. We come from eternity into physicality as agents of transformation, instruments for restoration and soldiers for Christ with a divine agenda for the expansion of the Kingdom of God. Our presence on this planet is part of a mission and we have all that we need inside of us to achieve it. God literally packed us with all the resources we need in order to impact the world and He wants to see us do better and fulfil the purpose for which He crafted us into physicality. All we need is enough focus so that we can discover, understand, develop and deploy our gifts to the world.

Being owned by God also has one major advantage. It gives us access to divine provision. Because God owns us He will provide for us. Any parent of a child knows instinctively that he or she has to provide for his or her children. This is both true for humans and animal and it is something that we have inherited from our creator. Knowing that God will provide for your destiny and your life plans is very important. It should give you confidence that even where the vision you have for your destiny may appear too big or too dangerous, God who is unlimited and all powerful will provide for and take care of you. You belong to God's family, you are part of the royal family and your father owns everything, therefore you need to be bold, confident and at peace.

Divine

Know your destiny, love it and "will" it into existence

God is love and we are an expression of His divine mind, which is centred on love. Additionally, the biggest gift that God has given us here on earth, besides our life, is willpower. Without it we would be like animals or plants. Our will is the second greatest asset we have received from God, after life, and it is the divine trait that needs to be treasured and developed the most, so that it aligns with the plan and vision of our creator. Your will is the instrument that enables you to "matter" in the physical world, as well as receive spiritual salvation from God. However, your will can become toxic and dangerous if it is disconnected from the love of God and His own will in your life. The two things must always go together. Love is the mother of life and will is the mother of purpose. God created us because he loved us. He used His will to serve and manifest his love. It is love that led God to want to create mankind and His will directed Him in manifesting love through creation. In everything divine, love drives and will directs.

In the journey for your delivery of your destiny you must learn to develop and manage your will so that you can do the will of God that is centred on expressing love in various ways. The will of God is all focused-on love, love for His purpose, love for His children, love for His Kingdom. In the same way the will of man should also be focused on love, love of God, love of God's purpose or destiny in one's life and love of humanity. Jesus said it all when he said that the biggest commandment is *"love your God with all your heart, soul and mind… Love your neighbour as yourself"* (Matthew 22:37). When you pray God to show you His ordained destiny for your life, you will probably hear Him ask you back "what do you love doing?" or may be "what would you love to do if you had all your other needs covered for you?". When you know your destiny, love it with all your heart, mind and soul.

Your destiny is divine: create love and receive love

God is God first and foremost because He is the creator of all that exists. His creator's trait is the most important one, because without it He ceases to be God and becomes a creature. When God created the world, His work did not end on the sixth day. He just left the rest of the creation job to mankind. He knew that man would need many things for his life and He did not want to do everything for him, He created the structure of nature and wanted man to "customise" the rest of the things needed to complete creation.

Dr Miles Munroe once said: "*God knew that man would need a chair, so he hid the chair in the trees*". God knew that eventually man would develop enough capacity to find ways to create a chair from the wood of the trees and make it as comfortable as possible for his own use. God also knew that every generation would have its own needs and He left it to people of that generation to seek for, design and create the solutions for themselves when the need arises. God wanted man to find fulfilment in perpetuating His creation work and He gave him enough brain power for that purpose. He expects us to create a new reality in mind that will lead us to focus on making a difference not just for our own lives, but for the good of the human family, as well as for the expansion of His kingdom on earth. In doing so,

Divine

God has provided every one of us with the ability to create our destiny on earth, using inspiration from Him. We are called to create ideas, concepts, tools, organisations, resources, opportunities and countless other things that align with God's purpose on planet earth.

A key component of our destiny has to do with our ability to develop and use our creativity skills in conjunction with our faith and vision. When we see things that we dislike in this world, we need to know that the awareness of such things in our spirit and mind and any burden of this in our heart is a call for action and creation. God expects us to respond to and create opportunities to show love, to give care, to elevate the divine in us and resit the devil's temptations. Only through our capacity to create that we can bring forth His love, deliver it to His people and transform the world in the process. However, most of us fail to meet this divine expectation, hence we fail our destiny. The reasons for this are many, including ignorance, distraction, poor spiritual leadership, love of money and propensity to sin. Your divine destiny is established in heaven. You can make it happen on earth if you focus enough to find out what it is, if you love it enough and if you design and develop a path for its accomplishment, relying on the help of God to guide you through the process. You are divine; hence you are expected to live, think, speak, work, love and behave divinely.

CHAPTER TWO

Keyword 2

Design

KEY POINTS
- You are designed as an instrument of God's will and purpose on earth
- Your destiny is connected to God's design. Know it and reproduce it
- Design and create your future with God's material and He will guarantee the outcome.

The beautiful design

THE BIGGEST SCIENTIFIC LIE OF OUR TIME IS THAT LIFE AND THE WORLD are products of serendipity. The existence of humans on earth is certainly not an outcome of "natural accidents" that gradually developed over time. Humans are the manifestation of a divine will and purpose. Humanity and the whole world are evidence of divine purpose, ingenuity and engineering power. Your life is not a biological accident. It did not start from some serendipitous event in ancient time that brought living cells together to evolve into an ancient monkey from whom our ancestors evolve.

Design

The Bible gives us a clear glimpse of God's design when it says:

> *"Before I formed you in the womb I knew you, before you were born I set you apart; I appointed you as a prophet to the nations."*
>
> Jeremiah 1:15.

When this verse is connected to Genesis 2:7 where God is reported to have formed man out of clay, the two passages put together provide a very clear picture of God's design not just in creating humanity, but also creating (forming) every person as an individual and original entity. No two people are exactly the same.

As you read these pages, you need to know that your life did not start as a result of a mere accident that took place when your Mum and Dad decided to have fun in bed. Your parents are mere instruments through which the supernatural agenda of God Almighty was executed in the physical world. Your life is a product of a very a beautiful love story that started before the foundation of the earth. Even in purely biological terms, think of the beauty that is present in the whole machinery that brought you into existence. Starting from when your parents came together for a moment of intimacy and enjoyment and through that process a masculine seed came into contact with a female egg and triggered the most amazing manufacturing process on earth: the development of a human body in the womb. Think of the marathon that took place when millions of sperms were catapulted into action and one sperm had to win the race for access to the egg, making you a winner from the get go. Think of all the divisions of the cells from a single entity into trillions of cells, arranged in particular ways to create all organs and members of your body. This is evidence that you are a product of heavenly engineering, designed and produced in heavenly places. You were designed in Heaven and delivered on earth with LOVE.

Beyond your biological structure, the process of consciousness formation is equally divine. Once you were born, the whole process of the development of your consciousness kicked in from the first day. As you grew physiologically, you developed another outstandingly and beautifully complex set of mechanisms that, although founded in biology, is not biological. Your consciousness as a human being is so complex that scientists and philosophers have been struggling for centuries to even be able to define it appropriately. You are more than what anyone can say of you, what makes you a consciously independent being is beyond human understanding.

All these processes as highlighted above are not just mind boggling, but they are utterly impossible to have come out of a compilation of millions of little "happy" accidents (mutations) that apparently took place over "millions" of years in undirected ways, as contended by some crazy scientists. The intelligent and all-powerful agent who made all these things possible is God and He alone knows why you exist and what your life is all about. He designed you with a purpose and for a purpose. When His purpose for your life meets your own plans for your life, you are on the right track for your destiny.

Partnering with God for your destiny

Your destiny has two parts: God's part and your part. You need to be clear about these two levels of responsibility that intersect and ultimately influence your life and destiny here on earth, as well as in eternity.

1 *God's part for your destiny*

God created you in His image and He started the whole process in the spiritual realm, long before you were conceived and birthed on planet earth. God is the master of creation and creation means the design, production and manifestation of something previously non-existent. Every design process requires contemplating and deciding upon the purpose, the look, the shape and the functioning of something new and useful. God has designed you with a mind, a spirit, a body, an established purpose and a destiny. God used His creative mind as the creator and His unlimited power to shape and produce human beings as part of His infinite ingenuity and wisdom. Whatever you have as part of your genetic capital, these are things that are from God and they relate to how He designed you, how He coded you into existence as an individual and for a particular purpose. It does not mean that you do not have any option to change what your genetic capital gives you, but it means you have limited options. There is only one of you in the whole history of the world and in eternity as well. God does not create copies; He only makes originals. Accept who you are as a child of God because there is beauty in you, even where other people do not see it with their naked eyes. There is so much beauty in the design that makes you to be who you are. God has designed and created you in your physical structure and everything that is linked to it.

In addition to your biology, there is also design in your mind. Your psycho-cognitive framework is a product of divine volition, even though this is something that is a lot more malleable and vulnerable to environmental influences than your genetic capital.

Psychology cannot exist independently of biology, therefore, even though we have a lot of power to alter our psychology or our intellect, there is still a lot in us that we cannot change. Science cannot explain why one person will be more interested in music and another in sport or in medicine. These are things of the mind, but they are connected to our hearts and our spirits. God designed the way human mind works and how it interreacts with emotions, as well as spiritual realities. Every individual can make changes in their "mental infrastructure" but only within the parameters set by God. Our designer gave us the ability to alter things in this regard, but only up to a certain level. You think the way you think partly because of your family, social and cultural environments (nurture) and partly because of your genetic capital (nature). A lot of what shapes your mental infrastructure (intellect, psyche, personality, feelings etc) is part of your genetic heritage and it comes in a package and you are limited in what you can change, no matter how hard you may want to try.

God also designed your spirit, which plays a very important role in your consciousness and identity. Science has very little to tell us about these things. Science is totally incompetent for our spirituality and when it comes to our mind, its competency is limited to the working of the (observable) brain, not much more. However, the human mind is more than just the output of brain activity and there is no evidence that the mind is actually inside the brain, as opposed to simply being connected to the brain in some ways not yet understood by mankind. Consciousness and identity are of significant interest to God. In the Bible, consciousness (in all its forms, including subconsciousness, consciousness and super consciousness) is referred to as the "heart". When the bible speaks of "heart" in many instances it is not about the "blood pump" inside our thorax, but the deepest part of us, where the intellectual, emotional and spiritual parts of us intersect and interact. All these things are all the 'intangible' parts of us, and they are part of how God designed us. He has done His work in creating us and giving us everything we need for our earthly experience. We simply need to connect with Him in a meaningful way and let him have His way in all that is part of us.

2 *Your part in your destiny*
Although God establishes our destiny in the spiritual realm, He expects us to deliver it on earth by using all the faculties and resources He invested in us through creation. God is the creator, He is creativity in a divine form. We, as His children, we are "creativity" in human form. We are creators too because He created us in His image, as the Bible describes it in the book of Genesis. Most people think that destiny is about the things that will have to happen in our lives, whether we like it or not. We link destiny to fate, which is often thought of negatively. But in the Bible, it is clear that man's will and his choices, decisions, work, and commitment are all needed for God's plan and purpose to be accomplished on earth. God is a gentleman, He does not interfere in our earthly affairs unless and until we let Him do so. The reason God doesn't interfere is not because He lacks the power to do so, but simply because from the very beginning of creation He established the framework, the environment, the laws and principles of how He wanted the earth to be and He gave man dominion over the earth. He delegated His divine authority over to mankind and asked him to manage "the garden of life".

It is interesting that in Genesis, God did not place man in the "bush", but He placed him in the "garden". There is a reason for that. Both garden and bush have the same material (soil, plants, animals), but the difference between them is that a garden is organised, ordered, cultivated and framed in particular ways, but the bush is wild, disorganised and even chaotic. This is why the bush is dangerous with many harmful creatures who pose danger to human life. The Bible says God planted a garden and placed man into it. In the same way, when we set out to live our destiny, we need to plant a garden for ourselves from the bush of life. Life is like a bush filled with weeds, thorns, wild and creepy creatures everywhere. Spiritually, since Adam and Eve were expelled from the Garden of Eden and wondered into the bush, life has remained "bushy" until the arrival of Jesus. With Jesus, through the obedience of our spirit and wilful and creative use of our mind we have the power to turn life into a garden by utilising the wisdom, understanding and knowledge that comes with the Gospel. The message of Christ guides us to connect with the mind and plan of God. That is the responsibility that you have when it comes to destiny living or destiny deployment.

Christian believers need to understand that there are three types of things that exist in life:
- What God has created and does not expect man to change
- What God has created and expects man to change
- What God left for man to create and change as he sees fit

The first category of things includes things such as natural laws, principles and the ecology. Anyone who messes up with these things can expect trouble, because it is a violation of God's laws. The second category includes natural resources such as trees, plants, minerals etc. We can change trees into chairs, plants into food, minerals into tools and machines. The third category is about the human reality and the social environment.

Design

God left it to us to create our own reality through our cognition and psychology and He also gave us the agency thru which we contribute to the creation of a social environment (such as when we do things in the community, take initiatives, promote or resist different things). The third category is where we exercise most of our freedom in designing and creating our future on earth.

The scriptures encourage us to harmoniously integrate our spirit, mind, body and soul for the purpose of serving God in our lives. We need the wisdom and help of the Holy Spirit to achieve this. God's spirit helps attend to the need of the spiritual person within us, at the same time as we meet the need of the mind and the body. We need God's wisdom revealed through the Bible and through divine revelation and inspiration. We should not seek to fundamentally change what God has established for us because we will never be wiser than God. If God creates you as a male, it is neither wise nor beneficial in a long-term perspective to want to become a female, even if modern medicine can help you to do a sex change operation and administer female hormones to try to change your body. Whenever we violate what God has established we create more issues, even where we think that we are just wanting to solve a problem that is troubling us. The humility to accept what one cannot fundamentally change in life is not given to all. Knowing that God designed us with His infinite power and wisdom gives us more power and increase our ability to live a more fulfilling life. It also improves our capacity to better deal with the challenges of living in a world environment that is permanently infested with evil, sin, corruption while focusing on our spiritual agenda. This is why we need to constantly interact with God as we walk through the journey of life, because He is the one who made us and who ultimately knows what is ultimately good for us and guide us through difficult times.

God has finished His job, start yours

It is important to know that God's part in the manifestation of our destiny is already completed. He has finished everything, and He is simply waiting on you to align to His will, purpose and destiny for your life. This is why He says:

> *"Ask and it will be given to you, seek and you shall find, and knock and it shall be open to you."*
>
> (Mat 7:7).

God did not say *"ask and it may be given to you, seek and you may find and knock and it may be opened for you"*. In this passage it is clear that if you ask God everything that is in line with His purpose, He will definitely give it to you. In fact, He has already given it to you, you just need to connect with it and download it into your reality.

A lot of time when we talk about destiny we tend to limit our understanding to just what happens during our earthly existence. But we learn from the Bible that life doesn't start with birth and it doesn't end with death. You have no control on the pre-birth and post death parts of your existence, but your life here on earth, your "earthly destiny", is an experience and a journey for which God has adequately equipped you and He expects you to take the driving seat for the journey. God expects YOU to design and create your earthly destiny with His assistance and guidance. God wants you to have control over your life and that control includes the ability to design how you want to frame your life to fit and use your freedom to serve His agenda on earth.

The world understands freedom to mean the ability to do what one likes to do, but in the Christian perspective, our freedom is about choosing how we manifest the best version of our identity into this world. It is freedom for self-manifestation in Christ, rather than what the French call "libertinage", which is freedom to do whatever passes through your mind without any considerations of what the rest of the society may think of it.

God designed us to be able to "make things happen" rather than just be at the mercy of what happens in our environment. Therefore, He gave us dominion. Although our destiny includes circumstances that cannot be controlled, but God did not just make us as mere robots, with no conscious experience and no free will. God put into us the very stuff that make Him God, namely consciousness, purposefulness and free choice. He gave us the power and ability to create and make things happen, just like Him, even though we may not match His ability in all areas. We can't speak things into existence instantaneously, but we can believe, speak, plan and work things into existence. Jesus told us that we could do even greater things that He did, if we simply believed.

The divine game of destiny

Your future on earth is the biggest thing that God expects you to design and create. He has equipped you for it by giving you the necessary spiritual, intellectual, emotional and physical resources. He stands ready to work with you, guide and support you, because in your future lies an important gift that He wants to provide to humanity. If you succeed, you get rewarded with a blessed, abundant and fulfilled life on earth, in addition to eternal salvation. Your earthly destiny is designed to be designed and produce based on the inspiration and revelations you receive from God. To the divine inspiration you need to add your faith, your decisions, your plans, your actions and your commitment to get the job done. Life on earth resembles a heavenly game where God hides from physicality, but remains accessible through faith and He holds the material and the instructions with which you must build your life. You must seek Him to access the material and He will test you from time to time and let you go through harsh circumstances as He gauges your ability to trust Him and keep your eyes focused on Him and keep progressing towards your mission. This is why your ability to see beyond your eyesight, open your "faith eyes" and transcend the physical conditions that you may find yourself in at any moment in life is a very important in the game of life. You cannot work with God without faith because that is how He designed the game and you cannot fulfil your destiny without allowing Him to guide, instruct, test and train you. As the master designer, God has programmed you to be the designer of your own "little reality" on earth. The way you conceive that reality over time will determine what you do. If you see yourself as destined for greatness and having a very important mission to achieve, you will spend your time and do things differently from someone who sees no hope in their lives and thinks life is boring and unfair. God is always ready to co-design and co-create our earthly destiny, if we allow Him and understand the process He has put in place for this purpose.

Design your path for fulfilment

Your capacity to create was embedded into your consciousness by God. It starts with the ability to construct your own reality in your own individual consciousness. This enables you to understand that you are alive, you exist as an individuated entity and you are part of a particular environment and a much bigger reality that transcends your own personal existence and what you can directly observe and understand. This capacity further develops as you mature, to enable you to connect to the spiritual matrix from which all things derive and remain connected to. From that point, it is all about "focus". Whatever you focus on, you magnify it and give it life and you also improve your knowledge and understanding of what it is.

When we study something or when we train ourselves for something, we are simply augmenting our level of focus on that thing in different ways and increase our capacity to interact with it successfully, based on the purpose we have in our mind. Human beings who have developed their ability to focus on things for a long time have been able to achieve outstanding things in life. But from God's point of view, the most important thing is to see us create our own future on earth that aligns with His heavenly plans for humanity. God is the owner of your life and you are simply the manager. You are given the mission to manage your life on His behalf and He will ask you to account for your earthly experience, at the end of the day. This is why your true fulfilment is in reconnecting to His heavenly-planned destiny and committing yourself wholeheartedly to the work required to achieve it.

Do we design or discover our destiny?

As Christians, our destiny has two parts, as described earlier. The heavenly-established part and the earthly-created part. We discover the first part and we design and create the second one. We discover the first one through our interactions with

God as facilitated by the knowledge of His Word (the Bible), prayer, revelations, our focus to His Will and our obedience to His commands. We will address the discovery part in the next chapter, but in this chapter, we will focus on the design part of our destiny. Designing our lives as Christians is simply using our spiritual and mental capabilities to shape our lives and craft our future on earth in line with the will of God.

Many people with a religious mindset actually think that we don't create our destiny, we just get one that is set by God and there is nothing we can do about it. They believe that our lives are set and we just need to obey God's commandments, worship Him as He commands us in the scriptures. On the other hand, the influence of new-age and post-modernist philosophies incorrectly leads people to think that we control everything about our lives, future and destiny. Neither of the above two schools of thoughts are in line with the Biblical truth. It is clear from the Bible that God expects us to exercise dominion over nature and this includes using our individual ability to shape our lives on earth. God gave us the capacity to exercise our free will so that we can either choose to be what He wants us to be or choose another path that leads to perdition.

When you read or listen to self-help material that is widely circulated today, there is a phrase that is repeated often which tells people that "they can be whatever they want to be" and their future is totally a matter of their choice. But this is not what the Word of God tells us or what God expects from us. For us Christians, we cannot be whatever we want to be, we need to be what our creator has created us to be, what He pre-destined us to be, because only Him knows truly the reason why He gave us life. God expects us to get the blueprint of our destiny from Him and then build our life based on it. Our destiny is achieved when "our" will to become the best we can be meets God's will for us to grow and become what He has pre-destined us to be. When these two wills collide, that is when we accomplish the mission, just like Jesus did.

Create like God

After we have discovered the blueprint for our earthly destiny, we need to go to the next stage and build the edifice. This is why Christian leaders need to provide clear steps and guidance to help the people of God connect to their destiny and become true agents of a heavenly transformation on earth. It is one thing to know what is one's purpose in life is, but it is another to actually do what needs to be done and do it well enough to turn the vision into a successful life accomplishment in the eyes of God. We know that children learn best in copying what they see from their parents and other influencers around them. In the same way, our design and creative potential is best developed and expressed when we learn from our Father. The scriptures give us the whole account of how God created the world and everything in it, including us. That account is in the book of Genesis and all the secrets of divine creation can be found within it. We can and should use the same principles used by God and create our future accordingly. We cannot create the past because it is gone. The present time (the "NOW") is also always too slippery and always gone too fast. But the future is at our disposal and God has given it to us. The future is all we have, because we can plan for it, we can visualise it, we can mould it and we can change it.

God tells Jeremiah (29:11),

"I know the plans I have for you, plans to prosper you and not to harm you, plans to give you hope and future".

It is clear in this passage that we have a divine future that is enshrined in the plans of our Father. Our job is to pull or download that vision from God and bring it on earth into our life. God plans for our lives are materialised on earth in many ways. He is the one who chose our parents, our place of birth, our DNA and genetic package, our mental infrastructure and other predispositions that we realise who we are. The things that happen to us from birth to early adulthood greatly influence what we become as mature and independent individuals. God works a lot to prepare us for His plans and He plants the seeds for our future with Him. Then from the moment we become mature we get a lot more power and increase our ability to align with His Will to make the choices that will either consolidate all He has placed in us or drive us away from His path, if we let the devil take place in our heart.

Principles of destiny creation

In order for us to design and create our future on earth, we just need to make sure we follow the plans of God and His process for creation. When God created the world, He left his fingerprints all over the place and we just need to capture the essence of His process and the principles that He established and transfer them to our own conscious effort to make things happen in our lives. Nature, as spelt out by God, is the greatest expression of engineering prowess imaginable and the book of Genesis describes how things came to be in detail. God is the greatest engineer of all time and He alone could have engineered the universe in a working order. Our human body gives us a glimpse of His divine abilities. What takes place in a human body to keep it alive and functional as conscious entity is extraordinary. The interaction between chemistry and biology in the human mind is literally mind-boggling.

God's creation model includes many things, but most of the elements are linked to His Word, His hands, and His breath. Let us analyse them in light of the Genesis account of creation of the world.

1 The Word

The story of Creation in the book of Genesis starts with God calling light into existence. Let there be light (Gen 1:3), He said, and there was light. God speaks and His Word brings things into existence. This tell us that in order for us to create anything of value we must refer to the Word of God. Without His Word, God is unknowable to human consciousness because we are unable to penetrate and read His mind. We only know God through His Word, which became flesh and came to live with us to reconnect us to Him. What is the Word of God in your life? What does God say about you, your identity and destiny? The process to create your future on earth starts with the above questions and you must investigate the answers in collaboration with God.

2 The Vision

When God calls light into existence, He has a purpose for it. Light makes it possible for things to be seen, conceived, understood and experienced. The purpose of light is to bring sight or vision, which is a critical element in the functioning of human consciousness. Therefore, in order for God to create "reality", He starts with light. In the same way, our journey to create our earthly destiny must include a vision that we receive from God the Word of God. We get that vision both from the Word as Logos (the scriptures, the letter) and the Word as Rhema (revelation). When God speaks to our spirit and our heart directly we experience His power through that process. Jesus is both the Word of God and the Light of the World (John 8:12). These two things are two sides of the same coin. Adam and Eve's original sin had brought darkness into the world and the arrival of Jesus on earth brings a new light for those who believe in Him. When Jesus enters our lives we literally see a new "reality" that was not accessible to us in the darkness of sin. With clear light, the design and crafting of our earthly destiny becomes easy as the new spiritual light allows us to see who we are, who God is, What He wants for us and how the devil is trying to divert us from our divine path. If you start building your future in the absence of the light of God, you are like a man building a house in darkness, it won't be long before things start crumbling.

3 *The Expression of God*

Throughout all creation, God speaks and things manifest into existence. We can therefore say that God engineered "reality" through His expression. When God speaks it not just the sound of his Word that matters, it is the meaning and power that comes with what He says. A word is supposed to be an expression of someone's intent, purpose and will. God's word in Genesis is His "expression" projected in the form of a pronouncement. The lesson to learn here is that in the same way nature is an expression of God's purpose, our destiny is an expression of our identity, projected on to the world. Crafting our destiny means figuring out how we want our life to matter or what we want to communicate to our generation in the name of God. It must express who we are and leave a legacy. This is why it is important to write your life purpose down and break it down into goals. One good way to do this is to write down your 12 most important life gaols that you want to achieve before you die.

4 The Separation

When God created things in Genesis, He did so in a sequence and after admiring each thing separately, He saw it as "good" for His purpose. He separated the newly created thing with other things. For example, He created light and separated it from darkness. (Gen 1:3-5). That Separation is very important, because the vision of God separates good from evil. In our lives the vision of God separates us from the world and takes us back to our true source and origin. When we decide to engage in our destiny deployment, we enter into a different dimension where we see the light of God, we live by faith (and not by sight), we set our eyes on Him and we focus on His will in us and not the desires of this world. This is why Jesus says

> He had come to separate people against each other.... families will be split, father will be divided with son and son against father, mother against daughter...
>
> (Luke 12: 51-53)

This tells us that our destiny deployment may separate us from our family, from our relatives and other people who we may be connected to, because destiny is deeply personal and profoundly serious. Our destiny also separates from the "evil" camp and put us in the "good" camp. As Christians, we cannot be confused about what is right and wrong and we are constantly aware of where we stand and where God expects us to be.

5 The Name and Identity of things

The Bible says *"And God saw the light was good. Then He separated the light from the darkness. God called the light "day' and the darkness "night"* (Genesis 1:3). There is a pattern that is evident throughout this chapter as God creates things. Regarding the light we can describe the following process: God calls light into existence (1), God sees light as good (2), He separate light from darkness (3) and He Gives it a name and then moves to the next thing to create. Name is linked to the identity of a thing or a person. Through a name we are able to identify or be identified as an individual person. Our identity is connected to name and character. This is also what happens in the spirt: when we receive Christ, He gives us a new identity and from that moment, we become co-creators with Him for a new individual reality. a new personality, a new consciousness, a new life, a new person in us, because the old one is gone. That new person must be seen as "good" and not "evil" in the eyes of God. This is also what God is expecting from us. He wants to see us as "good" creatures that give Him pleasure.

Our destiny deployment is about expressing or projecting "goodness" through our new Christ-centred identity. We do so through everything we think, say and do. We need to express our identity by affirming it clearly and loudly, expressing it powerfully with conviction, as if we were throwing it into the universe, like a genius painter throwing colour onto a canvas to create a masterpiece out of it. Let people think of "good" when they hear your name and let your destiny on earth be linked to an identity that reflect the very nature of Christ who is in you.

Design

Divine engineering

Mankind is a product of God's workmanship. The Bible says that God formed man out of clay. While the Bible does not provide the full details of the process that God used, it gives a clear picture of how God worked with His hands to form or shape man out of clay and then breathed into him to inject life in his newly formed body. This shows the engineering and transformation process that God used in bringing mankind into existence. In the same way, your destiny deployment involves workmanship. It requires an engineering or manufacturing process where you create your new self by using the image you get from God. You must plan for things with purpose. You will be required to use your hands, your mind, your energy and any other resources you have to engineer a new you, create a lifestyle and develop a work culture that will lead you to becoming the best that God wants you to become and achieve your destiny. Whatever you create, you must breathe life into it, like God did.

Breathing life into something (such as a project) means giving everything you have for it. Your breath is the most precious thing you have. It is the very basis and most fundamental aspect of life. If you lose breath, you lose life. Your destiny is as precious as your breath, you must give it all you have. God is the engineer of the cosmos and you are the engineer of your destiny on earth. He has given you the power and ability for the job, but you must ensure that everything you design and create as part of your destiny deployment is from His blueprint. If you pick things "out of blue" rather than out of the divine blueprint or if you just work with your own ideas, rather than God-inspired vision, dreams and desires, you will surely fail to meet God's expectations. You must use the blueprint from God and rely on the power of the Holy Spirit to inspire and support you throughout the whole process.

When one is building a house, he or she needs to know not just the material that is needed for the construction, but the properties of those material and the principles (both chemistry and physics) governing how different material can be put together to help create a bigger, more harmonious and functioning whole. For example, if you are building a house, you need to understand how bricks and mortar can be put together. You also need to understand the chemical laws and principles that are in action when making good mortar. If you make mortar using cement, sand and water and you don't respect the quantity and the correct process for the mixing, you will end up in trouble. In the same way, God expects us to be aware of both the spiritual and natural laws, principles and properties that apply as we mix things together in our consciousness, thoughts, feelings, behaviours and actions. In manufacturing our future here on earth, we must develop heavenly engineering and management qualities rooted in the Word of God. If we do so, we will produce quality outcomes that God expects from us. We must manage our time, our spiritual life, our family and friendship, our learning, training, work and income. Good management in life is crucial, because life is a business.

The engineering work for our earthly destiny must rely on inspiration from God. We cannot be successful in our destiny deployment unless we are inspired by our creator. God doesn't run our lives, we do. He is ready to lead us and inspire us, if we let him do so. God will not lead us until we start moving. We must be willing to move because life is movement. You can't drive an immobilised vehicle or lead a tree and God cannot lead you if you do not want to move forward in life. In this sense we work in partnership with God for our destiny, we do our best and He does the rest.

Many Christians today appear to be so comfortable proclaiming their faith, doing church every week, singing and praising, praying and fasting, but not many are really busy with their destiny work. Faith without action is dead, the Bible says. Action is not just about doing good deeds, it is primarily about the work we do in the name of God. This can be preaching, writing books, online publishing, teaching, charity work, promoting a cause or helping the needy, all in a consistent way and not just once in a while. Faith in God is good, but until we use it to influence and transform ourselves and impact the world, then it is just useless faith. We can worship God with words, songs and praises, but doing His work in our lives (both inside and outside the church) is the best way to worship Him. Seek divine vision in your life and design and craft your future with it and stay focused all the time. You can do this by reflecting on the following steps:

- Understand how God designed and created the world and the process He used to do so, as described in the book of Genesis
- Seek inspiration from God and capture His vision for your own life and let it influence all your life plans
- Mould God's vision in your life into a plan and break it into smaller goals that you can work on progressively. Always remember that your destiny is about work
- Create time and space for God in your life. Pray, study the word and meditate on it
- Identify and refine the gifts that God gave you and use them to impact the world. Don't take your gifts to your grave

- Act your faith and work hard for God. That is all that Jesus did when He was on earth.

One thing that will help you to focus on delivering your destiny on earth is how much desire you have to achieve the will of God in your life. In the following chapter we will discuss how our desires can lead us to discover our God-given destiny on earth and to work with God to design and create the work He expects us to deliver.

CHAPTER THREE

KEYWORD 3

Desire

> **KEY POINTS**
> - Know that God embedded His destiny in the "holy" desires of your heart
> - Search your heart and discover the gems that God has placed in it; they are the bricks for your destiny walls
> - Nurture and develop the destiny desires God placed in your heart
> - Condition yourself for Destiny Living through the management of the holy desires in you

"So, I say, walk by the spirit and you will not gratify the desires of the flesh"

(Galatians 5:16 NIV)

Desire to please God

DESIRE TO PLEASE GOD AND HE WILL GIVE YOU THE DESIRES OF YOUR heart. God works with those who believe in Him, trust in Him and have faith in Him. At the centre of everything we can do with God there are two critical things: will and desire. Our will enables us to decide on things and our desire pushes us into action. If you desire to know God and His destiny in your life, then God will surely reveal Himself and His will in you. This is because for anyone to want to know God and any of His plans, He must first have called the person. God chooses us first before we can choose to believe in Him. God is very happy when we connect to Him and He is even happier when we develop a strong desire to love Him, to trust in Him, to obey Him and focus on our heavenly Destiny on earth. The Bible provides all the information, knowledge and wisdom we need for the purpose of discovering and developing the holy desires in us and achieve our Destiny. In fact, the primary reason for the existence of the scriptures is to provide us with basic leadership and life management tools and concepts from God's perspective. Jesus came to lead us back to God and help us to live a purposeful life centred on the accomplishment of our God-ordained Destiny.

Managing your desires

We all understand that human life is governed by desires. Desire is at the centre of almost all human thoughts and emotions. It seats right in the middle of our consciousness. The pursuit of desires is in many ways what drives human behaviours. Most of our thinking is about processing desires and it can be said that life is really nothing more than a desire management exercise. Leadership is really about helping people to better manage their desires and the steps they need take to achieve them. Imagine your destiny being a building and the desires being the bricks with which you build the edifice. There are many words that we use in everyday language and those we use in leadership and management settings that connect with the concept of desire. For example: vision, purpose, goal, objective, dream, interest, passion, commitment, determination... all these words express some form of desire and this shows the importance of desire in our consciousness, as human beings.

The world is in a mess because many people are no longer able to police their egoistic desires. If most human beings were focused on desires that are connected to fulfilling their lives, helping others, building communities and improving societies in some ways, then the world would be a much better place to live. Just imagine, as an example, what would happen if everyone in the world happily donated 10% of their income to help less privileged people in the society, wouldn't this eliminate poverty? But this will be only possible if people have the desire to genuinely help, as opposed to being forced to hand out a portion of their income through tax or some other compulsory mechanism.

Wisdom is about managing one's desires and attending to the desires of other people living around us. The job of managing desires is made much easier when bad desires are asphyxiated at the source and good desires are given more oxygen in one's mind, nurtured and developed so that they can bear fruits. What we call desire is nothing but a form of energy that is emotionally charged and is manifested through the will in some form, either seeking pleasure or avoiding pain.

Desires don't always come in our mind, many of them actually come from our spirit. Understanding how the desire energy flows within one's consciousness is very important in the journey to achieve our God-given Destiny on earth. Desires are like ideas; but only emotionally charged. They can possess one's mind to the point where one loses control of themselves. There is a spectrum of longings from which desire derives. Often the energy starts in the form of a simple idea and, if it receives enough emotional investment, it develops into a desire and then grows into a dream that gets converted into a project and eventually ends as reality or physical accomplishment. What makes a difference between these various forms of desires is the amount of energy that one invests into them. The greater the investment of energy the greater the chances of seeing that energy crystallise into something palpable and real.

God planted His destiny plans in the desires of our hearts. For us to accomplish that destiny we need to develop those desires sufficiently and bring them into reality. The desires planted by God in us are a divine investment for our own good, but mostly for the benefits of our generation. They are resources which need to be recognised, developed and deployed as part of our great commission on earth. The Godly desires in us are gifts to the world and we need to nurture, package and deliver them to our communities when we are still alive. God plants holy desires into our hearts as assets sent to the world for the sake of His Kingdom. We are mere conduits for His desires to accomplish things on earth and through them God drives us into action, as part of our mission in the grand scheme of the restoration of humanity. It is through our desires that we are led into action, or rather, loaded for action. When we appropriately nurture the divine desires in us, we develop a divine character necessary for discharging our heavenly mission on earth.

The Origin of your desires

How do you know your desires are from God? There is no formula to know whether any particular desire within a man's heart is either from God, from Satan or simply from their own mental activity. However, there are clues that may help. We must always investigate our heart using biblical tools to test their origin. We also need to know ourselves well and understand how we function in our own consciousness. Most people who behave well are those who are often conscious of their own thinking and the desires emanating from it. We also need to read the environment in which we are living and how that environment is trying to condition us through social and cultural settings. Last, but not least, we need to know the realities of spiritual warfare, how the devil and his army of evil spirits and demons are continuously seeking to plant unholy desires in our hearts and derail us from our true Destiny.

Desires are like plants that grow out of our consciousness. Some of them are good for the garden of our mind and others are weeds, but they all come from seeds that were planted in the mind long before they could manifest in some fashion. In its simplest definition, a desire is just an idea with an emotional investment attached to it. You see something or think of something and you want to have it because of the pleasure or benefit you will get from it. The first step in recognising good desires is to simply raise one's level of consciousness and tune it to the God's frequency. Because most people live life on auto pilot, they don't question where ideas and desires in their minds are coming from. We hear God's voice through our desires, ideas and conviction that dominate our mind.

Destiny Living starts with our ability to "pay attention" to what matters in our life and become aware of ourselves, seeing ourselves thinking, acting, behaving and managing our lives. When we engage in Destiny living, we pay attention to who we are, what we want in life, who God is, what God wants in our lives and how we need to conduct ourselves day in and day out to live purposely. The word "attention" is very important in this context. Corporations spend billions of dollars to try to get people to simply pay attention to their products or branding. Sometimes, they even try to steal attention by embedding subliminal messages in their marketing tactics, to try to penetrate directly and sneak inside our subconscious and trigger emotions and get us to focus on or invest in the ideas they are presenting to us, all this without us even being fully conscious of what is happening. This is why the Bible says: *"Guard your heart, for everything you do flows from it..."* (Prov4: 23). In this passage, heart is not the blood pump in our chest, but our subconscious mind which sustains our consciousness and awareness of things, as well as the desires that can flow from it. When attention is invested in self-reflection, we see ourselves beyond ourselves, we look at ourselves from outside of ourselves and in the process, we connect to a higher realm of reality, a different level of our consciousness and identity.

Desires and Subconscious programming

There is no doubt that many of our desires come from our subconscious programming. The Bible doesn't use the word consciousness and any of its derivatives, because the word was not yet invented when the scriptures were written. In the Bible, the word that is often used to refer to what we now know as consciousness (especially, the subconscious) is the word "heart". The subconscious mind is essentially the workshop of our mind and the communication centre that connects our deeper self with the spiritual self. It also connects the "self" within us with the greater spiritual realm, which is a much bigger reality than we can possibly conceive. It is crucial to understand the working of our subconscious for to be able to better police and manage our desires in life.

God placed inside of us everything we need and all the tools to ensure that we don't have to struggle a lot to find out what He created us for. He provided us with all the equipment and the material we need to create our "personal/individual reality" that will enable us to function as individuated entities. Our desires are a great part of that personal reality. God "programmed" us with everything we need in order to accomplish our destiny. Many of us know that we all have deep desires that have started and stayed with us from a very young age. Such desires never really leave us, and we have to work very hard to ignore and suppress them. Using a computer analogy, when we are born-again (spiritually), we literally receive a new "matrix" or "motherboard" that runs a new "desire program" within us. When that program is activated, we get a new set of longings, a new awareness of ourselves, a new understanding of the world, new insights in life and a better understanding of who God is. All those things also come with a new energy within us. That new energy permeates all activities in our subconscious mind. It impacts on our consciousness and drive us towards the things that we either love and enjoy or things that we feel we have to do for God's sake, whether they are enjoyable or not, because they are part of our mission here on earth. If that energy is harnessed appropriately, it leads us to a superconscious level where we see our lives from a higher position. We get a new perspective where the ego within us is tamed and strives to embrace the plan of God, leading us to focus on the people and things of God. We yearn to serve God by serving His purpose and His people. The new divine new energy in us is lived or experienced through repeated and consistent desires to "matter", for God, to serve Him, to use our life for His purpose, to add value to humanity and expand His Kingdom on earth.

A new matrix for destiny living

Destiny living is about living a life fully focused on delivering God's destiny in one's life. It starts with knowing that you have a destiny and finding out what it is. When you ask God to tell you what your destiny is, He answers back with questions such as: what do you desire to do with your life? What "cause" do you desire to embrace as a lifelong commitment? What problem affecting humanity that you would like to help with? What legacy would you like to live for your generation? The answers to all such questions are not hard, because they are packed in your desires. All you need to do is put a plan together and submit it to God for guidance and get to work by deploying all your resources and assets (spiritual, intellectual, physical, material and financial) for the cause. This is why with God we all need to focus on "deployment" instead of "employment". The employment system in the world may be a good way to give people income, but it is a terrible system that is killing people spiritually and destroying their God-given destiny. (We shall address this issue in our latter chapters). Only when a new matrix for Destiny is Living is activated that we can focus on deployment and abandon the employment model of life.

The deployment of one's destiny is a very serious business. It is a business of a lifetime that for some people may start quite early and for others it may happen much later in life. It is something that is not always clear and straightforward except for a tiny minority of people who have been given a special grace from God to see a clear vision of their lives from a young age. Jesus himself, as a man (and not as God) is a good example. He knew what He was on earth for from quite a young age. He was going to the temple and teaching the scriptures with authority at the age of 12. Even though He started the active part of His ministry at age 30, He knew what His mission was and nothing could distract Him from that.

Some people are born to bring value to the world and they can do so even at a much younger age. They don't have to wait until they reach mature age or grow old. At the other end of the spectrum you have people like Apostle Paul who was almost forced into his destiny through a dramatic event and he never went back to his old life persecuting and killing Christians in the name of his religious beliefs, as a Pharisee.

In the midst of these two ends, we have the majority of human beings who take years and have to do a whole lot of things before eventually finding out what their true Destiny Mission is and committing to it. Often this is because people are born into communities and societies where they get "formatted or conditioned", based on their "cultural templates" and these templates take over their thinking process and their spiritual focus (if they have any). Even where someone may have accepted Jesus as Lord and Saviour, they fail to focus on their destiny and continue to live, knowingly or unknowingly, in the employment model of the world rather than the deployment one.

Focus on Destiny

All human beings start life with what we would like to refer to as a "General Life Template" (GLT), from which they build their identity or their "Personal Life Template" (PLT). The GLT is culturally specific and varies from country to country or even from one area to another. In the West the GLT reads as this: go to school to learn, graduate if you can, get a job, get married, buy a house or two, have children, retire and die. The societal and cultural pressure that is associated with this model of life is often so strong that not many of us can really escape from it. We are programmed from our very young age to accept this GLT as the normal course of life. It is how life is meant to be lived, so to speak. This model of the world is very materialistic and mundane and does not necessarily suit the needs of true followers of Christ, from a spiritual position. The influence of this GLT is such that sometimes opportunities will be knocking at our doors, calling us for higher purposes, but we will not recognise them because our focus is elsewhere and we will fail to embrace these opportunities because we are operating out of a particular mindset or paradigm that is not properly tuned to recognise spiritual callings and realities.

In the same way, a person may lead a criminal lifestyle for decades until when they meet Jesus and literally overnight their PLT or "Desire Template" is deeply altered through a simple prayer they are led to say by a pastor or an evangelist to accept Jesus in their lives. When Jesus enters that person's heart, they experience something in their consciousness that cannot be explained fully in human terms, because it is a deep spiritual experience. Through that process, all the criminal desires that have dominated the life of that person may be gone in a split second and all of a sudden, they develop a strong urge to testify of the goodness of Jesus, to praise and worship Him and celebrate how He has changed their life. Many Christians can connect with this, at least those who are born again and have been impacted by the Holy Spirit. There are cultural Christians who practice their Christian faith simply because they grew up in or have lived a long time within a Christian environment. Such people are conditioned to be Christians.

In contrast, being born again is a paradigm shift, a deep spiritual change that reconfigures our cognitive framework and removes egoism, rebellion and pride from our heart. It removes the feeling of emptiness and uselessness and reinstalls an understanding of one's place in the universe and the need to recognise and worship God, to speak of His love, His power and glory, as well as an urge to obey His commands and serve Him.

Holy desires and being born again

Jesus said that one has to be born again to see the Kingdom of God. It is the new birth that will generate the right desires within the person to know and serve God and achieve His destiny. The re-birth process replaces the sinful template that we have inherited from the original parents with a new PLT that is focused on Jesus and His will in our lives. Being born again is like undergoing a "spiritual surgical operation" where something is removed from within us and another brand-new apparatus is implanted. As a result, we shift our "spiritual genetics" from Adam's genetic code (original sin) to Jesus' DNA, which connects us to a new blood line. We become part of a new heavenly pedigree, which is actually our true spiritual nature. That new nature influences our spiritual, emotional and intellectual programming and, in the end, it affects our desires and behaviours.

Focus on Destiny

As described in earlier chapters, our destiny has two parts. The discovery and the creation parts. Both of these two aspects of our destiny are dependent on us being able to reconnect with godly desires. The discovery is done through prayer, revelations, ideas, dreams and vision(s) from God. It is through these things that we reconnect with God and through that reconnection, a new "spiritual software" is downloaded in us that enables us to know and understand our PHD and feel committed to it. We discover our God-given destiny through the Word of God, both from the Logos and the Rhema, the letter and the spirit of the Word of God.

God creates through His Word and He created us spiritually using the word, before we were given the opportunity to become flesh in the physical world. In the same way, the second part of our Destiny, the creation part, must be founded and centred on the Word of God and guided by the desires that manifest in our hearts when we focus on serving Him. When that Word is revealed to us, it gradually or suddenly, depending on the case, gives us more clarity on what we are called to do with the gift of life that we have. It gives us a vision of the foundation upon which our lives need to be built. When the vision is clear, action follows, day in and day out, to fulfil it.

As the author of this book, I have been led by God to talk to my generation about the need to focus on our destiny. This vision gives me the desires to write and publish a series of books, videos and other material to contribute and help equip the people of God. If I just have the vison and no desire to do anything to make it happen, it would be like someone knowing how to read and not doing any reading at all, which will make that person the same as being illiterate. When I look back into my life, I have always wanted to teach, educate and inform people and help them to learn. I haven't always seen the spiritual aspect of that desire, which became very clear to me only recently.

Life circumstances have distracted me for a long time, stealing my focus and pulling me into the world system where employment and career objectives have dominated my mind. I have also fallen victim, like many others, of the GLT that is prevalent both in my native Congo and in Australia, which has driven me to want to own a house, drive a good car and accumulate various gadgets. This has shifted my priorities and hindered my capacity to focus on my God-given mission on earth. Thanks to the grace of God I have awakened from the slumber and decided to disconnect from the "employment model of the world" and plug myself into the "deployment model". Three years before I started writing this book I quit my 9 to 5 job to do my destiny work. I did so after taking time to prepare for the change and ensure that I could still provide for my family, as a father and husband. Part of the plan was also to start a business so that I be able to manage my time better and manage my priorities as I see fit, despite the challenges that come with running a small business successfully. All this change in my life has come from the desire for me to serve God.

Desire filtration

As you read these lines, know that your destiny's blueprint is stored deep down into your desires. You need to do a bit of digging to access them. They are like diamond, gold, and other precious metals, you don't often find them on the surface. Every human being has a mine inside of their heart and if they take time to dig, they will surely find some wonderful and precious gems waiting to be discovered and developed. However, in order to best develop our godly desires, we need to study and understand how the energy of desires works in and through our consciousness. One thing that most people don't know is that most of the desires of human beings are actually from a spiritual source. The core nature of every individual's desire template is fundamentally spiritual. If you have ever wondered where do your desires come from, the answer is: mostly your spirit. The other sources for your desires include environmental stimuli, memory and projections in the future. Both God and the devil have access to our mind and our heart. This means if you are not careful enough, your desires may be coming from a satanic source and this can happen in more ways than one.

Throughout the years, I have personally been trying to investigate the source of my own ideas and desires. Many times, I realise that I am thinking of something that is quite strange and I starting wondering where the strange idea came from. When this realisation happens, I try to trace the idea back, to get an understanding of where it came from. A lot of times I am able to successfully identify the source of some of my ideas. For example, I could watch a photo that causes me to think of another person and then from that person my mind wanders off to the last location where I met that person and once I am back to that place (such as my high school), I start re-living some experiences that marked my time there and then I feel the emotion in my present time, which brings me back to my present awareness. In such a scenario, I am often able to go back step by step where the idea came from. However, in many other circumstances, no matter how hard I try to retrace the idea, I find myself unable to identify its source. Quite often I am convinced that some of the ideas and desires that penetrate my mind have just "dropped" into my consciousness from some unidentified source. It also happens quite often just before prayer or in the middle of a prayer that a strange and disgusting idea or image penetrates my mind from nowhere. I have a strong conviction that a big chunk of those ideas and desires are from satanic sources.

The effort in monitoring my ideas and desires has helped me considerably in guarding my consciousness, increase my attention to divine thoughts, as well as monitoring and policing bad desires that drop into me, but which are not from me. The spiritual origin of many of our desires and behaviours is what may explain why two children can grow up in the same family and be exposed to the same parental influences, educational experiences and environmental factors, but one develops into a serial killer and the other into a humanitarian. This is because the spirits of these two individuals ultimately determine the direction of their lives, regardless of their upbringing experiences. Science cannot fully explain the human mind because scientists cannot isolate and test our mind in a lab. We can all sit for tests or be examined by different machines that may reveal some aspects of how our mind works, but the totality of our mind is inaccessible to any scientific enquiry. All that science can do is to study our working brain, observe its activities in particular circumstances and with different types of stimuli.

I recently watched a crime investigation show on television where a 12-year-old boy killed both his parents in the US. The boy had never been exposed to any violence and lived in an affluent suburb of a large US city with his Christian parents and many of his siblings. When the Sherriff interviewed the young boy and he confessed to the murder, you could tell from the young boy's facial expression and the way he was talking about the whole thing and see the "devilish" nature of his spirit. During the show, the Sherriff mentioned that he had more than 30 years of police experience and had never come across someone like that boy, directly or indirectly. There was no doubt in my mind, when watching that documentary that the boy's mind was not just possessed but practically colonised by evil spirits. In such circumstances, it is understandable why science would not recognise this type of phenomenon as having a spiritual origin. Science simply has no adequate tools to do so, besides being limited in its analytical and methodological frameworks.

Refining desires

The Bible invites us to exercise discernment when exposed to ideas, concepts and teachings from various sources. This is important because these things influence our desires and behaviours. We must also discern our own ideas and desires that are generated from within our mind and heart. It is also important to differentiate between God's desires for us, our own desires and the devil's desires within us. The Bible tells us to submit all thoughts to Christ.

> 'We demolish arguments and every pretension that sets itself up against the knowledge of God and we take captive every thought to make it obedient to Christ"
>
> 2 Corinthians, 10-15.

The key message in this passage is about "taking captive every thought to make it obedient to Christ". This means we need to have a personal 'vetting system' where every lingering idea in our mind is checked to ensure it is right and spiritually healthy, otherwise it deserves no 'real estate" in our mind. Destiny living requires that all of our ideas are aligned with the Word of God and His vision and mission for our life. Any idea/desire/thought that is found to be contrary to the word of God must be either dismissed, washed away or reframed to be made obedient to Jesus.

We know that a desire is from God when it aligns with the scriptures and is linked to love and service to others. Such a desire will often point or lead to the achievement of higher goals that not only benefit us, but also add value to other people's lives. A desire or idea is from the devil when it is contrary to the Will and Word of God, and is centred in some egoistic objectives to satisfy us in ways that could ultimately separate us from God. The exercise to monitor and manage ideas, desires and energy with us is what we will refer to later in this book as *Spiritual Hygiene* and we will describe this in more detail in later chapters.

Desires, Prayer & Destiny

Prayer and meditation are very crucial in helping us to connect to and develop our Destiny desires. The reason why we are told in the Bible to pray ceaselessly is not because God wants us to rehearse or recite our Lord's prayer or any prayer a dozen times every day. God wants us to pray because that is the process through which we interact with Him and allow Him to lead us. Through prayer we submit our thoughts, desires, doubts and uncertainties to God and in the same process we enable Him to direct us accordingly. God is our source and our leader. He wants to lead us and He desires to guide us to reach our destiny. He is like our spiritual "mission control" and expects us to be constantly in touch with Him, in the same way a space ship needs to remain in constant contact with its Mission Control centre in order to fulfil its purposes. That constant contact is important for the ship to receive instructions on the direction, speed of the travel and other tasks to undertake as part of its broader mission into space. If a spaceship loses connection with its Mission Control permanently, it becomes useless. It is the same with us, because we are space travellers too, moving on planet earth while the planet moves through space.

The desire to pray is part of the signs of a new-born Christian, because there is a natural friction that occurs between the new spirit and the old one. It is not possible to be a good Christian and build a relationship with God without prayer. If you are not praying at least once or twice a day, there is something wrong with your spiritual life, especially if you are accumulating weeks with no prayer. Prayer is to the spirit what sleeps is to the mind (brain). Sleeps helps the brain to reprogram itself, which is essential for its normal functioning. If you spend several days without sleeping you will be creating a problem for your brain and your whole body will eventually be affected. In the same way, if you spend several days without praying, you will be preventing your spirit from having sufficient opportunities to reprogram itself and function properly. Prayer is the greatest source of spiritual strength, spiritual clarity and divine vision and motivation. Prayer fuels motivation and we all need motivation to keep driving towards our destiny. The greatest type of human motivation is spiritual motivation, which is made possible only through prayer and meditation, repeated many times over.

Prayer & Subconscious Programming

There is a dimension of prayer that is not talked about often enough within Christian congregations. That dimension is about the programming of our mind. We talk about the renewal of our mind, but we do not always discuss the process that can help us to renew our mind. Mind programming is the necessary process through which we clarify and re-affirm our beliefs, re-arrange our thoughts, recite our convictions and recalibrate our intentions. Prayer is such a powerful tool to help us to engrave our godly desires into our subconscious, where our mind connects with our spirit. When this is done properly, our mind re-aligns with our spiritual focus and we are re-energised for action that help us make progress towards our destiny.

Through technology human beings are able to create robots. We know that a robot wouldn't be able to function without its programming working correctly. Anything that malfunctions at the programming level will affect the way the device operates externally. In the same way, even if we are not robots in the eyes of God, (we have consciousness), but we do have a dual "cognitive and spiritual programming", which need to be maintained and updated constantly so that we can function properly. It is through the programming of our mind that we are able to learn, to acquire a culture and build a model of the world within our consciousness to help steer our lives. When we understand this, we need to proactively utilise prayer as one of the best tools under our disposal to program ourselves for divine success. Prayer is the only thing that, besides connecting us to God, it reprograms and updates us constantly to stay in touch with our creator's will and purpose.

We know from Science that more than 90% of the decisions

human beings make every day come from their subconscious mind. The same subconscious mind also runs all of our body's functions without us even being aware of it. What happens in our subconscious determines what thoughts, feelings, desires and actions we can produce outwardly, most of the time. If we program our subconscious correctly, it ultimately generates the right signals to shape and direct our awareness, focus and feelings to the right direction. Destiny Living requires that we build the right mindset from which we can expect to get the right type of desires and motivation to achieve our life goals.

Pray is not just a spiritual activity. It starts as a cognitive exercise before evolving into a spiritual reality. There is so much power in prayer, not just because it gives God a licence to intervene in our lives, but it also gives us personal power and drives us into action, from a cognitive level. For example, many people wonder why there are so many Islamic fundamentalists around the world who are not afraid to blow themselves up in the name of their religion. One important factor, amongst many others, that could explain such behaviours comes from the Islamic prayer regime, which requires believers to pray 5 times a day. Such a stringent prayer regime may be a significant contributor for to the behaviours we see displayed by some fundamentalists. It takes a lot of boldness to end one's life, but the discipline of faith linked to the power of prayer are two potent factors that can easily lead one to commit such acts, especially where there is a perception of injustice from an "ungodly" persecutor. Although there is no justification in any faith to kill innocent people in the name of God, those who cross that line are often encouraged by a strong desire, which is often nurtured through constant prayer, to defend their faith and seek justice in the name of God.

Unlike Islam, Christianity imposes no strict regime for daily prayers, even though the Bible says that we should pray ceaselessly. However, Christian groups with a strong prayer focus tend to be more fundamentalist in their beliefs and actions. They tend to be more active and radical in their faith than other congregations who don't have a strong prayer focus. The greater the prayer focus the more radical inclination there is. This is an indication that those faith groups that encourage more prayer by their members tend to produce a membership with more developed and refined desires to demonstrate commitment and loyalty to what they conceive as divine cause or divine mandate to do things, even though some of those things may be morally questionable.

There is no doubt that prayer releases an elevated form of energy within us as it enables us to examine and monitor ourselves in the name of God. When you pray, you are kind of breaking yourself into two parts, one part of you talking to God and the other watching and shaping what you say and pushing you to display your best behaviour before God. Because of this you not only control what you say, but you focus on the best things you can say and do to please God. You present your best intentions and desires to God for His approval and blessings and the repetition of these things end up driving you into maintaining the right behaviours. People who pray often for the right motives and with a holy fear of God end up developing a kind of "self-management program" inside their consciousness where the spirit is more in control than the carnal mind. As a result, they are shaped or formatted to think and behave their best and in line with their spiritual identity. They true become children of God and have predominantly godly desires that continuously drive them to think and behave righteously. They may still think of unholy things from time to time (because the flesh in them), but such ideas are often quickly starved of "spiritual oxygen" due to the presence and help of the holy spirit in their consciousness.

Last, but not least, prayer also works as an anti-virus program, shielding us against the many ambient spiritual viruses that are present everywhere and which could compromise our spiritual and cognitive integrity. We catch spiritual viruses everywhere we go, in the same way the body catches biological viruses from all types of environments. Spiritual viruses enter our spiritual system as 'small desires" and if they find a suitable environment within us, they grow and eventually bring spiritual sickness in us, hence disconnecting us from God and from our destiny. But if our mind is adequately programmed we grow the divine desires in us that help us to move forward with our destiny.

CHAPTER FOUR

Keyword 4

Discover

> **KEY POINTS**
> - You have a heavenly-established Destiny, seek it and you shall discover it
> - Discover yourself in the mirror of divine scriptures and divine revelations
> - Discover the real you by tuning yourself to God's divine frequencies
> - Discover the spiritual and natural laws that govern your life and your destiny.

The Three Dimensions of Destiny

THERE ARE A LOT OF DEFINITIONS OF THE WORD DESTINY. ONE WAY to define it is simply to think of it as "the combination of what happened to bring you into existence, what happens to you from the moment you are born, what you make happen in your life, as well as what you fail to make happen throughout your earthly existence", all put together. There is a strong connection between the word destiny and the verb "to happen". There are a lot of things that happen to us in life starting from birth till death.

Some of those things we control and others we don't. The most interesting thing is that we don't control the beginning of our life (birth) nor do we control the end of it (death). But we do have a lot of control over what we make happen between the cradle and coffin. We also have a lot of control over what we do because of what happens to us. So, one of the most important question in thinking about destiny is simply: "What do you want to make happen in your life, as part of the ultimate expression of your identity and your desired legacy on earth? This whole book has been written to help you respond to this very important question in your own life.

To help answer the above question, let us assume that Destiny has three dimensions that we propose to call: Fate, Escape and Shape.

1 *Fate*

Fate is about the things that happen to us and that we don't have any control over. For example, every one of us is born from parents that they don't get to choose. We also don't choose which country we are born in and what a genetic package (genes) we are born with. These things frame our consciousness and impact our existence significantly. When we realise that we actually exist as individuals, we are already loaded with stuff that we cannot fully remove or alter from our consciousness. We find out that we are already shaped in ways that we cannot completely undo. It is fate that determines whether we are born male or female, short or tall, black or white or yellow. It is also fate that gives us the type of consciousness we have, which significantly affect the way we think, feel, speak and behave as human beings, even if we can partially alter or reprogram our consciousness, to some degrees.

2 Shape

The second dimension of Destiny is the "Shape part", which is about what we consciously do, the actions we take in life, including both what we do right and what we do wrong, which end up shaping our lives in various ways. As human beings, we are born with spiritual, mental and physical faculties that give us the ability not just to be aware of our existence and identity, but to think, decide, act and make choices in life. These things ultimately lead us to an outcome that is a direct consequence of the thoughts, decisions, choices we have made throughout our life journey. So, we shape our lives through the things we make happen or create, directly or indirectly, consciously or unconsciously. We also shape our lives in the way we respond to events and circumstances, challenges and opportunities in our lives. David decided to fight Goliath and doing so shaped the rest of his life.

3 Escape

The third dimension of Destiny is the "Escape part". It includes the things that escape our consciousness simply because we are unable to comprehend them due to lack of maturity. Life is a very complex thing and there is a lot in it that the whole human race is yet unable to grasp. Such things still affect our lives despite us not being able to understand them or do anything to change them. It is a bit like what happens to a new-born baby who is totally at the mercy of what happens in its environment and can't do much to change things.

The Escape dimension is also about the things we fail to make happen, either due to ignorance, negligence, incompetence, lack of motivation or simply not being able to realise that we must do those things in our lives. There are many things that escape our consciousness simply because we are not focused enough. Most people on earth live life on "automatic pilot". Because of this, they end up living a miserable life as they are not active enough to make things happen. In Biblical language the terms spiritual death, spiritual slumber or spiritual blindness can be more appropriate. When people are spiritually dead, blind, or asleep, it is like they live in a parallel world with a different reality and they are completely oblivious to a whole host of things that can significantly change their lives in a positive way, as intended by the Creator. Moses witnessed injustice being committed on an Israelite and he did not let that incident escape his consciousness. He acted and sought to stop the Egyptian slave master who was smiting a Hebrew and from that incident, he ended up encountering God and being given the mission to lead Israelites out of Egypt. So many of us let important things escape our attention and focus. The accumulation of negligence, ignorance, inattention or laziness, all that affect our destiny on earth badly.

These three dimensions of Destiny enable us to conceptualise life and frame Destiny Living in ways that give us a clear picture of what goes into the mechanics of accomplishing our God-given Destiny on earth. Destiny is like a big machine that runs partly on its own program and that is also partly controlled by us. The part that we cannot control, we simply need to discover how it works, in order to get a better understanding of the machine and then use that knowledge to improve our performance on the part that we have control over.

Discover Yourself

The majority of people on earth, believers and non-believers alike, live their lives and die without ever realising their true identity, their real potential and their specific mission in life. Some spend a lifetime focusing on the wrong things that are not connected to what God gave them life for. Others may have some idea of what their chief life purpose is, but they get distracted by many things that divert them away from the path that God has set for them. For us Christians, nothing is more important than discovering our true identity in Christ. After receiving Jesus as Lord and Saviour, the next big thing in Christian life is about getting a clear vision from our Lord about who we truly are and what we are here on earth for.

Unfortunately, a lot of time is wasted inside our churches where religious considerations divert us from destiny living. These days, so many congregations spend so much time, efforts and resources into building mega churches and they forget about building people. They entertain believers spiritually and make them feel happy about themselves, instead of telling them the naked truth of the Gospel and the narrow way to self-affirmation and destiny deployment on behalf of God.

The Gospel is ultimately about connecting us to our true Destiny, on earth and in the eternal realm. Here on earth, the only way for us to discover our destiny is to connect with God and open our heart to allow Him to reconnect us with everything He deposited in us (all the holy desires, gifts, skills and talents). The desires in us will always be linked to the things that we see, which stir our hearts in one way or another. They are meant to drive us into action, based on our area of gifting. Many people see things that need to be addressed, but they ignore the voice of God in their heart that is calling them for action. If David did not step into action to fight a giant for his God and his people, he probably would have missed his destiny. The same also applies to Moses. Although these two biblical heroes were people chosen by God, the anointing of God alone was not enough for their life stories to have ended up the way we know. Their actions and their obedience of God's commands contributed hugely to the accomplishment of their earthly destiny.

As a matter of fact, most heroes in our societies are those who act, more from the standpoint of not accepting something (such as injustice), rather than promoting something, such as capitalism. Martin Luther King Junior became famous and changed both his own destiny and the destiny of American people in general and African-American in particular, because he wanted to take a stand against injustice in the form of racial discrimination.

Anytime an issue of morality, justice, integrity or charity keeps touching your heart, that could be a signal that you are probably equipped by God to help address such things and make a difference in that area. If you take no action, you could fail your Destiny. If you do, you may discover your true identity in the process and even end up becoming a hero, even though being a hero is not and should not be the primary motivation for Destiny Living. Investing time in prayer, meditation and the study of the scriptures helps to discover the way many ordinary people discovered themselves and were able to focus on the silent voice of God in their hearts, something that we should all do. But these things should not be done as religious obligations or rituals, they should be seen as tools that ultimately help us to the discovery, develop and delivery of our destiny.

Discover

Destiny as self-affirmation and self-negation

The part of our Destiny that is set by God in Heaven, which we must all invest time and effort to discover, is only the beginning. The rest of the job is much harder and requires a lot of sacrifice. Anything we do or build with God requires sacrifice. We must use the heavenly blueprint, as well as our physical resources (brain, sweat and blood) to work for a divine transformation of the world and the expansion of God's Kingdom on earth. That part of our Destiny, which requires us to create and build things, is about self-manifestation. It is a statement of self, an expression of identity, a value adding exercise born out of a conscious effort and commitment to reflect the divine nature of our identity and leave a legacy on earth, just like Jesus did. It requires making choices, hard choices quite often, in the name of who we are and who our Heavenly Father is.

Self-manifestation is also defined by the things we choose not to do, in additions to actions we choose to take. Every choice we make has an element of non-choice embedded into it. If you chose to go someplace, you are also choosing, at the same time, not to stay at the location where you are, when you make that choice. Our destiny therefore has both an affirmative and a negative aspect, it includes the "Yeses" and the "Nos" we say to things, as well as people and circumstances. The story of Joseph in the Bible is quite useful in this regard (Genesis chapter 39 to 41). Joseph said no to Potiphar's wife's seduction and invitation for adulterous sex. That no was a mighty "NO" that ultimately defined Joseph's destiny. Had he said Yes to the invitation, he probably would have ended dead prematurely without realising his destiny. The general he was working for would probably have killed him. He would not have met the fellow prisoner (Pharaoh's cup bearer) who introduced him to Pharaoh. This is a potent example how a "No" can take us to our destiny, even if it comes with pain, problems and prison attached to it, as it did in the case of Joseph. It was a mighty "No" for Joseph, one that brought trouble to his life temporarily as he ended up in prison unjustly, but in the perfect plans of God, the prison was a stepping stone for access to the Pharaoh's court, and ultimately his leadership position as the prime minister of the country.

Every true disciple of Christ must be prepared to the 3Ps: Problems, Pain and Prison. We must be prepared to say No to the world and some of our Nos will bring the 3Ps. Jesus experienced this situation too and so did Paul and most of the disciples during their earthly existence. God expects us to discover our 'heavenly-established Destiny' and then use the vision we get from it to create our earthly Destiny. In other words, we are expected to connect the supernatural to the natural.

Our heavenly-established Destiny is ordained by God in the spiritual world, long before we are born on planet Earth. When God said to Jeremiah that He knew him before he was in the womb of his mother and He set him apart as a prophet of the nations (Jeremiah 1:5). The Jeremiah that God knew before he was formed in his mother's womb is the "supernatural Jeremiah" whose destiny was established before the prophet Jeremiah was born on earth. The supernatural Jeremiah had a supernatural or heavenly destiny that the earthly Jeremiah could not fully change. Our supernatural destiny can only be discovered and not created. This is because we come on earth spiritually blind and only the Word of God brings the true light of His truth into our spirit to enable our mind to capture the true image of what God wants us to be. Once this is done (the discovery part), then we need to start the process of self-manifestation (the design part), which is about developing and projecting that identity outwardly, onto the world. We design our destiny through what we capture from God and the way we think, the action we take, the behaviours we display and the level of focus maintain in living purposefully.

Jesus knew His heavenly-established Destiny as the Messiah and Saviour of humanity. He took time to prepare for this and spent 30 years to get ready and then He gradually launched himself in self-manifestation to get His work done and save humanity. In creating our earthly destiny, we are expected to believe in God, understand His vision for us, do His work and proclaim His glory. Faith, action (work) and proclamation (articulation of our faith and values), all framed in delivering our God mission on earth, these are the things we need to focus on and it is all about how we conduct our lives. Christians cannot go with the flow of life. God expects us to invest time to discover and understand our chief life purpose. He also wants us to develop spiritual "agency", and act as agents for his transformation agenda. Spiritual agency is the capacity of individuals to be aware of and deeply understand their spiritual identity and its inherent value and capacity to make choices that lead to self-manifestation and destiny deployment. Spiritual agency ultimately improves our ability to manage our lives to meet God's expectations on earth. We must take our lives in a chosen direction according to the desires implanted by God in our hearts. We must grow our capacity for self-leadership under divine inspiration and be able to develop an unrelenting determination to accomplish God's will and purpose for our lives.

Focus on Destiny

Discovering Your Destiny

Dr Myles Munroe once said: "Your destiny is established in heaven, but it is not guaranteed on Earth". God's plan for our lives may not materialise on earth unless we fully play our part in making it happen. Here below, we are the CEO of our own destiny, even though the owner of the business (of our life) is God Almighty. He wants us do things according to His purpose and plan, but He expects us to be on the driving seat of our own lives. God willingly transferred His authority on earth to enable us to run this business with a high degree of freedom and discretion. As a consequence of this, He does not intervene in how we run the affairs of our lives on earth unless and until we let Him do so. Because He owns the business, He frequently knocks at the door of our hearts, seeking access to check how things are going and help us improve our management performance. But, ultimately, God is a gentleman and He generally would not break into our hearts, we have to let Him in and invite Him to lead us. If we do not open our hearts, prepare our mind and connect our spirit to Him, He will not intervene. He may keep trying to get remind us to give him access from time to time, for our own sake, but, in the end, if we persist in rejecting Him we lose the benefits of His leadership and become unfaithful and useless CEOs.

Here are key steps to hep discover your destiny.

1 *Understand your fate*

As described above, there is an element of fate in our earthly Destiny, which means there are things that we cannot control or change in our life. We must have the wisdom to know what these are and accept them. When something has happened or happens to us, which is outside of our control we must not dwell on it, but understand that *"all things work together for good to those who love God, to those who are called according to his purpose"* (Romans 8: 28). This no need to complain to God why we are short, tall, black, white or why we have the parents that we have or anything of that type. There is purpose and meaning for everything in our life that we cannot change and there is also purpose and meaning for "bad" things that happen to us and for which we see no direct responsibility. Joseph is a good example. He was sold by his brothers for no fault of his own. He also stood for what was right (not sleeping with his Master's wife), but he ended up in prison. He could have lamented and cursed God, for all those things. Just imagine him a few minutes in the prison cell crying: God why do I deserve being in prison for doing the right thing?

At any time in your life when you realise that you have to change your destiny, forget about everything that has happened to you in the past and why you are where you are with your life. Just trust that you are still part of God's plan and as long as you live in righteousness, trust that God will take you to your destiny. Joseph's destiny meant he needed to go to prison. That was part of God's plan for him to become a prime minister of Egypt.

Many servants of God throughout history were wounded, tortured, murdered because of their work for God. You need to remain faithful and hopeful, even in the face of great suffering that you may endure. Suffering and pain may give other people reasons to lose their faith in God, but for true disciples of Christ who are focused on their Destiny, these things are part of the "Destiny Equation", which include good and bad things, as well as many unknown factors. Some of the bad things that happen to us without us doing anything to attract them may be part of the training package that God puts us under to strengthen us for what is to come. All those things cannot be avoided and they have meaning and purpose in the grand scheme of things set by God. The example of Job in the Bible is also quite relevant here. A lot of bad things happen to him without him doing anything wrong, but as we know, his story ended very well with God.

2. Investing In Your Destiny

There is a universal formula for the manifestation of anything. That formula is the one we highlighted at the beginning of this book. Time + Space= Matter. If you invest time for your destiny and create space in your heart, spirit and mind for it, your destiny will matter or materialise. Your heavenly destiny is established by God. You need to download it onto your consciousness. This requires that you spend time and focus on interacting with God and knowing His plans. God's scriptures (the Bible) and your heart are the two main tools you use in this process. Through the scriptures, we are able to communicate with God and receive a vision that clarifies the reasons He created us as a species and are His plans for the whole of the human family. Then in your heart God will clarify His specific vision for you and the plans that come with it.

Imagine you want to watch a movie on your smart TV or your laptop. What will you need to make this happen? First, you need to download, install and activate a program that will allow you to download the video file that contains the movie. Even though there are hundreds of thousands of films that are available on the net, you will not be able to watch any of them unless you have the right program on your laptop or smart TV. In the same way, the program or software you need to install in you to enable you to download your "destiny file" from God is called faith. You need faith to interact with God and communicate in meaningful ways with Him. This is why without faith you cannot communicate with God. Besides, given that destiny is a lifetime matter, you will need to spend a great deal of time with God, because your "destiny file" is quite a heavy one with a lot of data and the downloading process often takes time. As long as your faith program is not compromised, the processing power will gradually improve and downloading will become faster in the process. The stronger the connection between you and God, the faster the downloading. You must ensure there is ongoing spiritual energy that powers the connection between you and God, in order for the downloading to be sustained long enough for the file to be fully downloaded. Sometimes things can take years, other times you can get a crystal-clear image of your destiny from God within days, minutes or even seconds. The energy that maintain the connection between you and God the father is the Holy Spirit, but the key or the link that gives you access to the file is Jesus. In the end, it comes down to three main things that we need to do to discover our supernatural destiny blueprint: 1- spend time with God (prayer, mediation) 2. create space for God's will and purpose in your heart 3. Study His Word (the scriptures).

3. Biblical and Scientific Tools For Self-discovery

There are many useful tools to help us engage with God and discover our Heavenly Destiny. These tools include, but are not limited to:

- Thoughts: self-examination, you are what you think
- Prayer: what do you pray about most of the time? Staying in touch with God,

- Dreams or visions: What you dream about and the vision(s) you get from God
- Meditation: be quiet and know that He is God.
- Bible study: knowing God's will through the scriptures
- Prophecies: What men of God tells you about your value in the eyes of God
- Revelations: insights, vision and understanding about what you think God is telling you.

It is important to analyse some of these tools to see how they may be useful in helping us to discover our true Destiny in God.

1 Thoughts and Self-examination

Proverb 23:7 says that *"You are what you think"*. God made us all with a powerful ability to think, deliberate, decide and act based on our thought process. God gave us a brain because He knew we would need it to make sense of both the World and the Word. We need to be careful not to let pride, selfishness and fruitless worldly philosophical speculations dominate our thinking process. We need to develop our thinking capacity to acquire, develop and refine our knowledge of the scriptures, our understanding of the world and the tricks and deceptive strategies of our enemy, the Devil. We need to develop a deep understanding of things that can help us to discover more about our own spiritual identity and utilise that knowledge for the purpose of achieving our God-given Destiny. The Holy Spirit reveal things to us, but our thinking ability can only develop through our own conscious effort to grow. We must make a conscious and consistent effort to focus on three things that are very crucial in helping us discover our supernatural destiny. Those three things include: knowing yourself, knowing God and knowing the world system. Your thoughts are the bricks with which you build your destiny edifice. Shape, refine and organise them well.

2 Prayer

Through prayer we elevate our thoughts to our divine Father and we naturally seek to project the best of ourselves in the process. What do you pray about when you pray for yourself? Write down your life plans and pray for them every day, you will witness the power of prayer in enabling God to guide you to discover the true you. So many of us pray about all sorts of things, forgetting to pray for our destiny. The more you ask God to reveal His will and purpose in your life, the more clarity you will get in relation to your destiny. This is why God tells us to pray without ceasing (1 Thessalonians 5:17). It is also the reason why Jesus was spending so many hours in prayer at the beginning of each day and then go on to teach with authority and perform miracles during the day.

3 Dreams and revelations

When God wants to talk to us and get us to do things for Him, He uses His Word. He also touches our heart in various ways. When God wants to convince us of something He may also use revelation to clarify His will and purpose for us. Unfortunately, most revelations are not communicated in simple and clear language. They come in many forms including dreams, visions, insights and new understanding of the scriptures. Any Christian who is serious about Destiny Living needs to be focused enough to pay attention to God's revelations in their lives, because one simple word from God can change a life. God is always revealing things to all human beings, but only some of us are awake and sufficiently focused to hear Him or capture His thoughts and vision for us.

4 *The Scriptures*

The scriptures are necessary to provide us with some reference in relation to the will of God for humanity. They enable us to know and be trained to understand how God operates. They open our minds and spirits for a new understanding, outside of common sense and scientific knowledge, regarding how God created the world and how He relates to human beings in general and to each one of us in particular. Everything we need to know about God, about the world/universe, life and spiritual realities is in the scriptures. The Bible says that

> *"all scripture is given by inspiration of God, and is profitable for doctrine, for reproof, for correction, for instruction in righteousness"*
>
> 2 Timothy 3: 16-17.

We must permanently expose ourselves to the light of the scriptures and draw the vision, knowledge, wisdom, understanding and insight that we need, to guide us through our life's journey. Because scriptures are multidimensional. One verse in the Bible can mean many things depending on what angle one is looking at it from. With the help of the Holy Spirit, we can discover the multiple treasures that every portion of the scripture encompass. Reading and studying the scriptures is essential and critical for Destiny Living and there is no alternative to this.

Just like God said in the beginning "Let us make man in our own image", investing the whole of His divinity in the process, we too need to involve the whole of our identity in making our destiny on earth. God made us in His image and we make our destiny in our image, as reflected to us from the mirror of divinity. We must be focused on opening our heart to the Word of God, searching for the truth of God, as it relates to our own specific life. We need to imbed ourselves with both the "Logos" and "Rhema" (the letter and the spirit) aspects of the Word. The Logos gives us knowledge and instructions, which is important because without it we perish. The Rhema is also very important because it gives us conviction, motivation, direction and peace of mind, all the things that we need to run and direct our lives correctly. We also need to develop a strong focus on God's plan for us if we want to discover what He has in His mind about our purpose and get busy to make it happen.

Searching is the keyword in the discovery of our Destiny. We need to search for the Logos through the Bible and also search for Rhema (the spiritual aspect of the scriptures) through our dialogue with God and our commitment to develop a strong and purposeful relationship with Him. That relationship can be manifested in our general interest in the things of God, meaning the time we spend with God, the space we create for him, the desire for His impact, the decoding of His work in our hearts and the materialisation of His vision.

We must be interested in the things of God if we want God to be interested in our life. But being interested in the things of God is not to be confused with being involved in the chores of the church. A lot of times people mistakenly think that being involved in activities at their local church is equal to being involved in the things of God. There are a lot of people who are quite busy at church doing all sorts of things, but they are not busy with what God wants them to do. Many such people are just interested in showing their piety and outward holiness, like the Pharisees were in the time of Jesus.

Additionally, there are also many people who confuse success with destiny. You can be successful in life but miss your destiny. You can be busy with your career and enjoying the prestige, money and security that comes from it, but totally missing the calling of God in your life. God tells us to seek Him and we shall find Him. When God says that we shall find Him, He means that we will not only know Him personally, but connect with His plans for our lives in a "destiny kind of way". In this sense, finding God is just another way of achieving self-discovery, true self-discovery. God is not human; hence we will not find Him somewhere waiting to be found or discovered as if he was playing hide and seek with us. We will find Him through a transformative event or process that changes our lives in a deeper way, such as when we accept Jesus as our Lord and Saviour and this results in a change of direction in our lives. One thing that is often missing in how Christian congregations around the world conduct their businesses in leading believers to God, is what I would like to call "Destiny coaching". In today's world, people need coaching for their Destiny, they need coaching for purposeful Christian living. They need tailored leadership, mentorship and guidance program for the sake of Christian maturity. Christian congregations that don't have destiny coaching programs are doing a disservice to their members.

5 Divine Spiritual & Natural laws

Knowing more about our heavenly-established destiny is very important. However, we also need to understand the spiritual and natural laws that govern life in both realms. Discovering these laws gives us more power and wisdom to navigate through life. When God created the world, He set up natural laws to sustain life and everything related to it. Before the physical world, God created the spiritual world where He exists and operates with many other beings such as angels and archangels. God also organised how the spiritual world can interact with the physical world by establishing relevant laws to govern these interactions. This means that anyone who understand these laws will be in a better position to better manage their existence. Those who are either ignorant of the laws or simply disregard them in some ways, are likely to have their lives negatively impacted by their ignorance. Destiny Living requires knowing such laws are and using that knowledge and the related wisdom to sustain the journey towards destiny deployment.

At the centre of life, there is only one thing and that thing is called "energy". Everything is energy, but expressed in different forms. God is a spirit and a spirit is energy. Therefore, God is an all knowing, all mighty and all purposeful and intelligent energy. The whole of the universe is nothing but a compilation of various forms of energy vibrating at different frequencies and all working harmoniously for most of the time. Knowing how "energy" works both in the spirit and in the natural world, means that one can place himself or herself in the best position to get things done, to minimise resistance and live a more fulfilling life. There are many natural laws, including:

- **Law of divine oneness**: we are all connected to one source
- **Law of attraction**: you will attract in your life whatever you focus on
- **Law of cause and effect**: what causes things, the effect you see have a cause
- **Law of action**: every action has a consequence
- **Law of compensation**: if you saw you shall reap
- **Law of relativity**: everything is only real by its relationship or comparison with something

- **Law of polarity**: everything is dual, everyone has poles or its pair of opposites
- **Law of rhythm**: everything goes through cycles, everything has a pattern
- **Law of perpetual transmutation of energy**: we have the ability to change the energy around us
- **Law of gender and gestation**: everything has its masculine and feminine principles and everything has a gestation/incubation period
- **Law of correspondence**: what we see outside is the manifestation what is inside of us
- **Law of Vibration**: everything in the universe is energy vibrating at some frequency

These laws permeate all aspects of life. Working with the knowledge of these laws can help anyone, regardless of whether they believe in God or not, whether they are righteous or evil in their lifestyles, they can reap the benefits that come from the blessings linked to those laws. In the same way, those who work against the laws will suffer negative consequences, whether they are saints or criminals. Only God is not bound by these laws and can override them at will. God can also allow some people to override these laws in miraculous ways. But miracles are exceptional and should not be relied on. No serious person can build their lives on the basis of miracles.

The laws listed above are also included in the Bible, even though they may not be described in the same wording. We will not go into detail to explain what each law means, but we may refer to them throughout the rest of the book. The reader is encouraged to research these laws as part of their personal discovery journey. In Joshua 1:8 God tells us to

> "keep this book of Law always on your lips, meditate on it day and night, so that you may be careful to do everything written in it. Then you will be prosperous and successful".

God expects us to invest time, energy and efforts to discover who we are in His eyes and what His plans are for our lives. Once we have the vision from Him, then the second thing that we need to discover is His laws and commandments. God has established these and He asks for obedience, not because He requires obedience from us, but because He wants us to maintain our integrity in the broader scheme of things. If we lose our integrity we go out of balance and self-destruct. He wants us to maintain our integrity and then move on to the next stage, when we pass away. Everything that God asks us is for our own good, not for His own sake.

Faith and Focus

Two things stand out in relation to how God may reveal His destiny for us: faith and focus. Our faith connects us to Him and our focus helps us to capture the message He is constantly giving us. Without faith there is no business with God and without focus we fail to understand God. If you already have faith but are not clear about your God-given destiny, then you need to increase your focus in your interactions with Him. We need to be very specific with God and ask Him over and over to reveal His grand plan for us, as individuals. He tells us to ask and we shall receive, to seek and we shall find and to knock and He will open the door. The biggest thing we can ask God is for Him to reveal His destiny in our lives and help us in accomplishing it on

Focus on Destiny

Earth. Everything else we can ask God is accessory. When we ask God to help us discover these things, we need to remember that He will respond, at the time and in a manner that He chooses. In the meantime, we need to continue to be busy with His work, remain focused and be guided by the light of the scriptures.

We must remember that God cannot lead us if we are not moving, because there is no need to lead immovable people or objects. Who wants to lead trees? They will never go anywhere. God will lead us when we are busy with action, studying His Word, His laws and principles and working towards some spiritually-inspired goals founded in our destiny plan. Regardless of what level of knowledge or spiritual maturity we may have, we will always need God's leadership. When we receive Jesus, there is a spiritual light that comes within us, triggering a transformation process for our spiritual restoration and our Destiny deployment on earth. In that process we receive some information and a heavy heart conviction about what God wants to do with our lives, even if things may not always be crystal clear at that point. From that moment, we need to start getting into action, practice our faith by doing things that make us useful in the family of God and contribute to the expansion of His Kingdom on Earth. We may start with one thing, such as helping at our local church, and then be led into another, such as going on an overseas mission to evangelise and perhaps we can even move onto another thing, such as creating charity organisation to help needy people in the name of Jesus. When we stay busy attending to the work of the Kingdom on Earth at any level of our Christian growth) and we focus on growing our relationship with God, we start vibrating at heavenly frequencies where messages from God become easier to receive. Once the connection is strong enough, God eventually downloads His high-resolution master plan for our lives.

Discover

True followers of Christ need to either be fully aware of their destiny or be busy seeking God's revelations about it. Those who don't know their God-given destiny are living a "default Destiny", a destiny that is a direct consequence of the cultural and socio-economic condition of the society in which they have lived and continue to live in. Default destiny is living life on auto-pilot and letting oneself be passively formatted by life circumstances, instead of God's plans. In the secular world, many people take confidence in their ability to create their future and their destiny. Nowadays we hear people everywhere saying "you can be whatever you want to be" and a lot of people buy into this. However, without a trustworthy reference point, people end up becoming anything that passes through their mind or anything they see in their society. For us Christians, life is not about becoming whatever we want to become, but becoming what God has called us to become. This can only happen if we build our lives with the right divine material and get inspired by God. If we use ungodly material to create our future, we are automatically off track and lost, even if we may appear to be successful in the eyes of men.

CHAPTER FIVE

Kewword 5

Decide

> **KEY POINTS**
> - Willpower is the biggest form of power that God has given to humanity
> - Decide to take ownership of your life and commit to "Destiny Living"
> - Decide to submit to Jesus' leadership and develop the right mindset for your destiny
> - Decide to focus more on deployment rather than employment for the sake of your Destiny

THE ABILITY TO MAKE BIG DECISIONS AND STICK TO THEM, AS A matter of faith and principle is one of the things that sets us apart from animals. God has given we human beings quite powerful mental abilities and the freedom to make choices and decisions in our lives and do so as individuals exercising their free and independent will, outside of the will of our creator. These attributes are from God, our Source, and they come with a huge responsibility.

As the Bible says, *"To whom much is given, much is required"* (Luke 12:48). As Christians, we have more responsibility to develop and use our mental faculties to support our spiritual focus in delivering our God-given destiny on earth. Our mental faculties are great assets deposited in us for the accomplishment of our purpose and destiny on earth.

From God's perspective, all our mental infrastructure (consciousness, awareness, will, as well as the ability to think, feel, focus, learn, understand and decide) is a package designed to enable us to make the right choices that lead us to accomplish God's plans on earth. Our willpower may be the greatest and most powerful gift we have from God, but it is also the most dangerous asset, a double edge sword that can harm us significantly, if we misuse it.

All our mental and spiritual infrastructure help us create both our own individual and internal reality (we literally construct reality through our consciousness). They also help us to contribute to the creation of a collective reality, a culture and an environment that facilitates the expansion of the Kingdom of God on earth. God wants us to be creators like him, but in a subjective dimension rather than the absolute dimension. To please Him for this purpose, we need to make decisions, big and small, but always consistent with His plans and His will. The power to decide is what gives us our creative ability to meet God's expectations in our lives. It starts with our decision to accept the call of Christ as Lord and Saviour and then it goes into the next level where we accept His mission or commission here on earth. Accepting Jesus and His mission in our lives means that we must create things, both tangible and intangible, directly or indirectly, individually or collectively, to meet His expectations regarding what He wants to us to deliver on earth before we return to Eternity.

Focus on Destiny

God will not decide for You

Many Christian congregations tend to encourage a religious mindset (directly or indirectly) where people expect that God will do things for them, instead of them doing and creating things with the inspiration and guidance from God. They teach about miracles and get excited about God's ability to make a way where there is no way. God certainly has miraculous powers, but it is not His plan that we His children should build our lives on the basis of miracles. Miracles are an exception, not the rule. The general rule is that everyone of us must think, decide, make choices and work to do the work they have been created for. If we do this, we will become what God expects us to be. God gave us all the abilities we need to lead a fulfilling and meaningful life and we must use these capacities under His leadership and guidance to make things happen.

The Bible says, *"You are what you think"* (Proverb 23:7). Churches must help people to improve their thinking ability in addition to improving their spiritual awareness and proactivity. The two things don't always go together. There are many people who are highly spiritual and said to be filled with the Holy Spirit, but when you get close to them you see that their thinking remains quite problematic. The Holy Spirit can help people get wisdom from God, He doesn't necessarily improve people's cognitive capacity. God does not directly interfere with our cognition (thoughts), as a matter of course. This is a domain that He left for us to manage as independently beings. The Spirit can inspire the mind and give direction, which ultimately can affect our thinking process at any specific moment in time, but the growth and development of our cognitive capacity (as a whole) is something that we ourselves must take care of. God doesn't dictate what we must think. If we don't try to develop our cognitive abilities, we should not expect God to do it for us.

The Bible says:

> "Do not conform to the pattern of this world but be transformed by the renewing of your mind. Then you will be able to test and approve what God's will is--his good, pleasing and perfect will"
>
> (Romans 12:2).

The renewal of our mind is something we are called to do through a personal effort to re-program and improve our thinking in the light of the scriptures and our desire to growth spiritually and serve God in the physical realm.

God created us in His image and that image is about His character, which is centred on three things: creation, love and leadership. God is our <u>Creator</u> and our <u>Leader</u>. He created us and placed us on earth, gave us instructions as part of his efforts to lead us to His destiny in our lives. He did all these things because He loved us. In the same way, as His children we have inherited His character and we are also creators and leaders and everything we do must be driven by love. We must decide to love God because He loved us. We must also help God create a new reality on earth and we must love what we are creating. When we decide to do this, we become leaders in our area of gifting. We show leadership through the decisions we make every day to take care of God's agenda in our life and impact our generation on His behalf.

Focus on Destiny

Decide with God's guidance

We all have this tremendous divine gift in our lives called "willpower". However, we often don't make a good use of this gift. In today's world, procrastination is endemic in most human societies. People are either not making decisions when they need to make them, or they make decisions unconsciously and do not have their mind clearly set on what they need to do with their lives. Willpower is the engine of life. The human mind is a powerful machine, the most powerful machine ever built on planet earth. We must study it and understand how it is structured and it how it works at various levels of consciousness and awareness. Christians who are interested in Destiny Living have a duty to study their own mind and know themselves better. No one can achieve anything great if they do not know themselves well. We must be able to monitor ourselves and be able to produce the best out of our mind, as consistently as possible. When we do so, we can expect to live a successful life in the eyes of God and men.

The human mind best learns through exposure and repetition. Our mind is structured by our character and personality. It is influenced by our exposure to various things that we see, hear and experience, directly or indirectly. Because of this we need to watch what information, knowledge and experience we expose ourselves to. We need to increase our exposure to what we want to learn so that the knowledge we gain in the process is engraved and strengthened in our mind. We know that knowledge is power, especially when it is applied wisely. God says that *"My people perish because of lack of knowledge"* (Hosea 4:6). This is an invitation for all Christians to love knowledge, not just knowledge of the scriptures, but all types of useful knowledge that can help us improve our thinking and our decision-making abilities for the purpose of destiny living. Everything we learn influences our willpower. We need the right knowledge that is useful for our destiny deployment and helps us to better understand who we are and the value and importance of good decision-making. Doing so is the only way we can create and deliver our destiny on earth. Our willpower must always be put at the service of creation, love and leadership. We must always ask ourselves what we are creating on earth on behalf of God, what leadership we are exercising and whether our decisions and actions are reflective of the love of God.

Manufacturing Your Destiny

Once we have discovered the specific will of God in our lives, which is what we call our destiny, we need to create both the internal and external conditions to enable us to design and develop our life and our future, based on that discovery. Before God created Adam and Eve, He created a garden out of the bush and placed them in it. We can call this the external environment. After creating mankind, God created a law that He communicated to Adam. The instruction or the law, to eat any fruit except the one from the tree of knowledge of good and evil was about creating internal environment inside man's consciousness for God's plan and purpose to be cultivated and achieved. In the same way, as we embark in Destiny Living, we must always attend to our internal environment, which is what we are thinking and processing spiritually, as well as our external environment, which includes the social, cultural and economic conditions in which we live. Both conditions need to be taken care of through our decision-making abilities. Given that we know about the consequences of sin, we must also ensure that our decisions are always in line with the divine legislation (the Word of God) that governs our lives. Any decision that is outside of the Word of God is not only illegal, but it is also ultimately toxic and detrimental to our long-term spiritual health. This is why it is important that we decide to build and develop new habits and routines to help ourselves train and condition the mind, not just to think, but to decide and act upon the instructions that God gives us as He leads us to our destiny.

Decide to partner with God

God is the manufacturer of mankind and we are the manufactures of our own earthly Destiny. This simply means that we create our future based on the choices and decisions we take. We all have a mandate from God to live purposefully by doing His will in our lives. The process of manufacturing our earthly destiny is not too complex.

Generally speaking there are four things that happen when one decides to manufacture anything:
1. The *purpose* one has in mind to achieve something or meet a particular need
2. An *idea*/vision/image of what one wants to create to meet the need or fulfil the purpose
3. The *willingness* or intention to make something happen
4. The *material* resources that are required to be put together to make the new manufactured product to take shape and materialise.

Decide

When God made mankind, He put all the above elements together. Every one of us comes to earth as a package of the purpose, power, idea, willingness and material from God, bundled together in a human body and delivered on earth through birth. By creating us in His image, God made us more than just simple products. He packaged us in a way that we encompass His very nature, as the creator. We all reflect that very nature. We are therefore creators by nature, primarily because we need to create our own subjective awareness of ourselves as individuated entities with a consciousness and with an independent will. The divine creative nature in us is manifested principally through our mind. We create or construct reality every day both in our waking moments as well as in our dreams. As a matter of fact, it can be said that life is nothing but a prolonged and conscious experience of the physical reality in a human mind.

Additionally, as much as we are an expression of God manifested in a physical body, we are also given the power and ability to express ourselves in life through what we decide to do and the way we want to live our lives. We can, if we want to, decide independently of God, the meaning we want to give to our earthly existence. God says, *"I put before your life and prosperity, death and destruction, choose life"* (Deuteronomy 30:15-20). This show the choice that God gives us to define and create our own Destiny. God has also made us with the ability to shape our character and express our identity through the decisions we take and the choices we make day by day. We are made to create meaning, make choices and make value judgements, all the time. Because of this, destiny can be understood as both an expression of God in us, as created beings, as well as our own expression or projection of self-identity in life (as independent beings with individuated minds capable of creating and influencing reality).

God did not want to have to define reality for us at every second of our lives. He gave us a mind that can generate reality within us and enable us to interact with other minds, as well as the physical world around us. He also gave us a spirit to shape and guide our mind. That spirit is the bridge between the spiritual and physical world. Our spirit and mind therefore work in tandem to produce reality and create an internal field of consciousness that is necessary to experience life and create our future, based on what we are receptive to. Through His leadership capacity God also put a burden in every man's heart for a cause that they can choose to champion, to contribute to the accomplishment of his plans on planet earth.

Jesus had His cross and all of us have our own cross too. We just need to be focused enough in our interactions with God to find what that cross is. Everything we have received from God, including our spirit, mind, body, gifts, passion, skills, abilities, and talents are all tools needed to help us carry that cross to the destination. Although not everyone always realises or discovers this "divine burden", but it is always present in every human heart. For those who are not spiritually attuned to the "burden", the feeling may be experienced simply as recurring concern or preoccupation, for something that is not quite right in the world. Many ignore that feeling or concern and go about their business of life. But for those vibrating in God's frequencies, the recurring concern in their heart drives them to do something and answer God's call for the transformation of humanity.

Martin Luther King felt the burden of injustice and acted to advocate for change. He did so know well the danger of his commitment within a racially segregated America. He lost his life, but he knew that his mission was bigger than his own life. Mother Theresa saw the rampant poverty in India as a concern and the burden was so heavy that she stopped her "employment" as a teacher and launched into her "deployment" as a humanitarian leader, dedicated to the cause of helping poor people in India. When she decided to embrace her poverty cause and devoted herself to it, she created a spiritual field from which divine intervention could be exercised and experienced not just for her, but for the people she was taking care of, as well as the broader human society. Her commitment to the cause led her to change and influence thousands of lives and educate the world about the need to help less privileged people, including those beyond Calcutta, India. She inspired many people to help others. She created her future and deployed her destiny on earth by listening to the voice of God inside of her and then make the right decisions to help create a new reality in the world, starting from her local community in India.

Decision Making & Destiny Living

Destiny Living is ultimately about making decisions and sticking to them, all with a focus on accomplishing God's mission on earth. To achieve our destiny on earth we need to refine our decision-making abilities and this requires us to make serious decisions. Some of those decisions include:

1 **Decide to serve God**
Decide to serve God by deploying all the resources He has placed in you. You are loaded with God's gifts in your life. These were given as resources to help you achieve your Destiny on earth.

Focus on Destiny

But you must first realise who you are, know what you have and be clear on what your mission is. An exceptional man in the Bible tells us about the need to decide to choose God. Joshua, a leader and outstanding general dedicated his life to taking people of God to the Promised Land, after the death of Moses. When dealing with rebellious tribes of Israel, he tells them what the Lord has said and he asks them to make a conscious decision, to choose if they want to serve the Lord or not. He says:

> *"If serving the Lord seems undesirable to you, then choose for yourselves this day whom you will serve…But as for me and my household, we will serve the Lord".*
>
> (Joshua 24:15).

This passage shows us a man who is clear and determined in his decision to serve God even in the context of a rebellious environment.

Choices are outcomes of decisions in our mind. The ability to make up one's mind and commit oneself to an idea or an ideal in the absence of any tangible and immediate benefit is something that most human beings don't have. Decision-making is an act of human will, it is about making a judgment about what needs to be done in any circumstances, what attitude to adopt or action to take in the face of something that one is not very sure about. Decisions are often influenced by thoughts and feelings or a combination of both. Often our decisions reflect the desires of the heart (emotions) and, as such, they tend to be a projection of our "sentimental attitude" towards something, rather than just pure rational calculations. When we make big decisions in our lives, we engage the whole of us; our thoughts, emotions, and the deep-seated convictions within us.

Decide

Accomplishing God's destiny on earth is a very big deal. As such it requires big, consistent and painful decisions to be make throughout one's life. Sometimes, such decisions can appear foolish or even mad, but they are the ones that that will ultimately lead us to an outcome that is in line with our God-ordained Destiny. In today's world three factors significantly affect the way most people make decisions and we cannot escape from these influencing forces.

The first factor is rational or logical thinking (as opposed to spirituality). We live in an increasingly rational world, where we are expected to make decisions that fall in line with logic, scientific or rational thinking. Science is the new God, it is said. Anything that is not scientifically logical is seen as irrational and it is frowned upon.

The second factor is information overflow. We are constantly flooded with so much information, especially in Western countries. We are and given so many choices about so many things to the point where making decisions has become a very complicated business, because too much choice makes decision-making a very difficult exercise. Too much choice kills choice, someone said. The third and last factor is the materialistic culture in which we are literally "drowned" in. We have been conditioned to think materialistically and encouraged to seek and pursue individualist and egoistic goals. Such goals are often directed at acquiring more money and material things rather than anything else of spiritual value. The result of this materialistic focus has created a consumerist obsession, which fuels the love of money in our hearts. Money obsession has become part of the culture and many don't even notice it anymore. We must remember that Jesus told us that we cannot serve both God and Money, we must choose one of them. We can use money to manage our lives better, but we must not succumb to the temptation to submit ourselves as wilful slaves to Money as the master of our lives.

The above three factors are significantly and constantly influencing our minds and impacting on the decisions we make, which shape our actions, influence our behaviours, create our reality, affect our future and determine our earthly destiny. It is in the background of this extraordinarily and complicated reality that we Christians are expected to consistently make the right spiritual decisions that will lead us to the accomplishment of our Destiny. Living a meaningful spiritual life in today's world is indeed challenging. The world is constantly pulling us down and preventing us from elevating ourselves to the spiritual mountain top, where God expects us to be.

2 Decide to focus on spiritual growth

Spiritual decisions are by their very nature non-logical. Our spirit is not regulated by logic, which is a product of our human mind. Therefore, many times unbelievers find spiritual things as 'illogical" and "irrational" and they discount or devalue them because they don't always make sense in their eyes. Spiritual decisions also do not align with the world's system either. This is why the Bible tells us that *"the just shall live by faith"*, which in today's world means that the just will need to make decisions that are not always based on visible evidence or human logic or scientific reasoning. The Bible defines faith as *"the substance of things hoped for, the evidence of things not seen"* (Hebrews 11:1). This means that as disciples of Christ many (but certainly not all) of our decisions will need to be based on the assurance of things unseen, invisible, unsubstantiated, but which come from God. Spiritual decisions are not about survival or egoistic desires, but they are about obedience to the Divine authority (even where things don't appear to make sense), expressing God's love and being a steward of God's grace to humanity.

A simple example of a spiritual decision in the Bible is when Jesus meets Peter first time and He invites him to follow Him. Peter accepted the invitation. Peter was a fisherman and fishing was a very good business to have at the time. Jesus who was asking Peter to follow Him had no job, no house, no property or any belonging of his own. If Peter had analysed Jesus' request rationally or logically, he would probably have said no, because logically it did not make much sense to follow a man had nothing and who was telling a prosperous fisherman (businessman) that He was going to make him a "fisher of men". I am sure Peter was wondering in his mind: "a fisher of men? How can someone make a living out of that?". What assurance was Jesus providing to Peter that the "fishing men" business was a serious enterprise? These are some of the questions that any logical and reasonable person would ask themselves if they were in Peter's shoes. There was nothing logical in the invitation made by Jesus to Peter, but Peter accepted the invitation, anyways. He focused on spiritual growth because he could sense something bigger than just fishing fish. He quit his fishing business and followed Jesus and went on to become the rock upon which the church was built.

The temptation of Jesus by the devil in the book of Mathew (chapter 4) is a potent illustration of the power of decision making. When you analyse the story in the Bible, the devil was only trying to get Jesus to <u>decide</u> to obey him. He just wanted Jesus to decide to agree with him and act accordingly. If Jesus had done so, Christianity would not have existed, the course of human history would have been radically different, and you wouldn't be reading these pages.

Decision-making defines how we discharge our Destiny here on earth, because one may know his or her purpose in life, but knowing is not enough, one must decide to act, to do the work that needs to be done, to carry the cross that must be carried. All these things are about making good decisions and sticking with them. Those decisions are mostly spiritual in nature.

3 Decisions and mindset

If you want to live purposefully, you will need to decide to build and develop a mindset for that purpose. Purposeful living is a life of decisions. In order to make the right decisions consistently, it is necessary to re-format the mind properly and have a clear and powerful vision that will pull you towards the direction of your Destiny. Destiny Living is like military service, you cannot be a good solider with a civilian mindset, you need a military mindset. Special forces in the army are trained as much for mental strength as they are for physical and fitness abilities. A mindset is a way of setting up or framing one's mind in a way that it processes all information with a particular filter that leads the person to feel, think and react in particular ways. Every human operates on the basis of their particular mindset. Most people adopt the mindset that is prevalent in the society in which they live, and they reinforce it throughout their lives through decisions and actions that are in line with the prevailing model of the world in that culture or society. When we decide to live a life dedicated to accomplishing our God-ordained Destiny, we sign up to become soldiers of Christ. Timothy 2:2 says:

> *"Endure suffering along with me, as a good soldier of Christ Jesus. Soldiers don't get tied up in the affairs of civilian life, for then they cannot please the officer who enlisted them".*

Decide

The Bible even talks about being *"prisoners of Christ"* (Ephesians 3:1). If we are serious in our determination, we need to develop an appropriate mindset using the scriptures, God's revelations and the best of scientific knowledge to develop a mindset for purposeful living.

In conditioning our minds for Destiny Living, the scriptures are our first point of reference, but they should not be the only reference. Another useful knowledge can be added into our "destiny toolkit", so to speak. Scientific fields such as psychology, neuroscience, leadership, business management, just to name a few, offer a variety of tools that can be quite useful for good thinking, problem solving and decision-making abilities, which are all very crucial and necessary for Destiny Living. It is important not to limit ourselves simply to what the scriptures say, because the best value we get from scriptures is in strengthening our spirit, improve our sensitivity to evil and giving us a direction for life. The wisdom of the scriptures awakens us spiritually, while scientific knowledge helps to better understand the natural world, the realities in the world and in our society. It also equips us in many ways to know how to deal with people and developing skills and competencies to perform tasks and lead organisations. Faith alone cannot resolve everything in life. We need faith, wisdom, knowledge, understanding, problem solving skills, leadership and business management skills, just to name a few things that are very important in today's world. We cannot simply believe that if we pray, believe and trust God, then God will make a way. The world is much more complex, life is an increasingly complicated affair. There is no doubt we do need other types of knowledge and scientific enlightenment. Science is not incompatible with faith. Science is useful to all humans, including Christians, as long as we remain aware of the limitations and dangers of scientific thinking in our spiritual life. We must not forget that the pioneers of scientific enquiries were mostly Christians.

4 Decide to manage your life like a CEO
The business of life is the most serious business anyone can manage. Everyone of us, by virtue of being alive, is forced to be the CEO of their own life. However, we are not always well trained, nor are we necessarily adequately prepared to run our own life in the best possible way. In the old days, life was quite a simple thing. People grew up in small villages where they lived on farming, fishing or hunting. People did not need money to live on, nor did they need to be employed in the way most of us are today. Most societies were very traditional and had one single reference as the model of life. Their cultural framework organised all important things in life including education, getting married, running a family etc. Today things are very different as we live in big urban areas with people from various backgrounds, culture and belief-systems. As life becomes increasingly more complex in today's world, all of us need to learn and develop strong business management and leadership skills. If we look at life in a business perspective, we can be more empowered to manage it well. God is the owner of the business (our life) and each one of us is a manager of their own life. Our job is to manage the development and deployment all the resources provided to us by the owner (God) to ensure the business is successful.

As you read these lines, you are called to manage your "business of life" and be the "leader of your own self". This requires you to have a vision, a mission, goals and objectives for your life. You also need to set up a plan and come up with adequate strategies to operate in whatever socio-economic environment you may live in. In running the business of life, you need to develop products for people and/or or offer services that can add value in their lives, from the value that you carry within you. The Kingdom of God on earth is your marketplace, you are trading value-added products with a focus on changing people's lives for the better, as a steward of God's grace in its various forms. Your key mission is not about making a profit, but pursuing a vision and achieving a purpose. You will need policies and procedures to enable you to adequately serve all the stakeholders who are linked to your business and do so from your heart and not necessarily from the perspective of making money, even though in general money should naturally come to you when you deliver value to people. The Bible says *"seek first the Kingdom of God and its righteousness and the rest will be given onto you ..."* (Mat 6: 33). If we get busy with discharging our destiny and contributing to the Kingdom of God, our Father, who is the great provider of all guarantees that everything else we need will be provided.

5 *Improving Your Decision-making Skills*

The ability to make the right decisions at the right time and be able to act on them appropriately, is such a valuable skill that CEOs around the world get paid millions of dollars, because of their skills in making the right decisions for the companies they are managing. Every day, the average human being makes hundreds of decisions in his/her mind. Most of these decisions are made within split-seconds, as part of the process that the brain uses to compute things, make sense of the world and enable the individual to navigate life. Just as an example, as part a morning routine, we make lots of micro decisions from when we wake up to the time we leave home for work. Such decisions include:

what time to get out of bed, whether we check our mobile phone, what we do when we open our phone and hold it in our hands, whether we need to pray or not and how long we pray, when do we take a shower, brush our teeth, eat breakfast and many other things that we can do. By the time one arrives at work so several dozens of small decisions would have been made within just the first two or three hours of the day. If we are driving to work even for half an hour hundreds of micro decisions are also made in the process of driving including steering, turning, accelerating, breaking, watching mirrors, listening to the radio etc...

It is a fact that most of our decisions in life are made at an unconscious level without much thought energy being invested into them. We program our brain to make such decisions. Unfortunately, many people who live life on autopilot, they navigate life making small decisions almost unconsciously, until they encounter something major that wakes them up. Therefore, in order to improve our decision-making skills, we need to attend to both the big rational and conscious decisions we make such as signing up for a university course, buying a house or getting married, as well as the micro decisions that govern our habits and daily routine. This requires attention being invested in a self-monitoring exercise where we "see ourselves thinking and deciding", both at micro and macro level, and we question and monitor our own thinking to ensure it is right and in line with our vision in life. Part of the reasons why the world is in so much trouble today is because most human beings do not see themselves thinking, feeling and behaving and they fail to monitor and manage themselves accordingly. We are too much attached to our thoughts and too driven to satisfy our own feelings and other personal predispositions. We just act out what is happening within us. This is a problem.

Decide

Decision making can only improve when we start becoming strategic in life. Strategy has to do with goals, which are informed by a plan and vision. When we become strategic, we start analysing and interpreting information before us to ensure it connects with what we want to achieve. Interpreting or constructing reality as we move about in life is a very big job. We get exposed to so many things and we need to make sense of so much data in front of us. This means we need more focus. When we decide to aim high in life and discharge our Divine Destiny on earth, we cannot let our subconscious mind make decisions willy-nilly. We need to train it and program it so that it can work in harmony with our vision and life goals. We must ensure our subconscious doesn't sabotage our resolutions and our commitment for self-affirmation and destiny deployment. When we decide to steer our lives towards a particular direction, we need to develop relevant habits and routines that will support such decisions and drive us to the desired destination. The guidelines below can be helpful for anyone seeking to develop a good decision-making template in their mind and improve their decision-making abilities.

6 Seven Steps to improve your decision-making abilities

1. **See yourself thinking and police your own thoughts**
   - Learn to watch yourself thinking and question your own thoughts.
   - Be aware of how your feelings are interacting or interfering with your thoughts.
   - Learn to laugh at yourself and put yourself on trial in your own mind.

2. **Practice your decision-making ability and build mental muscles.**
    - Start small by planning to do small things and ensure you do them as you plan them. For example, decide to walk 30 mins every day for 30 days and stick to it no matter what.
    - Challenge yourself regularly by gradually increasing the level of the commitment you are asking from yourself. e.g.: Walk for 45 mins hour instead of 30 minutes.
3. **Organise yourself and plan things before you do them**
    - Plan to do things and review your plan on a regular basis.
    - Plan your next day before you go to bed. Keep a diary or notebook on your bedside and write things down as they come to your mind. Taking notes reinforces memory and improves decision-making
    - Organise your work material to enable you to locate what you need when you need it.
    - Prioritise things and do one thing at a time.
4. **Adopt clear resolutions to govern your thoughts and behaviours**
    - Decide not to think negatively and not to engage in behaviours that express negative energy, even where you are hurt. (e.g.: don't retaliate).
    - Write down your own "personal commandments" and commit to obey them. (e.g.: if you want to develop a character of integrity you can say "I will never accept corruption").
    - Avoid procrastination, neglect and over-commitment

5. **Monitor and audit yourself regularly against procrastination and neglect**
   - Avoid over-committing yourself to things that don't add much to your vision, even if they may sound good.
   - Pay attention to the things you decided NOT to do because of your vision. Write your "hate" list as a declaration of what you are not going to do in your life
   - Learn to say No to people or projects, you can't do everything in one lifetime and you can't please everyone either.

6. **Monitor and audit your own decisions and your thought processes**
   - Write down positive statements about yourself and rehearse them regularly. For example: I am a woman of integrity, trustworthy and committed to excellence.
   - Pray over your plan every day. Prayer reinforces and strengthens your positive mind and it also invites God to guide and lead you.
   - Read and Teach. Read the stories of people who help changed the world through their actions. Focus on your role models in your line of interest
   - Emulate good examples you read about or see in real life.

7. **Teach what you want to learn.**
   - Create opportunities for you to teach what you are learning.
   - Find a coach and/or a Mentor to guide you in your learning and teaching

The above guidelines are not a guarantee for making perfect decisions all the time. They simply help to provide a fertile ground on which good decisions become easier to make. If we plant the right ideas in our minds, we harvest good decisions. Often, we make bad decisions in life if we have no clear vision, no sense of direction and no tool for the type of decision that we are called to make. We also make bad decisions when we are ignorant about things we are dealing with or perhaps we get caught unprepared in some situations. Sometimes we also get driven by things in our environment, rather than our own sense of purpose and a determination to achieve something of value with our lives.

Decisions are like bricks we use to build the walls of our lives, we need to make many of them, but we simply need to build one on top of the other with consistency and alignment, as part of a plan. At times, we may need to make big decisions which require a lot of thinking and careful consideration. But for the most part, it is the little decisions we make every day that really shape us as individuals and impact our lives significantly. Life changing decisions require courage, vision and perseverance. Destiny Living is about making a choice to live for a divine cause and continuously make the right decisions to promote that cause and stick to it, even where things are tough. Nothing of great value comes easily and people who succeed in life are those who stick to their decisions and focus on hard work, smart thinking and everyday commitment, at the service of their vision.

7 *Decision-making and Problem-solving skills*

A large part of our mental energy is spent in trying to resolve problems that we encounter in our every day's life. Having good problem-solving skills is critical for success. Solving problems is about making good decisions. Our education system does not always prepare us sufficiently to be able to solve all the big problems in our lives. Some disciplines such as engineering and management do better than others in offering good problem-solving techniques templates and insights. A good engineer will have problem and troubleshooting solving skills to help address various engineering issues and a manager will be trained to resolve management problems, but there is not enough attention in our education systems to prepare people to live out their God-given Destiny and address all the spiritual, emotional, intellectual and physiological issues that we can expect to encounter in life.

The education system in most countries remains focused on preparing people to be responsible adults and give them skills to help them find employment. From a purely intellectual perspective, problem-solving requires a variety of skills and everyone who is serious about living life purposefully needs to develop these skills. Having poor problem-solving skills in life is a recipe for a mediocre life. Spiritually speaking, the Bible provides us with divine wisdom and insights into life, but it doesn't provide us a magic formula to solve all problems in our lives. We therefore need to know the scriptures on the one hand, as well as learn and develop good decision-making and problem-solving skills in our socio-cultural and economic context, wherever we may live.

There is no magic formula for solving problems in life, but generally, good problem-solving strategies involve the following steps, which are listed in no particular order:

1. Identifying issues at hand (What is the problem exactly?)
2. Researching and investigating what one is dealing with (What is involved in the problem?)

3. Analysis and evaluation (What the problem means and all its possible effects)
4. Developing alternatives (What are possible ways to solve the problem?)
5. Creative thinking (Can the problem be solved in new ways?)
6. Decision-making (Acting and tackling the issue)
7. Communication (What is the best way to communicate both the issue and the solution to it?)

Biblically speaking, we know that a great deal of our problems in life come from a spiritual source. When the spirit is dead, sick or disabled, the mind is also affected and the decisions that are made in such situations are often problematic in many ways. In fact, most of the issues we deal with in life come from seeds that we have planted long time ago from a spiritual standpoint, which take time to germinate and show up in our life. For example, greed, dishonesty, immorality and egoism are all spiritual problems and they are the roots of many of the issues that people deal with in life. Christian's maturity requires that we build our own Bible-based and Spirit-inspired personal problem-solving template to enable us to make good decisions. Such a template will work like a formula that we can use to make the decisions we need to make.

Here is a simple problem-solving template that you can use. It is called the *ABCDEF* problem-solving template:

Ask yourself what type of problem you are dealing with
- Is it spiritual, emotional, intellectual, technical, financial, communication issue?
- Ask God to show you what the real problem is.

Decide

Correctly diagnosing a problem is half the solution, the rest is finding an appropriate remedy

Be clear on the ideal solution you want
- Focus on the solution and not problem. There is no use crying over spilt milk.
- Visualise the solution in your mind and imagine what it would feel like

Check with God
- God's solution is always the best. What does His Word say about your problem?
- Make Jesus your advisor. What would He advise you in relation to the issue at hand?
- Get God's direction by submitting your thoughts to Him through prayer and meditation. Ask God's people in your network (such as a church leader) if you trust them enough.

Discover the opportunity inside the problem
- Every problem is an opportunity to learn and grow
- Every problem is also an opportunity to help others. We deliver value in other people's lives and in the society by helping to solve problems.

Examine options and consider relevant information for each of them

Consider the possible alternatives to solving the problem
- Study the implications of each option and seek God's guidance in selecting the best out of the bunch.

Fix it or freeze it
- Get into action to solve the problem, because thinking or praying alone won't fix the problem.
- Plan what to do: take timely action and implement it in the right way. It is not just about what to do, but when to do it, how to do it and who's best to do it.
- if you cannot fix a problem immediately, freeze it and be patient until the right opportunity arises to act on it. Timing is as important as the solution itself.

Plan your decisions

Good decision-making requires planning. As the saying goes, "failing to plan is planning to fail". Planning enables us to put all of our resources in a decision. When we plan, we engage our mind, our spirit and feelings into the decision. We cannot know the future with any certainty, but we can plan it and because the Bible says that *"you are what you think"*, this means that if you plan your "thinking" well and think about your plans constantly, you can become what you plan and get the future you want. If your thinking mostly gravitates around your life plans and how to implement them, you are bound to succeed. Even God has plans. He told Jeremiah;

> *"I know the plans I have for you, plans to prosper you, not to harm you plans to give you hope and future".*

In this verse lies the secret for divine planning.
1. We must *plan for our future.* Failing to plan for the future means we are not serious about it and don't

want to take whatever comes our way. Even animals plan for future needs

2. We must plan with the intention to make ourselves and others prosperous. Whoever wants prosperity must plan for it, not just wish for it
3. We must not plan for anything that may harm us or others. Doing so is not only foolish but also evil
4. We must *plan with hope,* because we know that God is our side and He has promised us that He will make us prosperous. Hope is important because it gives us patience to wait on God's time and not be desperate and lose faith.

The Bible also says *"commit to the Lord whatever you do, and He will establish your plans"*. (Proverbs 16:3). It is important to note that in both these verses (Jeremiah and Proverbs) and many others in the Bible God is talking about "plans" not "plan". This is because there are many aspects of life that require planning and we need to have a plan for each of them. We need a plan for spiritual growth, our intellectual development, our finances, our physical health, our family and many other things. However, we must ensure that all our plans need to be coherent, harmonious and have one direction, which is the direction of our God-given Destiny. Plans also need to be expressed clearly and broken into smaller goals, including short-term, medium term and long-term objectives. Whatever you decide as part of your Destiny Living, make sure you support your decisions with a solid plan and invite God to look into it, approve and bless it. That is the only way for Him to lead you and transform your life. God can't lead you if you don't have plans. Make plans for your life and take them to God in your every day's prayers.

CHAPTER SIX

Keyword 6

Do

> **KEY POINTS**
> - Do what God created you to do here on earth, that is your destiny
> - If you have faith in you, there is action waiting to be taken outside of you
> - All God's work involves sacrifice. Find your cross and carry it to the mountain top
> - Do everything with purpose and conviction and do not do things just to please people

ACTION, NOT JUST FAITH WILL DEFINE YOUR EARTHLY DESTINY. As you climb the ladder of Destiny Deployment, the problem shifts from faith and knowledge to action and deployment. Most people perish because of lack of knowledge, as the Bible says, but many Christians miss their destiny, not because of knowledge, but because they fail to do what they know and act out their faith. A lot of people know what to do, but only a few people do what they know. Procrastination is a widespread disease of the mind and the spirit in today's world and Christians are unfortunately not immune to it. So many people lack power inside of them to move from thinking to deciding and then taking action.

In the Bible, when God created the world, He simply spoke things into existence. But for mankind, God decided to "do" something rather simply "speak" something. He did something with his hands, the Bible says. He used clay to shape man before breathing life into him. Although God was very much capable of simply "speaking" man into existence, but He chose to work with tangible material (clay) and invested some practical efforts along with His divine power to shape man and breathe into him to bring about human life. By doing so, God was telling us that if we want to create something of great value we need to act, do something beyond just speaking. Our destiny work is the equivalent of what God did in creating mankind. Whatever God did in creating us is what we need to do in creating our earthly destiny. If we want to live out our Divine Destiny on earth, we need more than believing, thinking and speaking. We need to do things, design and shape things and breathe life into them. We need to perspire after we have been inspired. It is about creativity in action.

Plan Your destiny

The accomplishment of our purpose in life is dependent on by faith-inspired action. Destiny is an assignment, it must be done and completed through action. That action needs to be planned appropriately to make things happen, otherwise both our faith and knowledge become useless. Knowledge becomes power only when it is put into action. Faith means nothing until it is translated into action to change oneself, to change things and change the world. If the Almighty God did something tangible to create mankind, whatever thing a human being wants to create, he or she must "do it", work for it, just like God did. Whatever you have decided you need to do for God, for your Destiny, just go ahead and do it. When you start doing it, things will start happening. You will probably encounter difficulties, make mistakes and learn from them and then get better and better by refining your actions.

The Christian community around the world is plagued with a disease that I call the "proclamation disease". This spiritual illness is a symptom of the religious mentality that is increasingly infecting the Church of Christ today. You see a lot of people declaring or proclaiming lots of things in the name of Jesus and getting excited in the process. But when you look closely, so many of believers are quite hollow in their Christian life, with no substance to show for their faith. They have nothing concrete in their lives other than some confidence in the power and love of Jesus Christ. The Bible is clear that faith without action is dead. Faith is intangible and invisible. It is only by doing that you can translate the spiritual or supernatural power into physical realisation. So, don't just proclaim that you live for Jesus. Do things that show you mean what you say. We can't talk or shout or proclaim our way to our Destiny. We must do the work that is required to teach, preach, coach, mentor, help, heal and care for others as instructed by God. All destiny work involves working with other people in the name of God and for a mission that is centred on restoring the human family.

The inspiration and revelation of the spiritual truths that we get from God in our journey to our Destiny is only the first step. God can only accomplish things in the physical world through physical beings like us. This is why in the Bible, whenever God had to do anything, He always asked people to take some type of action first and then He would add His supernatural might into it. In Exodus 4:2 God asked Moses what he had in his hand and Moses responded that he had a staff and God asked him to throw it onto the ground and it turned into a snake, which brought relief to the Israelites in the desert who were being tormented by other snakes. Even when Jesus was performing miracles, He always asked for something practical from the people. For example, He asked that to have jug filled with water before He could turn it into wine, He asked for few pieces of bread and then multiplied it to feed multitudes. When He needed money, He asked for someone to catch a fish and then extracted a coin from it. There must be a foundation upon which God can add His divine providence and help us to make things happen. That foundation can only be built through the work that every Christian must do.

As highlighted in the previous chapter, when we are talking about a whole life journey, we must plan our actions so that we can give God a chance to guide and lead us in the process. Even though faith can help us to do great things from time to time, only through planning we can achieve a successful destiny deployment. Without planning we are at the mercy of our own thoughts, emotions and impulses as dictated by the environment and the circumstances we find ourselves in. The Bible says *"the just shall live by faith"*. This means when we get a revelation from God about who we are or about any particular mission that we need to accomplish, we must not just believe and trust what God is telling us, but go ahead and start getting things done. We must do that even when we seem to have no resources or no obvious capacity to do what we are being told to do. We must trust that once we start getting into action, God's hands will operate and we will prevail in the end. Just imagine Noah building an ark that was going to be used to save creation from total destruction. He had no capacity, no resources and no support from the community. But he proceeded and with God's help, he was able to complete the job

With planning, we have a chance to review, assess and reassess what we are doing from an intellectual perspective, because God gave us a mind for a reason. It goes without saying that it is crucial for us to seek God's guidance and leadership in the planning, strategising, as well as in the tactical steps we take to get things done. At times, we may just receive a revelation from God (we must be prepared for this) to act immediately and we must do so without having to plan for anything, because God has His ways, which are not ours and may not necessarily appear logical or reasonable. But in the absence of any clear vision, revelation or instruction from God, we must use our brain power and our wisdom to plan and strategise our actions and leave room for God to intervene anytime and lead us to our destiny.

Growth and action

If you are not busy with God's mission in your life, you are disobeying God and disobedience means death, spiritual death. Disobedience is not simply doing the contrary of what God asks you to do, such as fornicating when God's commandment says that you shall not fornicate. Disobedience is also about not doing anything, through ignorance or laziness, when you are expected to take action. There is no doubt that God is very disappointed when He sees many of His people spend a whole life on earth without even being aware of their life purpose. When God sees His people missing their destiny completely, He calls it a wasted life, which is also another form of disobedience in His eyes.

When we receive Jesus in our heart, His presence within us often comes with a burden in our heart, a burden to do something for Him and for His Kingdom here on earth. Working for His Kingdom means doing work to help transform humanity and expand His Kingdom by positively influencing people to move in the direction of God. That burden is the cause for which we must dedicate our lives, it is our cross that we must carry until we die. Everyone one of us has their cross. Carrying a cross is about doing work with a plan and purpose. It is different from doing good deeds such as helping the poor here and there occasionally. When Jesus asks us to carry a cross and follow him (Matthew 16: 24-26,) it is about embracing a cause and then working, sweating, enduring pain and sacrifice to see it through. That often involves investing time and money, to take that cause to the mountain top. This is what Jesus means by asking us to carry our cross and follow Him. Some of us realise this quite early in our Christian journey and we dedicate ourselves accordingly. Others either remain ignorant, negligent or get distracted for many years until something heavy hits them in the face and they have no other option, but to serve God, a bit like Apostle Paul. The best way to grow our Christian faith is through action directed in a particular spiritually-inspired cause that we choose in the name of Jesus. We need to be busy for Jesus, once we stop the "doing" we start losing focus and ultimately, we may end up losing our faith.

For example, even though keeping sabbath is not a requirement in the New Testament, keeping the tradition to attend church every week enables people to grow their faith, because it gets people together in the name of their faith and also keeps them busy in doing things for God, at least once a week. The tradition gives many people opportunities to be useful in the congregation. There will be a lot fewer Christians in the world without Sunday church services, not just because of preaching and teaching (which we can get from our electronic devices these days), but because of the fellowship and the work to organise it and make it useful for the community of believers. The only way to remain obedient to the will of God in our lives is to remain in action. That action can start from our own family and then evolve in our local church, our community and beyond. We must create daily routines, develop habits, plan things, based on clear goals, take steps and develop a commitment around the things that we are called to do.

12 Practical steps to develop an action plan for Destiny Deployment.

1 Create an environment that will encourage you to pursue your vision in God

Once you a have clear vision of your Destiny Mission, create a personal environment that encourages you to get into action. Continually expose yourself to people, images and sound that add value to your spiritual and intellectual life and encourage you to excel. Cut out anything in your life (including friends) that is not helping you to grow spiritually and grow your God-given gifts. Create order in your life and set up personal boundaries that keep you focused and busy.

2 Set up a personal prayer regime

Pray several times every day and pray for your Destiny plans and goals more than you pray for anything else. Prayer moves God and helps to mobilise spiritual energy within you. It also sets the universe in motion to deliver things to you into the physical world at the time that is right with God. Prayer is a licence allowing you to invite and allow God to move into your life. God is a gentleman, He likes being invited and He always delivers more than what you expect, if you stick with Him long enough.

3 Build and develop a Destiny mindset
Embrace the pursuit of excellence in your area of gifting. Whatever gifts and talents you think you have received from God, decide to develop them and excel in them. Build a mindset focused on growth, as well as high spiritual and emotional wisdom. Train and program your mind by praying repeatedly, as a means to exercise dominion in your own spiritual and cognitive environment. Prayer enables mind programming and facilitates the development of a new mindset focused on God.

4 Create habits for success
Build suitable habits and routines that will help you to progressively utilise your gifts, talents and skills in line with your Destiny vision and mission. Build a daily routine that helps you get things done little by little. Rome wasn't built in a day and your destiny is a lifetime business with God. Monitor and assess your own progress regularly and make changes where you see the need to or where the spirit of God is leading you.

5 Learn something every day
Ignorance kills and the only thing that kills ignorance is education, especially self-education. Educate yourself and try to learn something every day. Spend time reading and studying the scriptures. At the same time, seek advanced knowledge in your area of expertise (professional skills) and focus on developing

any other talents and gifts you may have. Aim to develop some expertise in your area of gifting by learning as much as possible. One hour every day on any given subject will make you a subject matter expert in that field in just 2 years.

6 *Diarise your learning experience and revisit it regularly.*

Plan your learning and do one task every day that will get you closer to achieving any goal that is connected to your Destiny Mission. For example, if you have ever wanted to write a book, decide to write half a page or one full page every day. Before you know it, you will want to write more and finish the book quicker and possibly write more books.

7 *Nurture companionship and relationships for your destiny*

The first companion for your destiny is your spouse, if you have one. Make sure he or she can see clearly the vision you have and how he/she can support you for it, at the same time as you support him/her as well. The best thing is for the two of you to work for one vision.

Create your "Destiny Companionship" with like-minded friends, elders in faith, coaches and mentors to help you. Build a team and a network that supports your Destiny work and invest in it too. Value all people and add something to their lives whenever you can, you never know who God can use to lift you up to your next level.

8 *Teach to learn*

Whatever you want to specialise in, create opportunities to teach what you are learning, it is the best way to learn. Read, watch or listen to expert material in your chosen field every day for at least one hour. Use technologies such as wireless headphones and a mobile phone to learn through audio books, videos and other digital material. You may also want to use social media platforms and blogs to share your learnings and, when ready, promote your expertise widely as a means to create impact.

9 Seek coaching and mentorship proactively
Seek coaching and mentorship actively and don't hesitate to pay for it if you can't get it for free. It can cut years in your learning journey and save you a lot of pain. Identify biblical characters or reputable Christian leaders and read their material continually. Speak to your Pastor about regular Destiny coaching sessions.

10 Renew and re-program your mind
Recite and rehearse your vision, life goals and key bible verses every day. Sing praises regularly to lift yourself up and train your mind to revere and worship God. Learn songs that connect with your Destiny Mission. Songs are powerful motivators.

11 Fast and pray for your Destiny Mission on a regular basis.
Attend to your destiny mission every day. Ensure you can see, hear or feel something about your Destiny Mission every day. Stick a picture on your desk or office wall or use anything visual so that you remind yourself several times every day. Break your Destiny work into goals and objectives with a specific timeline on it. Time is a limited resource. Find a way to do even very little tasks daily (e.g. write one page a day, if you are an author) and reward yourself in the process. Take steps to organise an accountability partner to monitor your goals and ensure you do what you set out to do.

12 Think and do charity

Whatever you do, there is always room to help other people. Charity is a must for Christians. It can be done individually, through your local church or other organisations. Go beyond money and reach out to people who need help. Don't just give money, go where the needy people are and talk to them, touch them and hold them if you can and tell them about the love of Christ. Join a charity organisation (there is strength in unity) or create one if there is none that fits your idea of deploying your Destiny Mission, it could be the reason why God created you.

CHAPTER SEVEN

Keyword 7

Dominate

> **KEY POINTS**
> - Dominate the world through leadership, love, compassion and creativity
> - Exercise dominion through your fruitfulness and multiplication
> - Develop a dominion mindset: you have a mandate to dominate on behalf of God
> - Dominate on behalf of God, not for your own glory

"God said: be fruitful and increase in number, fill the earth and subdue it. Rule over the fish in the sea and the birds in the sky and over living creature that moves on the ground".

Genesis 1:28

AFTER CREATING MANKIND AND PLACING THEM IN THE GARDEN of Eden, God did two things: He gave Adam instructions not eat fruits from the tree of the knowledge of good and evil. He also blessed Adam and Eve to "be fruitful, fill the earth and have dominion over creation". These two things are extremely important in understanding and achieving our God-given destiny. Firstly, God legislates His authority over mankind. He establishes boundaries and instructs man on what he is allowed to do and what he is not allowed to do. Secondly, we see God mandating humanity to take charge and dominate the earth as His agents working under His authority. That authority is exercised when man devotes his skills, gifts and talents to help create a reality on earth that is in line with God's will. The biggest lesson in this passage is that as long as man remains under the law and leadership of God he has a mandate to dominate creation, he is blessed with fruitfulness and multiplication.

Primary and secondary creation

By giving us dominion over creation, God wanted us to manage His creation, as well as continue the creation work, not in terms of "speaking new things into existence" like He did, but using our intellectual, physical and spiritual faculties to cultivate new things, replenish the earth, manage creation and produce new things that add to the beauty of God's creation. When we do so we create beauty, add value to and help make life a more enjoyable and fulfilling experience for ourselves and for people around us. In this sense there is primary creation and secondary creation. Primary creation is God's creation that brings about natural things such as plants, soil, the sun, water and other such things. Secondary creation is when we use our faculties and abilities to create new things out of what nature makes available to us and in the process, we add value to humanity.

An example of a secondary creation is when a garden is created out of the bush by planting various plants in some new and orderly fashion that creates beauty and harmony that goes beyond what we can observe in the wild. God Himself showed us an example of this by planting a garden in Eden, where He placed Adam. It is important to note the way the Bible has worded things by saying that God "planted" the garden, not "created" the garden. God did not "speak" the garden into existence. It suggests that God had to do something extra in planting the garden, he used His will and purpose for the achievement of a particular goal.

Just like God, we need to create or build things that are "good" to see. Such things will not just be beautiful, but they will connect with the divine purpose for creation and enable us to exercise the stewardship we have been given over it. Additionally, because of sin that wrecked God's original plans for mankind, we need to do things that contribute to the restoration of humanity. Dominion in the Bible is not about dominating other human beings for egoistic or evil purposes, it is about showing a dominating level of care, leadership and excellence in one's "field of divine gifting". When God gives us gifts, these are meant to be used to serve His purpose on earth.

Live and work like Jesus

In this chapter we will focus on God's instructions and blessing for man to dominate the earth and how that relates to what God expects us to do in relation to our destiny. There is no dominion without action. We need to remember that faith is from God and action is ours. Our faith comes from God, He gives us faith and what He expects from us is that we give Him action, which speaks on behalf of the faith we have in Him. The purpose of faith is twofold: to rebuild our relationship with God and to inspire us for action that connects with His plans for humanity. By action, we don't just mean "good deeds" or "living a righteous or holy life", but we mean a life dedicated to the achievement of one's life purpose and destiny, as ordained by God.

As stated previously, Jesus' main life purpose was to carry the cross and His destiny was to become the spiritual saviour of humanity. Both of these things involved action, not just isolated action, but a long-term focus, work and investment for the sake of impacting the world. The work of Jesus also included a level of suffering and sacrifice that was intrinsically attached to His existence on this planet. To achieve His purpose and accomplish His destiny on earth, Jesus was focused on the work of His Father. He even equated it to food in John 4:34 by stating: *"My food is to do the will of Him who sent me and to finish His work"*. Jesus worked hard day and night and He was never tired of the work He was doing. By analysing the Bible, we find 7 activities that dominated Jesus work on earth, besides prayer:

1. Preaching
2. Teaching
3. Leading and coaching (the disciples)
4. Caring for needy people
5. Healing
6. Delivering people (from demonic possessions).
7. Performing miracles

Jesus did all these things with authority, which gave Him dominion over natural laws and spiritual powers, alike. All Christians are expected to live like Jesus and imitate what Jesus did. Although not all of us can do everything Jesus did, each one of us is gifted in some ways by God. The only difference is that many people need others to discover the gifts they have from

God. The 5 ministries that are listed in the Bible (pastorship, apostleship, prophesy, teaching and evangelisation) are all about the church helping people to reconnect with God and discover their true identity, their mission on earth and the gifts they have been entrusted with. Not everyone's destiny is linked to the above 5 ministries, but all Christians have abilities and gifts to make an impact in the world. Such impact can be done through sharing knowledge (1), leading others (2), caring for the needy (3) and demonstrating dominion over supernatural forces (4). Jesus has already done His Job by investing in us and He is ready to bless and anoint us when we stand ready to impact the world in His name. He requires dedication and boldness from us. Christians are called to dominate the world as leaders, and this can only happen if people are focused on their area of gifting as preordained by God.

Once we understand that we have been wired by our manufacturer to dominate the world, we must seek His help and know His plans for the work we need to do here on earth. There are three parts in doing anything with a sense of purpose: knowing what you must do (1), planning what you must do (2) and working tirelessly until the job is done (3).

Let us examine these three things in more detail:

Genesis dominion: a packaged deal

When God blessed man to have dominion over creation, He was sending him to work and giving him a licence for the management of the garden and everything that was connected to it. That was the original destiny of man: to manage creation with the blessing, authority and dominion of God. Because Destiny work is mandated by God, it is important to understand what sort of mandate it is. We need to know what we are being asked to do, what is the purpose of it and why it is necessary. When these things are clear, then we can plan our work and perform it with a strong faith and an unwavering commitment.

God blessed mankind in the Garden of Eden to have dominion and we will refer to this as the "Genesis Dominion". It is important to analyse the Genesis dominion properly and break it down to its various components to draw all important lessons from it. What type of dominion did God mandate mankind for? Why does God want man to have dominion over the earth? How does God expect man to exercise that dominion? What prevents people from achieving their God ordained dominion? These are some of the questions that need to be addressed in looking at dominion.

First, it is important to note that the blessing that God gave to mankind to 'have dominion" over the earth and subdue it, this blessing was multiple and multidimensional. The blessing for dominion, the blessing for fruitfulness and the blessing for multiplication. It was a "packaged deal" and needs to be understood as such. Dominion, fruitfulness and multiplication, they were all offered in the same divine uttering and cannot be disassociated from each other. There are two lessons to learn here: firstly, our ability to dominate nature and all other circumstances of life is connected to our ability to be fruitful and show multiplication in our lives. Secondly, the full package of the Genesis blessing is a product of growth and maturity. Human beings, animals and plants can only multiply and produce their own kinds once they have achieved a certain level of physical growth. If you can grow, you can become mature and maturity will equip you for fruitfulness, which automatically comes with multiplication.

Dominate

When you look at nature you notice that in the beginning there is a seed, a seed grows into a tree, the tree grows into maturity, which in turn triggers the fructification process. The beginning is singular but the end is plural. A single seed can bring about thousands of fruits. At the two ends of the process you have a seed and fruits. In between the seed and the fruits there is a growth process that is governed by a number of supernatural and natural things, including genetic coding (1), environment/ecology (2) and nutrition (3). The genetic coding is the program that is embedded in the seed and which tells the seed what to do and guides it through the growth process towards maturity and fruitification. The environment or the ecology enables the seed to take shape and source its nutrition, without which the seed is unable to survive.

When God created mankind, He planted one single seed and that seed was meant to bring blessings to generations, on the condition that the environment and the nutrition is right. This is the same for our Genesis dominion. God has planted the seed for the dominion in us, but we must take care of the environmental and nutritional needs in order for us to fully experience and benefit from the dominion. God's seed in us is the gift of destiny (life with purpose). At the centre of our destiny there is a gift. Every one of us has a seed for a special gift that has God has placed inside of us. We simply need to provide that seed with a good environment, i.e. good soil with water and sufficient exposure to sunlight and the "magic of God" that is in the gift will take its course and everything will develop from the genetic code that is implanted within the seed. No one tells a seed to germinate and grow. It knows what to do based on what is contained in it. When the seed of a tree is planted on fertile ground and the baby tree shoots off the ground, it gradually grows to the point that it naturally dominates the area around it. Therefore, it is rare to see another tree of the same size grow in the shadow of a growing tree, because as the tree grows it naturally colonises the ground under it. Grass and other smaller plants can grow under it, but not another tree of the same calibre. This shows that dominion is a product of growth which is a God-ordained process, a type of divine software that tells the seed what to do, how to interact with nature and what to produce at different stages of its development.

All believers in Christ have the seed of greatness and the blessing of dominion deposited in them by God. As long as you give the seed within you what it needs to grow, the rest of the growth process is taken care of by the "divine program encoded in the original seed" and that same growth process brings the dominion with it, as long as the environment and the nutrition are healthy. Everything about the growth process that is encoded in the seed, including the size, direction, number of branches, number and size of the fruits, all these things are taken care of by the genetic code inside the seed, which was deposited by the Creator of the seed. God who gives us the seed of our destiny has encoded everything within us, we must take care of the environment we expose ourselves in and what we feed ourselves with and the rest of what we need is automatically provided.

10 ways we can exercise dominion here on earth

1 Dominion through fruitfulness
Agricultural metaphors are all over the Bible. They are very good tools to help illustrate God's role in designing plants and their purpose in nature. They also show the role of man in investing physical energy (work) to cultivate the plants and gain significant benefits from them. There are approximately 34 verses about

fruits in the Bible. The fruit analogy is quite powerful as it illustrates the value that things and people are expected to bring into the human family. Fruits are products of a tree or a plant. Every fruit also has seeds that contain the genetic material or information that is necessary for activation, germination growth and reproduction (multiplication). Fruits are the multiplied products of the gift that is placed in a seed. In order words, fruits are gifts of the gift.

Fruit trees are food manufacturing machines. Trees don't eat the fruits they produce, they don't benefit directly from their fruits, but people and other creatures in the environment do. Trees may receive secondary benefits from their fruits, such as when birds come to eat the fruits and drop their manure on the ground to fertilise the soil, which will make the tree healthier. The main lesson here is that our gifts to the world are not primarily designed to benefit us, we must simply focus on delivering them to those who need it. As we do so, anyone who needs our gifts will usually bring something to us that will benefit us in some ways. The more fruits we have, the more people will want to come to us and the more benefits we will receive from them, directly or indirectly. What we produce to the world from within us not only enables us to dominate the world through fruitfulness, but it also indirectly brings us provision for further growth and subsistence.

If a fruit tree has no fruit it becomes useless. The story of Jesus cursing a fig tree (Mark 11:12-25) is quite powerful in illustrating how God expects us to bear fruits. Jesus knew very well that fig trees only bear fruits in season, therefore it was not the tree's fault that it did not have any fruits when Jesus wanted it to have fruits. If the tree could talk, it would probably say to Jesus "Master, why do you want me to bear fruits when it is not my season to do so?". However, Jesus was trying to make a point that the tree was useless without fruits and this lesson applies to humans too. He also said that *"you will know them by their fruits"* (Matthew 7:15). In this sense the fruits we produce is a projection of our identity.

The fruits of our work are a manifestation of who we are. This is why our work should primarily be an expression of identity, not just an instrument for income generation. The world has conditioned us to think of work as an income generation exercise. But in the beginning work was a platform for the manifestation of our God-given identity. Adam did not need to work to survive, the garden provided everything he needed. God gave him the work to manage the garden or creation, which was a fundamental aspect of his identity as set by God. This shows that it is through work that we fully become what God wants us to be. It is through work that we become one with Jesus and He becomes one with us.

Many times, in the Bible Jesus linked the work of His father with His identify as the son of God, who was one with the father and the father one with Him. Whatever work we do ends up reflecting our inner self and our very identity, as a person. You can look at the faces of two people, one being a soldier and the other being a priest or minister of God. If these people are really good at what they do and they have done it for many years, you will surely be able to recognise who is who, without knowing them. Their work will show on their faces. A good soldier, like a commando, will surely have a face that will look different from that of a very good minister of God.

Fruitfulness in the Bible is about work, but not work as most people understand it. In the capitalistic societies that we live in today, we see work as something we must do to earn our living and pay bills. While this may look normal to most humans, in the eyes of God, work is not primarily about paying bills. In the garden of Eden, before the fall of man, work was about a divine mandate to be useful in the bigger scheme of God. God mandated Adam to manage the garden. That work was connected with Adam's self-affirmation, framed in the obedience framework. Adam's obedience to God was meant to enable him to become his true self. When one finds their true calling in God, dominion comes naturally because it is mandated by the creator of the universe.

In many of his preachings, Dr. Myles Munroe used to differentiate work with job. He said that our "job" is about earning an income and our "work" is about our divine mission on earth. This is a very good way of looking at how we use our time on earth and the meaning we assign to our various occupations. Ideally, we must always strive to live from our work, but if we must have a job, we need to ensure it does not overshadow our work. Apostle Paul was a tent maker, but his life was dedicated to building churches and preaching the Gospel to gentiles. He naturally dominated the world and is remembered for his (gospel) work, not for his tent- making job.

Our behaviours, our utterances, our attitudes, our dreams, visions and work, all these things are fruits coming from the seeds that are inside of us and that we have provided good soil for during many years, consciously or unconsciously. Because of sin, all humans have both good and bad seeds within them. Whatever we give good soil to naturally grows and produces fruits, good or bad, within us and without. Whatever we plant within us and give good soil to ends up dominating our identity. When focusing on our destiny work, a key question that we must all ask ourselves is: "what am I producing as fruits for the human family?".

Focus on Destiny

The western culture in general and American culture in particular is dominated by individualism and consumerism, which are all birthed by capitalism as the mother ideology. At the centre of this ideology the focus is on "having", rather than "being". It encourages people to pay more attention to what they want to acquire or possess in life, what they want to get for themselves in an individualistic or egoistic sense. But the culture of the Kingdom of God is inviting us to focus on the "Be" and not on "Have". There is a reason why we are called human "beings" and not human "having". Jesus wants us to be people who can produce fruits, in the name of God, so that humanity can benefit from them in a true altruistic sense of the word. When we do so, the very act of providing fruits also brings provision to our own lives, because fruits are attractive, delicious and nutritious and people will come to us to fetch them and leave something in return.

Fruitfulness and process
Before a tree can produce fruits, it must first deploy all its parts both underground and above ground. It must grow to maturity through enough interactions with its immediate environment. There are many things we can learn from the process that leads to fructification. Let us look at the following five things that relate to fructification:
1. Seed planting
2. Germination
3. Growth
4. Maturity
5. Seasonality

These things can teach us a lot about our destiny deployment, because it is all about bearing fruits for God.

Dominate

A tree must first be born of a seed before bearing fruits. Being born is the first step and then the tree must grow enough to reach maturity and be ready for fructification. Besides maturity, there is also seasonality. A tree can be mature but have no fruits because it is not the right season for it to produce fruits. Destiny living also follows these same patterns and the life of Jesus illustrates things quite well. Jesus was conceived from of a divine seed (1) that was deposited miraculously into Mary's womb. He was born like every human (2) and then grew up (3), but He did not do much until He reached maturity at the age of thirty (4), as per the Jewish customs at His time. When He started His ministry, He told His disciples about the need not to tell people about His messianic identity until when it was the right time to do so (5). He went on to develop a team of disciplines in the same way a tree will grow branches before producing fruits. It is through the disciples that humanity has come to eat of the fruits of the gospel. This is multiplication, as He multiplied Himself as a human being through His disciples, who were expected to deliver the fruit of the gospel to the world. Jesus Himself did not need the gospel, but humanity did.

Many of us today want to get everything too quickly and be out there and successful in no time, forgetting that God who created this world has set rules and principles in place that we must abide by in order to satisfy Him and be truly successful in His eyes. God took six days to create the world and this tells us that even God wanted creation to be part of a process that takes time. This means there is time for everything. Farmers know that the best fruits are those that are produce by the tree at the right time or season. Fruits that come too early or too late (out of season), taste differently and often are not the best.

We must live our destiny on earth with the full knowledge of the principles that govern the fructification process. We need to identify, assess and develop the skills, gifts, talents that we have, both those that are inborn and the ones we acquire through learning and training. We need to invest time and effort to develop the skills that are necessary for our destiny deployment. Skills are useless unless they are put into action for the achievement of a particular goal. Skills must be at the service of a vision or they can become useless or even harmful for the soul. Christianity is not just faith, understood as a belief system, but it is a mission, understood as work geared towards the restoration of humanity. God gives us faith and we pay him back with our work and worship. He invests faith in us and expects to see us get his work done on earth, because He has removed Himself from physicality and wants to work with us who are rooted in the physical world. God gave us dominion over the physical world and expects us to do work to deliver value on His creation. Every man since Adam, including Jesus Christ, has been part of God's plan for the restoration of humanity. That work has involved the harmonious combination of the spiritual with the physical. Christ was spiritual and Jesus was physical and together, they delivered the saviour on earth.

Fruitfulness outside of the church
For God's plans to come to past and His Kingdom to expand on earth, it requires work. Unlike what many Christian believers think, much of this work is actually outside rather than inside Christian congregations (churches). There is a reason why Jesus did not build any church building. For Him the whole world is His church, which needs to be restored. God so much loved the world that He gave Jesus. Our work on behalf of God enables us to transfer value from the spiritual realm into the physical

world. We get inspired spiritually, our mind gets impacted, our consciousness is transformed and our hands get busy with work so that we can produce good fruits. If we do this well, dominion comes naturally in the process and the vision of God materialises, as a consequence. If Jesus Himself came on earth to accomplish restoration work, then we should not be just talking with our mouths, singing praise and getting excited inside the four walls of our congregations. Each one of us has his or her own work to impact the world. Every Christians must investigate what their work is as they interact with God every day. However, as for everything in our spiritual life, the life of Jesus offers us a mirror we can look into to see our spiritual self-reflected. Jesus made us leaders, all Christians are leaders who are expected to lead in their area of gifting and conviction. Our Christian congregations should be training centres to equip believers to develop their faith and deploy their gifts as preachers of the gospel, teachers of the scriptures, healers of the sick, carers of needy, liberators of the oppressed, leaders of God's peoples, financiers of the work of God and problem-solvers of various kinds who make a way where there seems to be no way, because of the power the one who lives in them.

2 Dominion Through Multiplication

Multiplication is another principle established by God, as a means to execute His will in the physical world. Most people think that when God blessed Adam and Eve and told them to multiply, He was talking about procreation only, but this is not really the case. God certainly wanted humanity to reproduce itself and He built all the mechanics of reproduction in the biology of man and woman to enable reproduction. In this sense, the first parents did not necessarily need extra blessing for procreation because the blessing was built in the biology. But if God commanded man to multiply, this is because He wanted not only to ordain or command the biological mechanics to be set in motion for procreation to take place, but He also wanted man to deploy everything that was invested in Him and create abundance of all types. The blessing of multiplication goes beyond biology. It is also spiritual, intellectual and physical.

Today, neuroscience informs us that that every time we learn something new we create and multiply new connections in our brain and the more we learn the more connections take place between the brain cells (neurons). The sum of the all the connections in our brain makes our intellectual capital. This tells us that learning is multiplying connections in our brain. The more we learn, the more authority we build in our field of learning. If we do it long and seriously enough, we end up naturally dominating the field in question and becoming an authority in our community and beyond. In the Bible, God says that my people perish because of lack of knowledge. Because knowledge is acquired through learning, we can say that people of God perish because they fail to "multiply" their knowledge capital that has been invested in them. We all have a duty to grow and multiply our God-given knowledge capital.

Spiritually, the law or principle of multiplication also applies. We multiply our spiritual capital through awareness, attention, intention, and action, which can all be expressed in the form of focus, meditation and prayer. We can only connect with God through attention and the more attention we pay to God in terms of His will and His work in our lives, the more spiritual abundance we attract in our life. This is why Jesus says He had come to give us life, life in Abundance. By multiplying our attention to God, we produce the fruits of the spirit and those fruits generate benefits that we can enjoy in other aspects of our lives.

True spiritual growth is not about knowing the scriptures, even though this is important. True spiritual growth must lead one to become aware of self and God and then act, behave and work for a higher purpose than their own "self". As mentioned earlier, Jesus said: *"You will know them by their fruits"* (Mat 7:15-22). Here Jesus is drawing our attention to the fact that our very identity is based on or reflected through what we produce as fruits that people can benefit from. Jesus never monetised His teachings and miracle works. While in today's world it is not necessarily a sin to draw financial benefits from the things of value that we can produce from our spiritual blessings, the difference is in how much focus and the degree to which we prioritise money over service to humanity, as we serve a higher purpose.

3 Dominion through and attention and focus

It is important to note that the multiplication blessing as described above, is attached to "attention". The moment we start paying sufficient attention to something is when we start multiplying the brain resources within us to help design and produce the work for it. Then with work comes the fruits. The Bible says in 1 Timothy 4:16: *"Pay close attention to yourself and to your teaching; persevere in these things, for as you do this you will ensure salvation both for yourself and for those who hear you."*. Attention must be developed into focus and when you focus on something you give it life and you magnify it. If you focus on your purpose for life, you automatically give life to it and if you work on it long enough, you create your destiny out of it. This is why this book is titled "Focus on your Destiny". It is designed to

Focus on Destiny

help you give life to your destiny by investing attention and focus into it consistently and appropriately.

The ability to pay attention to and keep focus on things is what makes a difference between success and failure. It is through human attention that ideas and concepts are formed, inventions are developed and technologies are created. Nothing can be conceived, achieved or realised by a human being without proper attention. If a human being permanently loses his or her ability to pay attention to anything, they cease to be human. The people in our communities who pay attention long enough to what matters in the society often end up being our heroes and our leaders. Wherever your attention goes, the whole of you follows. Unfortunately, our ability to pay attention, as a human race, is dwindling due to, amongst other things new digital technologies and many other factors. Many of us are victims of "Divided Attention Disorder" (DAD) and this condition diminishes our ability to focus and deliver good work. The direct consequence of this situation is that most of us do not grow enough, hence we become unable to produce the fruits that God expects us to deliver to humanity, as part of our destiny mission.

Although many of us Christians have become more knowledgeable of the scriptures, the great majority of us do not invest enough time to focus on God's commission in our lives. The scriptures are meant to give us knowledge as light to use for our journey, as we get busy with our divine mission on earth. There is a big deficit of fruitfulness in the lives of many Christians today, despite the increase in the knowledge of the scriptures. God doesn't give us faith just for us to know Him or just for our own benefits. He gives us faith primarily to enable us to transact with Him and enable us to make ourselves available to Him so that He can help us and lead us into our destiny on earth, to make sure we can play our role in the expansion of His Kingdom. God certainly gives us a lot of things as our provider, including peace of mind, good health, wisdom, material abundance and many other benefits. However, all these things are primarily meant to equip us to do His work on earth. If you are not doing your "divine work", God is not impressed with your prayers, worship, fasting and any other such things. Your life on planet earth needs to be centred on your divine life assignment. It is not about religious activities designed to simply revere God, to fear and acknowledge Him and live a holy life. All these things are good, but if you are not focusing on your destiny, you are missing the most important thing in your relationship with Him, you are focusing on what is accessory in the eyes of God. This is why many people may actually be very successful in what they do, live a holy life, but still completely miss their destiny.

Many congregations today are struggling to even just get their believers to pay attention to the sermon being delivered on Sunday morning services. Often the preacher is competing with believers' mobile phones for attention. Our generation is now addicted to being distracted all the time. In such a context, getting people to pay attention to their destiny mission becomes a mammoth challenge. Destiny deployment is a very serious business.

Another thing that is not helping believers is the fact that many preachers inside congregations are not offering sufficiently mature teachings to their congregants. The rise of Pentecostal churches has also brought about an increase in dramatic and spectacular scenes inside churches, with lots of sloganeering, dramatic prophesying, tongue speaking and miracle deliveries. As a result, our churches are becoming some sort of "spiritual bars", where people go to "get high" and feel good about themselves and about God. More and more churches leaders are just preaching the message they want their members to hear rather than what they must or need to hear for their spiritual growth. They do this because they want their members to be excited so that they can stick around, give money to the church, and bring their friends and relatives to help the congregation grow. Churches are no longer a place where people are given solid spiritual knowledge and nutrition for Christian maturity. They have ceased being platforms for coaching believers for discipleship and the accomplishment of their God's destiny in their lives. Most of our churches today have become some sort of "spiritual massage parlours". Because of this, people's attention to what matters or what God expects of them is being diverted or diluted into many things designed to please them and make them feel good so that they can help to grow the ministry. The main focus has shifted from spiritual growth into ministry growth. Building church buildings rather than building people. There is not sufficient "attention to Christ details" in these congregations, hence believers are neglecting their destiny assignment.

Your attention is precious in the eyes of God, because that is where everything begins, including consciousness, identity, willpower, faith, obedience, purpose and work. Once you invest in your attention, it develops into a focus and focus leads you to action, which then develops into work and that brings transformation and restoration. This is what Christianity is really about.

4 *Dominion and Maturity*
In a fallen world, Genesis dominion can only come as a by-product of spiritual/Christian maturity. It is important to note that spiritual maturity cannot be ordained or decreed, it must be developed and earned in practice, through the exercise of our

faith, the acquisition of knowledge, our obedience and trust in God, discipline and determination, as well as the use of all the resources that God has deposited in us. We learn these things, not only through the study of scriptures, but the best way to learn things of God is through direct experience, as we navigate life. Head knowledge, though important, does not necessarily give maturity, it must be combined with lived experience. Christian maturity must lead us to discover our Purpose-driven and Heavenly-inspired Destiny (PHD). Jesus warned us in Matthew 7:21 that:

> "Not everyone who says to me, 'Lord, Lord' will inherit the Kingdom of Heaven, but those who do the will of my Father who is in heaven".

The question that follows from this is "What will was Jesus talking about?". I recently asked this question to my brethren when teaching the word at my local Church. Many people responded by saying that what Jesus was referring to as the "will" of his father relates to God's laws and commandments in the Bible and whatever else God wants them to do. Most people appeared to take the view that through that passage, Jesus wanted people to be obedient to the Word of God and not just profess their faith verbally.

While the above answers are not false per se, in this book we submit that the "will" of the God in our lives goes beyond obeying the laws or commandments in the scriptures. The will of God has two aspects to it: the general will (for the human family) and specific will (for each individual person). However, it is through the specific will of God that His general will can be accomplished. What each one of us does with God enables Him to accomplish His will for His Kingdom. God has assigned a will to every individual human being on earth. He created all of us with a purpose. He brought us from 'eternity' into 'physicality' because He has something that He wants us to do on earth with our physical life. That something is our divine mission. It is the work that He wants us to do for Him and that no one else can do quite like us. His will is that we do that work on this planet and do it fully and diligently, just like Jesus did when He lived on earth. When we do that work, we accomplish our "destiny" and God gets more value from our lives. If God did not have any mission or assignment for us in the physical world, He would have kept us as spiritual beings in the eternal realm.

5 Dominion through Leadership

When someone develops Christian maturity, they are automatically pushed into action, they seek to be impacted by God's anointing so that they can impact the world for His sake. Maturity breeds leadership and leadership generates dominion. Jesus said in Mat 5:14-16:

> "You are the light of the world. A town built on a hill cannot be hidden. Neither do people light a lamp and put it under a bowl. Instead they put it on its stand, and it gives light to everyone in the house".

When we are fully in Christ, He lets His light glow in and through us and we find ourselves dominating our environment in the same way light dominates darkness. Light does not dominate darkness to benefit from it, it simply dominates because of its very intrinsic nature. When we are born again through Christ, we automatically get a mandate of leadership, to show the light of

God and chase darkness out of this very dark world. When this is done, we bring about a better reality in the world, in the same way light brings a better reality and an improved experience of things compared to darkness.

6 Dominion and self-leadership

Dominion through divine leadership requires a number of things. Firstly, a vision from God so that we can use His guidance to lead ourselves and to lead others. No leader can be truly a leader if they can't lead themselves first and foremost. The management of self is a very serious business and most humans are not very good at it. The self in us is dominated by the desires of the flesh and the conditioning of our culture. When we discover our true spiritual identity/self, we must tame the biologically driven "self" that other people refer to as the "animal" in us. We cannot live without God's leadership and we cannot adequately lead ourselves without help from the one who made us. When God gives us a vision, the power of that vision will provide enough force to help drive ourselves to a position of leadership and divine dominion. Divine vision and leadership are needed to transform you, so that you can help to transform the world by transferring the benefits of your own transformation to people around you and beyond.

7 Dominion and management.

Leadership goes together with management. Every leader is a manager, even though some manager are not leaders. Whatever leadership goes, management must follow. God gave mankind a job in the garden of Eden to manage creation, cultivate the land and take care of all creation. Every man must learn leadership and management, because we all lead a life of some sort, we are all leaders of our own lives and every leader is a manager. This means every human must learn good life management skills. Whatever gift, skills, talents and resources that God has given to us, they need to be managed well. If we fail to manage well, we lose what we have been given. Good management is the reason why, at least materially, people in Western countries enjoy a better life than those in third world countries, even though there are more natural resources in third world countries. God has established the principle of good management as an avenue for His blessings to materialise in the physical realm. Because of this, whatever we manage well will flourish and whatever we mismanage will be lost or taken away from us.

Our churches should be places where we learn life management skills. Life management education includes many things, such as knowing and expressing our identity, self-leadership/development, understanding socio-cultural conditioning, mindset programming and re-programming, emotional intelligence, relationship management, communication (intrapersonal and interpersonal), planning and goal setting, strategic thinking, problem solving, wealth creation (business), healthy living. Christians are not just leaders by virtue of receiving the light of Christ in their lives, they also need to be good managers of their own lives, their own families and their own affairs. When good leadership is combined with good management, dominion comes naturally.

8 Dominion and Communication

There is no effective leadership without good communication. Communication is both the easiest and the most difficult thing in life. Human beings communicate all the time, both directly or indirectly, willingly or unwillingly. They do this with words, writings, gestures, body language etc. However, many issues in our lives come from lack of communication or simply poor communication. People in any community who master the art of communication often become leaders, because they know how to capture the deepest desires and fears prevailing in their community and are able to craft words that connect with the feelings, hopes and aspirations of their people to the point where the rest of the community is naturally inspired to follow them, respect or even revere them in some circumstances.

Jesus impacted His generation by preaching and teaching the gospel. It was all about communication. His message lingers today not just because of its spiritual power, but because it was communicated in a way that conveys profound meaning and life wisdom across various generations. The depth of the Gospel has touched and will continue to touch the human soul to the core for many more generations to come.

If God is the Father of Creation, then maybe communication is its mother. Because in the beginning God spoke, He communicated and commanded nature to birth things from nothingness. There is power in God's utterances. When God communicates, creation follows. Whatever God affirms gets translated into reality. "Let there be light" and light was. The physical world came into being because God communicated and ordered nature to come into existence. Once man was created, God communicated to him as a means to lead and guide him by establishing the rules in the garden and releasing various forms of blessings in his life. In the same way evil came into the world through communication, when the Devil talked to Eve and tempted her to disobey God. Then Eve communicated to Adam and the rest is history. Throughout the Bible, the key word that summarises everything is communication. All scriptures are a form of communication between God and humanity, which is why we call the Bible the Word of God. A word is a verbal or written expression of something, which is meant to communicate a particular 'reality' with another person.

We live in a sick world and Christians need to be able to communicate the diagnostic and therapeutic powers of the Gospel. Destiny living requires that we learn to strike a chord with people whom we are called to serve so that we can better connect with them and bring them to the light of Christ. Using the right communication helps to build a "power field" where love, support and progress can flourish, the Holy spirit can move and people can grow. Our great commission to preach the gospel is nothing more than a communication assignment. We must be clear and coherent, in our communication, not just using words alone, but express love, display good behaviours and show deeds that convey the love and fear of God. When we communicate the gospel and our faith in it and we do so with the whole of our lives, we are in a better position to dominate any field in which we are involved. God works with us when we act as His agents for divine transformation. Every agent must learn to communicate appropriately and effectively on behalf of his or her boss.

We also have the power to dominate the world and the enemy within it through words. The power of the tongue is well documented in the Bible. Provers 18:21 reminds us that *"life and death are in the power of the tongue, and those who love it will eat its fruits"*. We can bind spirits on earth through words and we can give God a licence to act in our lives using our tongue. We develop a relationship with God through our tongue as we pray more and invoke His name. When we befriend God, He gives us the power to tell the mountain to move out of the way and the mountain will oblige. That power resides in us and we must speak it, voice it, communicate it to nature and to the world.

9 Dominion through Destiny Living

People in the world live normal life, but us Christians we are called for "Destiny Living", which is a different paradigm. It may take a whole life for us to move from one to the other, but we are called to keep moving from "normal work" into "destiny work", from "employment mode" into "deployment mode", from skill-based occupation into gift-based occupation. Skills can be learned through schooling and training, but gifts are given by the creator, they are not really learned, but they can be perfected through learning and training. Destiny living doesn't mean that we all must become pastors or preachers or church leaders of some sort. A car mechanic can do destiny work by fixing people's cars and a doctor can do "destiny work" by providing care to patients. This is possible by incorporating the gospel principles in the work and demonstrating the love of Jesus through it, as long as one is truly being led by God in the process. For example, a doctor may offer to treat disadvantaged people free of charge at his/her private clinic on a regular basis where there is such a need in the community. He or she may regularly travel to a less developed country to do charity work and offer medical treatment in the name of God. In the same way a business man can provide regular financial resources to good churches and other charitable organisations, as well as coach and mentor other believers in business and wealth management, in the name of Christ. Whatever area of work that one is gifted in, there is always room for God, because it is God who provided the gift in the first place and who sustains life for the person with the gift.

However, God doesn't expect us to simply include Him in our plan, He wants us to include ourselves in His plans. This means that there must be a time when we decide, based on our growth and maturity in faith that we either quit our job (career, occupation) to do our destiny work (divine mission). This means quitting work that is done simply to pay bills and accumulate material wealth and start work that is fundamentally about a statement of who we are spiritually and our effort to help expand the Kingdom of God and leave a legacy in the world. Once we understand our work in God, just like Jesus, Apostle Paul or Peter, nothing has the power to stop us. We may find ourselves enjoying our work so much, because the energy in us is so strong and the motivation is so high to the point where it doesn't feel like work anymore. We may even endure trials and tribulations in the process, but still go on. When we get busy with the work of God we have God's blessing to dominate the world with love, leadership and care and we effectively exercise that dominion that God talks about in the book of Genesis. Every gift we have, every talent, every amount of intelligence, wisdom and energy may need to be invested in our destiny work. If you are still struggling to get up in the morning to go to work and you continually suffer from "Mondayitis", that could be a sign that you are not yet connected to your destiny work and destiny living.

10 Dominion through thoughts

Besides spiritual knowledge and revelation, the Bible also teaches us how to think properly so that we can be right in the eyes of God and accomplish His work accordingly. Philippians 4:18 says: *"Whatever is true, noble, right, pure, lovely admirable, if anything is excellent and praiseworthy, think about such things"*. There is no doubt that if we can constantly occupy our minds with truth, nobility, righteousness, purity, excellence we will not only elevate ourselves to greater heights intellectually and spiritually, but we will find favour with men and with God, as well. Our ability to please God and add value to the world is greatly impacted by our ability to think well and think holy.

The Bible also says:

"Each one of you should use whatever gift you have received to serve others as faithful stewards of God's grace in its various forms"

(1 Peter 4:10).

We must develop our thinking ability and continuously refine it through education and self-leadership. Proverbs 4:23 and Proverbs 23:7 are two important verses that remind us about the importance of thinking well. The first verse says *"be careful how you think, your life is shaped by your thoughts"*. The second one says *"for as a man thinks in his heart, so is he"*. For us Christians, the quality of our thinking will be determined by a combination of three things: education (schooling or cultural), the knowledge and Wisdom of the Word of God, as well as our own efforts to renew and develop our mind. We must always constantly seek to improve our thinking and submit our thoughts to the authority and leadership of Christ in us.

Practical Tools for dominion

1 A Spirit of obedience
God's blessing for mankind to dominate the world is first and foremost a spiritual blessing. It requires that we keep our

relationship with Him healthy and remain connected to Him. When we lose our connection to God, we cut the source for the spiritual blessing even though in the natural world things may not be visible. We must cultivate a spirit of obedience and learnt to listen to and obey and trust to God. When we do so we keep the flow of spiritual energy that gives us a vision, motivation, power and wisdom, the combination of which generates dominion over what life, the world or the enemy throw at us. Obedience brings blessings and blessings produce anointing and dominion. Obey God and get power to dominate life.

2 A Mindset of Excellence

Mindset is relatively a new word that is quite present in the personal motivation industry. The Bible talks rather about renewing our mind, but in the end, it is the same thing. The renewal of the mind is meant to help us to develop a new "mindset" to support our spiritual vision. God can have a powerful vision for your life, but if your mind remains all over the place, it will not be able to support the vision. This is why we need to "set your mind", in the same way we need to set concrete as a solid foundation before we build anything heavy on it. By renewing our mind, we develop a new way of seeing things, a new way of communicating with our self and others, as well as a new way of thinking, behaving and doing things. The Christian mindset is anchored in love, enlightened by a vision and dominated by the desire to serve Jesus. Is your mind set for Christ? If so, what are you building on it?

Renewing your mind means more than just reading the scriptures or preaching the Gospel. It seats at the intersection of spiritual wisdom and intellectual development of the person. It involves learning, re-learning and un-learning things. It requires knowing just as much about the "Word" as it does about the "world" and the ways of the devil. We need to know enough about the main ideologies, philosophies, cultural precepts and spiritual movements of the world so that we don't let ourselves fooled by them. Renewing our mind also means actively pursuing excellence in our thinking, our work, our communication, the management of our emotions and our interactions and dealings with people. All of these things are important for us to build a "destiny mindset". The holy spirit can help us renew our mind. But we must be at the driving seat and be in charge of the whole process by proactively exposing ourselves to the right teachings, the right influence and the right knowledge and information.

3 *Heartset of love*

We cannot lead and dominate the world, as Christians, unless our heart is pure, and our mind is sound and set for service, in the name of Christ. When we set our heart right and guard it accordingly, we can exercise compassionate and caring leadership. This is what God wants from us and what the world needs. We need to set our heart right for our destiny, because it is from the abundance of the heart that our mouths will be speaking most of the time. We need a "heartset" of love, care and compassion so that we become more conscious of the deep desires and emotional attachment to our beliefs. We need to program our heart, so to speak, to create an internal motivational drive that is constantly propelling us towards our mission for God. When our heart set is right, we harbour the right desires and we pursue them with conviction. Our heart is always communicating to us. It always gives us signals so that we know when to move and get something and when to stop and let it go. As people of God, we cannot always be logical, because logic is the language of physicality not spirituality. Listening to our heart gives us the benefits of a Godly inspired wisdom. When we have the right "heart set" we may aggressively pursue our Destiny work, but we will not do so by trampling on others or worse wrecking other people's lives, just because we want to achieve our own goals.

If your heart is right, it will kill all bad desires before they grow and multiply within you and become toxic. Christians are not immune to bad ideas or unholy desires; our hearts are as much exposed to evil ideas and desires as anyone else in the world. However, the Holy Spirit helps us by warning us of these things, usually through some signals in our heart. A heart that is set for Christ and destiny living will often refuse to give life to evil desires within it. It will simply nip these ideas in the bud, as the saying goes. This is why the Bible says *"above all else, guard our heart, for everything you do flows from it"* (Proverb 4:23). We best guard our heart when we build a subconscious program (just like a mindset is also a subconscious program) to help us quickly identify and reject evil and unhelpful desires entering our consciousness.

As highlighted in previous chapters, most of the deep and recurring desires in our hearts are expressions of our spiritual identity. A serial killer has recurring desires to kill so much so that it is incomprehensible when we looked at things from a purely intellectual level. Why would someone desire to kill so much and display so much cruelty against other humans for no reason? Many serial killers kill people they have never met before. They just enjoy killing. It is also the same when we hear of a paedophile leaving his wife at home and going out to have sexual intercourse with children, perhaps even abduct and kill them after raping them. Why would someone do this? Science would call these things as "mental disorders" and will not be able to explain what causes them. However, in the light of the Word of God we know that it is the spirit that controls the mind in the same way the mind controls the body. Most strong and recurring evil desires are actually expressions of evil spirits inhabiting the mind of the person and expressing themselves through hideous actions and behaviours. Because science is incompetent when it comes to spiritual matters (it cannot test them in a lab or conduct experiments), it calls all these things as mental disorders.

Renewing our mind is as much important as guarding our heart. When we accept Jesus in our heart and receive the Holy spirit, we not only have a new mind, we also have a new (spiritual) heart. We must take care of both, as the two most important instruments for a conscious living and for a spiritual expression of our identity. A right heart set will make it easy for us to vibrate to a divine frequency and we be able to start downloading the divine energy, wisdom and blessings that we need to have in order to exercise dominion on earth. There is a lot of focus in the self-help industry to get people to focus on mindset alone. While mindset is key to any transformation of the person, the feelings and desires are part of the equation. This is because thoughts and feelings work in a loop. Thoughts generate feelings and feelings do influence thoughts. Scientific investigations have also demonstrated that most of the time, the mind is at the service of emotions and the heart is the centre of feelings and emotions.

4 *A Skillset for transformation*

Many of us may be spirit-filled, tongue-speaking and blood-washed Christians, but we cannot dominate the world, if we are unable to demonstrate skills and competency in whatever we are doing on earth in the name of Christ. Jesus had great communication skills and the Bible mentions many times when He was speaking with authority and He commanded attention and respect when addressing crowds. This is why the Jewish establishment saw Him as a danger and started opposing Him. This shows that Jesus' divine powers were not the only ones He relied on, He had a skillset that enabled Him to deliver the gospel effectively and powerfully.

All of us have skills and gifts from God, even before we are saved. In the old days, Christian leadership relied mostly on the power of the Holy Spirit to help them deliver the gospel to communities and make a difference in the world. However, in today's world we need more than that, given the increasingly complex nature of the world and the dominance of scientific thinking. Science is the "new god" today, therefore it becomes imperative for all Christians, especially Christian leaders to educate themselves and, build a solid skillset that is needed to navigate and impact the world today.

We must know the world to change the world. We need knowledge and skills so that we can speak the language of the world when it is necessary for us to have meaningful conversations with the people we are dealing with or preaching the Word of God to. When we do this, we can then gradually lead them toward Christ using the language of the scriptures. In today's world, any spiritual leaders need to educate themselves in various fields that are relevant to the lives of their congregants. In develop economies this may include leadership, business management, education, philosophy, psychology, sociology and cultural studies. When a leader is too ignorant of the world, often they lose authority on the face of both educated believers and unbelievers. The exercise of spiritual leadership within churches is becoming a more complex business. Skills bring money, impact, influence and all these things are needed for the work of God on earth, if they are used with wisdom and guidance from God. If you are focused on your destiny deployment, you must be able to identify your skill set, develop it and use it appropriately for the discharging of your divine assignment.

In addition to the above, in most western countries, the media has painted quite a negative image of religion over the last few decades, depicting it as some form of superstition or an irrational set of beliefs. Because of this, believers are being seen by the rising atheistic movement and many scientists as foolish people who believe in an imaginary God and have no scientific understanding of the world or refuse to accept scientific facts. Through social media we get to see images around the world about church leaders and believers doing very weird stuff. I recently saw some church leaders asking their flocks to eat grass, craw like sheep inside the churches and many other similar things. All these weird things reinforce a bad image of Christianity. The many sexual scandals that have been exposed by the media in relation to some Catholic priests around the world have also tainted the whole of the Christian family globally. Even people who believe in the existence of God have been affected by all these things and some have lost their faith. Because of all these things, we need highly skilled Christian leaders who can make a rational case for Jesus in this century, in addition to the spiritual aspect of things. This is why people like the late Ravi Zacharias are so much needed in today's world. Ravi's eloquence and philosophically sound argumentation for the superiority of Christian world view has been so influential for many young Christians. New generations of Christians will need more Ravi Zacharias to emerge and occupy the public sphere.

More educated Christian leaders are also likely to generate more faith in the church, as well as more growth, both numerical and qualitative, inside the many Christian congregations around the world. Because Christians are the light of the world, we must educate ourselves more than the average person. We must use the benefits of our spiritual insights, anointing and blessings to complement the knowledge, talents and skills we have to help promote God's agenda on earth and accomplish our destiny in the process.

5 Dominion and Spiritual hygiene

We live in a fallen world, infested with all kinds of evil spirits who are trying to corrupt us and derail our efforts to grow spiritually so that we don't accomplish our destiny on earth. As we are being exposed to all types of crazy ideas, ideologies and lifestyles in today's societies, all these things affect our minds and corrupt our spirits. In the same way our physical body is constantly being attacked by all types of viruses and harmful bugs, our spirit is dealing with spiritual pathogens. In addition to this, the processing all types of energy (physical, mental, spiritual) within us generates substances and residues, some of which need to be removed so that they do not cause us harm. For example, as we move around, the biological mechanics generates substances such as sweat, oil, gas and other such things that we need to get rid of in order to maintain good health. We call this personal hygiene and it involves washing our hands, body, months etc... all for the purpose of or remaining healthy, fresh and presentable in the eyes of other people in the society. Otherwise, if we don't do these things, we may get infections, stink, look unclean and drive other people away from us.

Spiritually things also work the same. As our spirit operates in conjunction with our mind, it generates spiritual energy, which interacts with other types of energy in our environment and beyond. In that process, it can potentially catch what we can refer to as "spiritual viruses and bacteria", which are simply different types of negative energy. This is why Destiny Living requires us to practice "spiritual hygiene", which is a process through which we take time to notice what is happening with our spiritual energy, what is affecting it negatively and what needs to be done to clean ourselves of the spiritual impurities that are generated by the processing of spiritual and mental energy within our consciousness. As we process ideas, desires and feelings in our daily activities, we spend energy and generate residues and impurities, on the one hand, and we also catch spiritual pathogens (viruses and bacteria) which penetrate our consciousness from the environment, from our dealings with other people, as well as from the master distributor of evil, the devil. All these things negatively affect our mind and spirit and if they are not taken care of, they affect our mental and spiritual health by creating fear, insecurities, worries, stress and many forms of toxic energy that end up making us sick and creating big problems in our lives. Mental and spiritual impurities and pathogens are just as real and omnipresent in life as physical ones.

The conscious process to attend to these potentially harmful things is what we call spiritual hygiene. It involves many things and requires taking time and using various tools and resources to actively remove negative and unhelpful spiritual energy from within us. When we do so, we refresh our spirit and keep ourselves clean and presentable in the eyes of men and God. It is our responsibility to minimise the accumulating of bad energy with in us, which may end up causing spiritual sickness and/or mental derangement. Spiritual hygiene also involves psycho-cognitive examination of ourselves. In practice, it can be done in many ways such as through prayer, affirmations, introspection, bible-based meditation, fasting and visualisation of our life goals. In order to rid yourself of negative energy, you must be able to examine yourself quite deeply. You need to look at yourself from outside of yourself, be able to separate yourself from your body and mind and then look at yourself from a distance by examining your interactions with your own self through your thoughts, ideas, feelings, desires, aspirations, behaviours and reactions to things.

You also need to look at how you have interacted with other people who have directly or indirectly penetrated or affected your field of consciousness. You must see yourself operating as an individual in whatever environment you may be in or have been in recently. You also need to look at all the thoughts, feelings and desires that you have harboured and have opened yourself to and realise how these things have affected your core spiritual identity first, as well as any other impact on your level of focus for Destiny Living. Spiritual hygiene is also about looking at the interactions between your mind and your spirit, especially the ecological balance between your bodily desires, your thoughts, your feelings and your spiritual identity and goals. Doing this on a regular basis enables us to remain spiritually and mentally healthy and minimise anything that may end up disturbing our progress towards our God-given destiny. A spiritually hygienic person is less likely to suffer mental illness because he/she is able to quickly rid themselves of negative energy that end up creating depression and all sorts of mental conditions. There is no doubt that if people practice spiritual hygiene the mental health pandemic that we are seeing all around western countries and other advance societies will be greatly minimised if not eliminated.

Spiritual Hygiene Tools

1. **Mind Programming**: this is about visualising and reinforcing your spiritual identity through the programming of your thoughts. You must be able to have a clear picture of who you are spiritually and how you are projecting that image and identity outside, on a daily basis. The programming also requires loud and frequent affirmation of who you are, as well as loud and frequent rejection of anything that is not you. See who you are and say it loudly many times and state what you are not and will not do. For example: I am destined to be a great teacher of the word of God. I am called to impact my generation. I will invest time to learn from the Lord so that I can receive from Him and pass it to my generation with power and impact. I will not sabotage my destiny.

2. **Strategic prayer**: this is about elevating one's deep-seated desires to God, expressing gratitude for His leadership and asking for His assistance to bring those desires into fruition. Many of us pray for a whole lot of things, but we forget to pay for own life goals regularly. We must write down our life goals from both a spiritual and material perspectives and ask God's intervention in refining those goals and bringing them to fruition. You must pray for your life goals every day, if you can. Start by listing at least 12 major life goals for yourself and ask God to lead you in the process.

3. **Emotional stocktake**: this is about reflecting on your feelings over a period of time (like 24 hours) and realising how those feelings have affected your thinking and spiritual goals. Good emotions need to be reinforced and bad ones released, but all

from a high spiritual standing where you are in control and your higher self is managing and controlling the lower parts of yourself.

4. **Watchful thinking**: it is about being conscious of your own subjective thinking and being able to monitor and police your own thoughts to ensure they remain in line with your spiritual identity and goals. Watchful thinking is a bit like self-parenting for the purpose of your spiritual development and destiny deployment.

5. **Vision fertilisation**: this is about meditating on your vision in life and through your thoughts and feelings provide that vision with enough spiritual, mental and emotional nutrition and reinforcement to help it grow. It is a bit like planting a garden in the bush of your mind and you need to continually take care of it.

6. **Scriptures programming**: reading the scriptures with deep investment of thoughts and feelings, as well as a focus on how the scriptures speak to your vision in life. You must attach scriptures to all your life's goals and repeatedly pray for those goals citing the scriptures that you have identified.

7. **Therapeutic Forgiveness**: it is about making a conscious effort not to hold any grudge against anyone and forgiving and releasing people from your mind, to remove negative energy from yourself, which may hold you back in one way or another. Not forgiving people, blocks the free flowing of positive energy within you. It may eventually make you fall

sick and it definitely prevents the Father from forgiving you for your own sins.

8. **Spiritual nomenclature:** this relates to a proactive effort to name, label and categorise things in your mind based on your spiritual identity and also adopting adequate attitudes vis a vis those things. For example, you can label TV as a dangerous device for your spirituality. Because of this you can then be very selective about what you watch on TV and you can even get rid of it all together, because you want to use your free time in something else more productive and useful for God.

Most of our problems in life come from things that we left unattended or failed to pay sufficient attention to for a long time. Without a conscious effort to clean up one's spiritual energy and environment, it becomes very easy to get infected and develop various spiritual pathologies or maladies that will impact one's life, not just spiritually, but also intellectually and eventually physically.

Every Christian who has truly received Christ has a mandate to exercise dominion over creation, and this means showing God's power, authority and love through our lives. The divine domination given to us is only possible if one is fully spiritually healthy and able to exercise all the responsibilities that comes with the management of his/her own life and stewardship over creation. You cannot dominate over nature if you are unable to manage your own self. Divine dominion is also set to help us dominate the circumstances of life, as well as enable us to show love, leadership, excellence and care at the highest level possible. After the fall of Man, as described in Genesis, the mandate to dominate is now intrinsically linked to the contribution each one of us can make for the restoration of the entire human family and the rest of creation. The restoration work will always be filled with adversities, including the devil's plans to rob, kill and still what God has put into us. This means our dominion will need be exercised in the spiritual world where we must use the power given to us by Jesus Christ to keep the devil and his accomplices under our feet. Beyond our own individual lives and the unending attacks of the enemy, the divine dominion given to us need to be directed towards a relentless effort to reform the ungodly cultures, ideologies, philosophies and lifestyles that continue to keep human societies under the bondage of the enemy. To whom much is given, much is required and the blessing of dominion that we have been given requires us to use it extensively as a powerful tool for the delivery of our earthly destiny on behalf of the one who created us.

CHAPER EIGHT

Keyword 8

Discipline

> **KEY POINTS**
> - Self-discipline is the best tool to shape your character
> - There is no greatness without self-discipline
> - Self-discipline is the secret of all great leaders and masters in history
> - Christians are called to be soldiers of Christ and need discipline to execute their duties
> - Self-discipline and self-leadership are the two biggest pillars of destiny living

"Join me in suffering, like a good solider of Christ Jesus. No one as a soldier gets entangled in civilian affairs, but rather tries to please his commanding officer."

2 Timothy 2:3–4

THE BIBLE TALKS ABOUT DISCIPLINE, MOSTLY WITH THE CONNOTATION of regulating one's behaviours and not succumbing to sinful desires of the flesh. While this is very important, in this chapter we will talk more about discipline as a tool for self-leadership, self-affirmation and destiny deployment. We will focus on how discipline can be used, not just to avoid sin, but to propel us to our God-given destiny.

Discipline is one of the best tools to help shape the character of a human being. All good parents know that they need to instil some level of discipline in their children if they want them to grow and become responsible and successful individuals and citizens. As we discuss discipline in the following paragraphs, we will focus more on self-discipline, which is the ability to control one's feelings, overcome one's weaknesses and impose oneself a set of measures to facilitate growth and development in different areas of one's life.

The Bible teaches us that as children of God, our character has both divine and human traits. Discipline enables us to tame the human in us and focus more on developing the divine part of our character. We have a plural identity that includes our spiritual self, intellectual faculties and biological drives. These different parts of us create friction as they operate within us. They don't always work in the same direction and in harmony. In Matthew 26:41 Jesus tells his disciples "…the spirit indeed is willing, but the flesh is weak…", showing us that even Him experienced the gap between the spiritual longings and the biological limitations. A spiritual focus in life means elevating one's desires and submitting them to the celestial leadership, even though the body will always be pulling us down to earth and closer to sin. Self-discipline comes handy to help us to train ourselves to subjugate our fleshly desires and make them slaves to the spirit, which is led by God's vision.

Self-discipline is very important for personal development and spiritual growth. Those who are serious about living their God-given destiny understand the value of self-discipline. It is the engine for spiritual elevation and intellectual growth and one of the most important intangible assets that one can have in life. In the army, discipline is one of the most important values. Without discipline it is very difficult to achieve serious outcomes in learning and in discharging one's responsibilities. We need to learn and work hard, work smart and show discipline and commitment in what we do. God wants us to make good use of everything He has given us so that we can discharge our destiny duties and leave a legacy in the world.

Self-discipline in many ways is actually more important than intelligence, because self-discipline can help someone increase intelligence through learning, practice and hard work. On the other hand, intelligence without discipline can be dangerous. Often very smart people who lack self-discipline end up being locked up, because many of them tend to use their intelligence wrongly thinking that they can get away with anything, until they are caught. Discipline is also important for morality, because it is through discipline that we learn to police our egoistic or evil thoughts and stop them from corrupting our mind and influencing bad behaviours towards others.

Self-discipline or self-control is one of the spiritual fruits that Apostle Paul mentioned in the Bible in (Galatians 5:22). Although the term "self-discipline" is not widely used in the Bible, but there is no doubt that it is a critical attribute of the Christian identity. The devil will always tempt us to do and choose evil and God will always encourage us to do good and choose life. As we get confronted with these two things, discipline will determine how we shape our consciousness to obey mostly God or the Devil. In the old days, religious monks used to spend a lot of time training themselves for self-discipline, because they knew its power and its importance in living a purposeful life focused on spiritual attainments.

Focus on Destiny

Today, the Christian believers need a lot of teachings regarding self-discipline. So many people call themselves Christians these days, but they live like pagans and are not much different from any regular person in the society. This is because there is a lack of good teachings and spiritual leadership in our congregations. We must train ourselves for self-discipline. The Holy Spirit can help us to live a holy life, but He cannot do everything for us. God gave us a spirit and a mind for a purpose, and we need to develop these through discipline, as we strive to grow from believers to disciples of Christ and become leaders and agents of divine transformation of the world.

It is regrettable that we have a breed of Christians today who are quite vocal, but not moral enough. They are spiritual, but not sufficiently ethical. Many shout out Jesus! Jesus! during Sunday service, but as soon as they get out of the church they go back to the "normal self" and engage in questionable behaviours. When you look closely into this phenomenon, you realise that these people may know the Word of God, they may have faith (they are not always pretending, although some do so) and have the best intentions to live their faith, but what they lack is self-discipline and self-leadership. They don't have enough self-discipline to police their thoughts, control their feelings, shape their habits and elevate their desires to the level that God expects them to do. A lot of Christians today are not properly fed spiritually, especially in an environment where we talk more about the grace of God than delivering our destiny on planet earth. People are being conditioned to feel good about things of God, but the good feelings don't necessarily make them grow spiritually. Because Christians are not nourished appropriately, a lot of them suffer from what we can refer to as "spiritual Kwashiorkor". The only way to heal this spiritual disease is to instil a sufficient dose of self-discipline and self-leadership in their consciousness.

Self-discipline and Knowledge

Self-discipline is about being at the driver seat of your own thoughts, feelings and desires to help achieve your predefined goals. A man with self-discipline has inner strength and the ability to control what is happening within himself to ensure he does what he must do and not just what feels good. Without discipline children grow without the ability to control their desires and they end up thinking and behaving as if the world owes them everything they want. In the school system, good educators also understand that without discipline it is not possible for students to learn well and use their knowledge responsibly and ethically. Discipline helps us to conduct ourselves well in the society, it also enables us to achieve our individual goals in life. In today's world, people know a lot of things, but not many of them use their knowledge to accomplish anything remarkable. Because of access to information and new technologies, such as television, digital telephony and the media in general, we are exposed to a lot of information than any other generation before us. The information overload has increased our "head knowledge" on so many things, but we lack practical knowledge. Knowing is one thing and doing is another, and self-discipline can help us to decide what knowledge we need for what purpose, as part of our vision. Knowing without doing is useless and doing without knowing is dangerous. When you are self-discipline you manage knowing and doing accordingly to make it easy to reach your destination.

Discipline and Vision

Self-discipline works better where there is a vision. When you know where you are going, you develop motivation to drive yourself to that destination and self-discipline helps you to keep focus and keep making progress until you get there. One of my teachers used to say: "you must first do what you must do, before you do what you need to do and then eventually do what you want to do". This distinction between the "Must", "Need" and "Want" is very useful for someone who has a clear vision, a sense of purpose and duty, as well as clear goals to achieve in life. The regular person in the street who is going with the "flow of life" and taking things as they come does not need to worry much about what they must, need or want to do. Usually, they just do what they want to do until they are forced by someone or some event in their lives to do what they must and need to do. But as soon as someone gets a clear vision in life and they decide to engage on the road for self-actualisation, then the distinction becomes very clear between "must", "need" and "want". Self-discipline is what is needed to the various needs of each of these three areas of personal responsibility.

Discipline is like the policeman inside your head with the job of maintaining your own self-imposed internal "law and order". It is also like a manager within, helping us to manage our inner world and drive us into useful behaviours, habits and actions to help us achieve a particular vision and transform our lives for the better. Whatever goals or plans you have in life, you will require discipline to achieve them. If you want to climb Mount Everest, you need discipline to train yourself, otherwise you will fail. If you want to save money and build a school for disabled children, you must have discipline. As soon as you identify an important goal in life, self-discipline becomes a crucial personal asset for its realisation. For us Christians, self-discipline is useful to help us control the machinery of our inner world when pursuing our vision and living our faith on earth. The Bible clearly says that "the Just shall live by faith". It is a big challenge to live by faith in a world that is increasingly more materialistic, egoistic and chaotic. To overcome this challenge, nothing works better than a high dose of self-discipline and self-leadership that will help you stay the course even when the going gets tough. Self-discipline works better when it is at the service of a clear vision and mission for which one consciously decides to dedicate their life.

When you are self-disciplined in life, it means you are doing what you know you have to do, you do it consistently even where there is no immediate result or benefits, doing it at the right time (not just whenever you feel like it) and in the right way, in order to get the results or outcomes you want to get. Many people have great ideas, ambitions and plans to do things, which they believe to be important in their lives, but only a small number of people are disciplined enough to summon their internal energy, motivation and drive to actually go ahead and do these things. How many of us make new resolutions at the beginning of every year and we start to do things, but only for a very short amount of the time until we forget about it? The majority of people do this, mostly because of lack of self-discipline. This is why many good ideas die premature death, because those who birth them don't have a strong sense of self discipline to nourish them appropriately until they bear fruits and bring success.

Discipline and Goals

Once we understand that self-discipline is important for our vision, we need to put it to use by directing it to specific goals that we have identified as milestones for our vision. When you have clear specific goals, focus and discipline can help you achieve them more easily. For example, if you want to climb Mount Everest, you need to be physically fit to do it. This means you need to prepare your body for that challenge and to exercise accordingly to raise your fitness level, before you start climbing. A strong level of self-discipline will enable you to keep you going to the gym day after day, even when you do not feel like it, because you know that you "must" be fit to reach your goal. Discipline also has a lot of indirect benefits. A friend of mine use to tell me "half of what is needed for success is just showing up". If you want to get fit, showing up to the gym is half the job done. Once you are able to get to the Gym and start exercising you may realise that exercise is actually fun and you can enjoy it. You may have started exercising with the intention to lose weight, but you could end up enjoying or even being addicted to trimming your body and, in the process, meet people at the Gym who may teach you things and even add value into your life in some ways. You may also start developing particular fitness abilities that are relevant for mountain climbing, as opposed to simply losing weight or getting fit. You could learn extra things such as what type of exercise works better for what fitness purpose and what machine or exercise regime are relevant. All these things are additional benefits that one can get simply by exercising discipline for something as simple as showing up at the gym two or three days a week.

Discipline and Good Ideas

We are all capable of producing good ideas, whether educated or not. I read somewhere that ideas are the cheapest commodities in the world, because everyone has them in abundance and can produce them on demand and at no cost. Every one of us can generate tons of ideas in our head, but only a small number of people are able to nurture and grow ideas to turn them into successful enterprises. Good ideas are not enough to succeed in life, nor is knowledge, because there is a long way from a good idea into a successful project or endeavour. Success comes when we nurture an idea, grow and mature it, plan it and build a strategy for its implementation before working hard to make it happen. If we act on it and follow things through with consistency and determination we can convert ideas into successful achievements which requires many things. Intelligence, self-motivation, emotional intelligence, planning, strategising, communicating and interacting with people are also important to turn good ideas into successful projects, but self-discipline is what will connect and cement all of these things inside of us to keep pushing us forward until we become successful.

Biblical insights about discipline

There are over 20 verses in the Bible that emphasise discipline in life. This demonstrates the importance of this very crucial skill in life in general and destiny living, in particular. Apostle Pauls deals extensively with this issue when writing to different churches that he was establishing and he also reiterates the need for self-discipline to his protégés. The main benefit of self-control or self-discipline from a biblical point of view is about overcoming the desires of the flesh and elevating the desires of the spirit in our lives. The Bible says:

> *"Purify yourselves from everything that contaminates body and spirit, perfecting holiness out of reverence for God"*
>
> 2 Corinthians 7:1

Apostle Paul also tells the church in Rome:

> *"offer your bodies as living sacrifices, holy and pleasing to God,"*

All Christians are aware of the constant battle we face between the desires of the spirit and those of the flesh. Many times, we set out to please God, only to find ourselves dragged down by fleshly and worldly desires. This creates an inner conflict and those who lack self-discipline easily succumb to the temptations to put these desires before God's will. If the spiritual in us is unable to dominate the flesh, we become easy prey to the enemy who knows how to entice us and lead us astray from our destiny. Unless you are spiritually mature, the desires of the flesh are always more compelling and strongly attractive. Destiny living requires a lifestyle that is similar to an athlete in training for the Olympic games. It requires a lot of discipline and a stringent exercise regime focusing on the goal to win a medal. Apostle Paul says in Corinthians 9:27: "*I beat my body and make it my slave*". This show how determine he was to ensure that his "carnality" did not destroy his "spirituality".

Although self-discipline starts with a strong desire of the mind, but it also requires help from the Holy Spirit. We cannot count on our will power alone to remain on the path of our destiny, because our enemy is quite powerful and without the help of the Holy spirit it is not possible to keep the devil under our feet most of the time. In 2 Timothy 1:7 Apostle Paul says: *"God did not give us a spirit of timidity, but a spirit of power, love and self-control"*. All this clearly indicates that the assistance of the Holy Spirit is required for us to remain disciplined in life, but we must work on it every day and this is why Jesus asks us to pray every day, because we need God's help constantly to stay focused.

Ways to build and develop self-discipline

1. *Secular strategies for self-discipline (mind exercise)*
   - Be clear on your vision and break it down into smaller, but specific goals and objectives that you can start working on step by step, day after day
   - Build a routine with daily tasks/actions that gets you moving towards your vision
   - Develop a growth mindset and embrace a personal culture of excellence, strive for excellence in everything you do or you are involved in
   - Do something every day which connects with your vision. Gradually increase the time you do it until it becomes second nature
   - Inundate your senses with sound and images about self-discipline and self-leadership. Use technology to help condition yourself for your vision and goals. For example, buy a pair of headphones and listen to podcasts or motivational material when commuting to

work, driving around, doing your daily walk.
- Decide to build expertise on self-discipline as you go, so that you can eventually teach or coach others on it. The best way to learn is to teach. If you decide to teach self-discipline you will force yourself to learn to develop it.

2 Biblical recommendations for self-discipline (spiritual exercise)

- Pray without ceasing. Establish a strict prayer and meditation regime. Nothing lifts the spirit more than prayer
- Write down you vision and life goals and read, rehearse and pray for it with passion
- Renew your mind by studying the scriptures and linking it to your divine mission
- Create opportunities to help others and practice whatever God is showing you in your vision
- Seek a spiritual/coach/mentor and ask them to hold you accountable for your spiritual goals. You can start with your Pastor or Church elder as mentors, if you trust them enough
- Fast regularly, to enable your spirit to subjugate your body and help your mind to focus on your spiritual needs
- Decide to develop self-discipline geared towards your destiny deployment. You can achieve anything through Christ who strengthens you.

If you are disciplined enough, it becomes easy to grow your faith and walk by faith. Your destiny journey will be more

Discipline

fulfilling if you develop the discipline of great spiritual masters. You can do great things with a little bit of faith and a great dose of self-discipline.

CHAPTER NINE

Keyword 9

Drive

> **KEY POINTS**
> - Living purposefully means driving your life towards the destination that God has set for you
> - Learn the mechanics of self-leadership and spiritual motion
> - You are the driver of your own life, God only gives you directions, but you must do the driving
> - Trees don't need to be led, but humans do. Keep moving and let God lead you.

What is driving you?

WHAT IS DRIVING YOU IN YOUR LIFE? HAVE YOU EVER ASKED yourself this question? What is the main motivating factor that is leading you to do the things you do, day in and day out? What is your primary motivation that is leading you to live your life the way you do? What is it that you are running after in your life, is it just making a living and getting by or is there more to your life than that? Do you have an overarching motivational drive that is influencing your daily routine, your behaviours and your habits? Or perhaps you are just going with the flow of life and living on automatic pilot? You may or may not have ever asked yourselves these questions before, but for anyone who is serious about leaving a valuable legacy on earth by discharging their God-given destiny, these are fundamental questions that need to be asked and answered not just once, but quite regularly, as a way to take stock of one's life.

Everyone of us has some internal motivation that is driving them in life. The habits that define our character are often products of a deep-seated motivational drive that is linked to our spirit. Spiritual motivation is the highest form of motivation. It is not always evident and cannot be studied scientifically, but biblical wisdom tells us that it is the spirit that drives the mind and the mind drives the body. Understanding the workings of our internal motivation (spiritual, emotional or intellectual) is very important. Almost all great spiritual masters and philosophers throughout the ages have encouraged their disciples to work on knowing themselves better. You must know thyself well in order not to be your worst enemy.

Christian motivation

In many spiritual belief systems, including Christianity, people tend to talk about submission to a higher power (God) and the requirement or obligation to obey that power. Often that obedience is explained as a requirement from a spiritual authority, because we are the subjects and God, as the Master, requires obedience from us, therefore we must do what that authority requires. In this sense, motivation is not talked about much in the bible, because it is of a lesser value than "obedience". We are told to obey God, because He is God. We are not so much told about being motivated to do the will of God, we just have to do it, otherwise we will be disobedient and disobedience means death. However, at a higher level of spiritual enlightenment, we come to develop enough motivation within ourselves to submit ourselves to God fully, not because we must do it to avoid hell, but because we connect to God in a meaningful way and understand He alone has the key to our true Destiny. God is the only one who can help us live purposefully, meaningfully and abundantly. He doesn't actually "need" anything from us, because He is and will always remain God, whether we obey Him or not. He comes to us to give us life and life in abundance.

Motivation is defined as "internal force that moves someone toward action, something that provokes or stimulates a given behaviour or action that can be observed outwardly". Motivation is a very important element of the human psyche and it deserves serious attention for anyone interested in human achievement in general and destiny living in particular. As this book is about helping people to focus on Destiny, then motivation plays a very important role, because it is crucial in pushing people forward towards their Destiny. The core motivation of true Christians is not and should not be the same as the motivation of the people of the world (unbelievers). We are in this world, but we are not of this world, the Bible reminds us. Christians are supposed to be driven by faith and guided by divine inspiration and revelation. Our motivation comes from the unseen, from the spiritual world, while the motivation of unbelievers usually comes from the material world with all that it can offer, such as money, material possessions, sex, power, pleasures of all types.

David spoke of his motivation in Psalms:

> "I desire to do Your will, O my God; Your law is within my heart"
>
> (Psalm 40:8).

He also said:

> "Whom have I in heaven but you? And earth has nothing I desire besides you"
>
> (Psalm 73.25).

Throughout the book of Psalms, we get exposed to a man's heart (David's) which is driven by the desire and motivation to be in the presence of God, worshiping Him, obeying His command and doing His work. David was driven by a very powerful overarching desire to serve the Lord. He exemplifies what all of us Christians need to look up to. He was a King and he had a lot of power and a lot of material wealth. He could have let himself be influenced or even corrupted by those things, but he did not. It is said that power, money and sex are the three most powerful forces that drive the human mind. These three things are said to make the world go around, within a secular understanding of things. But in the Bible, we see David who has the position of a King with access to all those things, but he stayed focused on God, seeking Him assiduously and longing to serve Him.

Filling the motivation gap

As an observer of Christianity, I see a growing gap between what people believe, proclaim and profess, and what they actually do in real life, how they behave and interact with others on a day to day basis. Christianity is fundamentally about living like Jesus. In the book of John 4:34, Jesus said: *"My food is to do the will of Him who sent Me and to finish His work"*. Jesus was so focused and motivated by the need to please His Father through His work, so much so that He equated it to food, which is something that we need many times every single day and without which we cannot survive. Apostle Paul also was motivated by the need to please Christ and he dedicated his life for that. At a higher level of faith, we come to understand that our motivation as Christians should be expressed through our dedication to God's mission in our life, rather than simply professing our faith and living a holy life, but in an ordinary kind of way. Christians are people on a mission and our primary motivation in doing anything godly is to do everything we can every day to get that mission accomplished. Living righteously is a good thing, but dedicating our lives for our God-ordained destiny on earth, should be the greatest motivation of all mature Christians.

The question then becomes, what is causing this gap to grow between our beliefs in God, on the one hand and our limited motivation to do His work in our lives, on the other hand? There are many things to consider in answering this question. Firstly, there is a "knowledge gap" that is affecting us. The Bible says *"my people perish because of lack of knowledge"* (Hosea 4:6). This means we must know the scriptures through and through and connect that knowledge with our purpose in life. Once we fill the knowledge gap and know what we ought to know, we need to look at the "action gap" that also exists between what we know and what we do with the knowledge we have. "Action gap" or "Work Gap" is the amount of time and energy that we fail to invest in making ourselves useful to God in expanding His Kingdom on earth, helping with the restoration of humanity.

Drive

It is one thing to know what to do, it is another to actually do something with what you know.

Most people in the world are motivated by self, they want to take care of themselves, feed their ego and get personal pleasure and satisfaction, whatever it may be. However, the Gospel teaches us not to be self-centred, but rather serve others with love and care. Jesus said: *"the greatest among you will be your servant. For whoever exalts himself will be humbled and whoever humbles himself will be exalted"*. (Matthew 23:11-12). Through this passage, the Lord is showing us they way to greatness. Greatness is linked to purpose and destiny. Greatness comes through action, work and service to others. It takes a lot of motivation to do all of these things and in order for us to satisfy God, we need just as much knowledge as we need motivation to put that knowledge to good use. Knowledge tells us what to do and motivation pushes us to do it.

The Holy Spirit is not the panacea for our motivation problem. The spirit of God certainly helps, but He does not do all the heavy lifting for us. We have to use our own personal will to extract motivation from within us and continue to stand firm when the going gets tough. This is why Jesus says that *"the spirit is willing, but the flesh is weak"* (Matthew 26:41). It is also the same reason why the disciples of Jesus could not sustain the watch in prayer in the Garden of Gethsemane. If it was all about the Holy Spirit, He would have kept them motivated to pray. Motivation must come from deep down in our spirit and mind. Christians are destined to greatness and it is not only biblical to seek greatness, but it is just human nature that we all want to be great in some ways, even though some people would not admit this. The difference between the world and Christians is that our greatness lies in serving others in the name of Christ, not in seeking fame, wealth or self-satisfaction. Christian motivation is about being dedicated to the work of restoration of humanity and making oneself available, as an instrument through which God distributes His grace on planet earth.

Motivation and destiny

> "Each of you should use whatever gift you have received to serve others, as faithful stewards of God's grace in its various forms"
>
> (1 Peter 4:8 NIV).

This verse complements what Jesus said by asking us to be servants of others as a way to achieve greatness. How do we serve others? By using "whatever gift we have received" from God and living as "stewards and agents of God's grace in its various forms". This is the minimum that God expects of us and one of the two main reasons why He gave us faith, the other reason being that He simply loved us and wanted to enable interaction with us. When we become agents of divine transformation and distributors of divine grace on earth, through our work, it becomes easier to understand why Jesus died for us and why He said in Matthew 16:25 that *"For whoever wants to save their lives will lose it, but whoever will lose his life for me will find it"*.

One way to help improve the motivation for Christian work is to translate the deep spiritual truths in the Bible into motivational concepts that can be conceived rationally and be used practically. In fact, this is the job of pastors, evangelists and teachers. They need to communicate spiritual truths in ways that captivates the mind of the believers, in addition to impacting their spirits. Faith becomes mature when it no longer just relies on doctrines and dogma (which must be believed whether one understands them or not), but it is understood clearly and can be explained rationally. When this happens, the motivation to live it becomes more robust.

Christian motivation rests on two main things. The first one is "purposeful /destiny living" and the second done is "transformational agency" which is the ability to act or work for a divine transformation of the world. The two are connected because our purpose is tied to us living and working as agents for heavenly transformation of the earth. As you read this book, how much appetite do you have for the things of God in your life? Are you just trying to live a normal or ordinary life and eventually retire, go to a nursing home and die? Or do you see more in life? Do you see yourself as having the seed of greatness in you? Does your mind connect to any cause, any desire for service? Do you want to be great the Jesus way? Do you catch yourself thinking of something for which you would like to contribute your time, energy, money and other resources to, as an expression of who you are, spiritually? Is there anything for which you will be prepared to sacrifice your whole life? If you have clear answers to these questions, you do have answers to what your Destiny is about.

People who have a sense of Destiny have a feeling that they are destined or called to do something significant, something of a great value for humanity. They may not be able to explain this feeling in clear terms, but they get a sense that they are meant to do something quite valuable before they die. Such people have their mind constantly thinking about the future, which they see as being greater and brighter than their past and their current circumstances. Some people have a clear idea about their destiny and others may not have a sharp picture of things, but they just know it.

People have a seed of greatness and a sense of Destiny when they take interest in doing things for the benefit others. They live for others and they are driven to act to help others such as addressing injustice, defending a given cause, starting a charity or getting involved in something that help less privileged individuals in the society. The sense of Destiny provides a great deal of motivation to such people and they are very much interested in improving their own lives through their interactions with God, as well as through self-learning, personal development and self-leadership. They don't want to just live a normal life.

Society's Motivational Matrix

Today, in most countries in the world, the motivational matrix is one that encourages people to go to school to learn so that they can get a job in the future and earn good money for living. There is very little encouragement for people to learn, as a means for self-discovery, self-development and self-manifestation. The school system also does not really prepare us to live our Destiny on earth, in a spiritual sense of the word. It is a machine designed to create employees to power the economy in our capitalist societies. Formal schooling does not sufficiently prepare people to become agents of positive social transformation, creators of wealth and masters of their own destiny. The socio-cultural script or the General Life Template (GLT) of life has remained the same for hundreds of years: go to school, get a qualification, get a job, get married, buy a house or two, retire, go to a nursing home and eventually die in peace.

Imagine if the script was something along the lines of: got to school to learn how to learn, get a qualification if you can, but focus on self-learning and personal development, as instruments for self-manifestation and the achievement of your vision in life. You can get a job if need be, but only as a means to learn how to manage work and then move on and use your skills, talents and God-given gifts to solve problems, create value in the world and accomplish your Destiny.

What if people were encouraged to work always, not for the money, but for self-affirmation and legacy building until the last moment of their lives? There is no doubt the above two scripts will create radically two different types of societies and the latter one will certainly be better.

I grew up in the Democratic Republic of Congo (DRC), before migrating to Australia at the age of 27. My life experience in the Congo has enabled me to understand life from the perspective of a third world country, the DRC being one of the poorest countries in the world, even though it is potentially the richest piece of national real estate on the planet. On the other hand, my life in Australia has exposed me to the highest standard of living that human beings can enjoy on this planet. I have lived in Melbourne for 20 years and Melbourne has been nominated many times as the most liveable city on the planet. These two experiences in the DRC and in Australia (two extremes in terms of standard of living) have given me very deep insights into life. In developed countries such as Australia, people are busy with work, family, studies and striving to earn more and do better in a market driven society. In poor countries a lot of people are busy trying to simply survive in an environment where there are limited structures to help them lead a normal life. In both these two groups, most people have little motivation asking themselves what is driving them. They just find themselves busy in a vicious cycle of things that are part of the system and the culture in which they live.

Mature Christians need to remove themselves from the systems of this world and the socio-cultural framework that is framing it. They need to look at the world from the point of view of the Kingdom of God. This means detaching yourself from the world system and all of its cultures and connecting to the culture of the Kingdom and His will and Work, as described in the scriptures. It is for this reason that the Bible says we are in the world, but not of this world. The Bible also calls us to live by faith and not be driven by the attractions of this world. This can only be achieved if our primary motivation in life is reprogrammed both spiritually and intellectually to serve a larger vision in life that is not focused on accumulating material wealth or having fun as the world understands this.

Driving your "self", the Jesus way

There is no bigger challenge in life than driving "self ". We all have a big vehicle that we are driving every day, it is called "self". It is always on the move, it never fully stops, even when we are sleeping. The drive metaphor is ultimately about how we conduct our lives, how we see the future and what steps we need to practically take so that we can keep moving forward to achieve our vision in life. Everyone in life is moving towards some direction, willingly or unwillingly. Nothing that has life stays static. In fact, nothing in the universe is static, everything is moving or vibrating in some ways. Most people on earth are simply being driven by the flow and circumstances of life and they act and react based on their cultural template and the model of the world that they harbour in their mind. These people may not be necessarily aware of the internal and external "forces" that are driving them, because they rarely take the time to think of such things.

Every yes and every no from a man's mind is a step towards some direction in life. It is important to examine the forces that drive us internally, because such forces explain why we have the passion that we have, why we tend to do some things more often than others and why some things attract our attention and focus more than others. When we do so, we start paying more attention. We can then make a more conscious effort in understanding how we can direct our lives in a specific direction and achieve particular goals that we have set ourselves, as conscious beings, first and foremost, even before we bring our faith into the equation. The outcome of every persons' life is a result of both the environment and the circumstances that have shaped them, on the one hand, as well as the decisions that they have taken consciously and unconsciously in their everyday life. More success is achieved when we increase the amount of conscious decisions that we make to lead and manage our lives in line with our life goals.

Jesus lived by faith and we must do the same. Faith enables us to format our consciousness and direct our lives, not on the basis of what we see around us (the environment) or what happened to us (the past), but to live on the basis of a divinely-inspired vision of life and stick to it as a primary motivation factor for our lives. It also means living in the light of the Spirit of God and the knowledge of His will, as revealed through His scriptures and through personal revelation. Last, but not least, living by faith means living with a focus on what our Creator has given us life for and deploying all that He has deposited in us to help us achieve His purpose. When we understand these insights deeply enough, they create a strong internal thrust that can keep propelling us forward towards God's plans in our lives and maintain the momentum within us for a long time.

Living by faith means spending a great deal of time in prayer as Jesus did. Unfortunately, most Christians struggle with prayer as we lead an increasingly busy life, especially in the Western world. Prayer goes beyond communicating with God, it is also about talking to ourselves and programming our mind, examining ourselves, filtering and arranging our thoughts, activating positive emotions and generating a spiritual field in and around us that can lift us up and takes us close to God. This is why prayer is such a powerful driving force. We literally drive ourselves to our Destiny through prayer and work. The more we pray, the more we strengthen our connection with the divine energy and the stronger that connection, the more progress we can make in life, in the right direction.

Driving your "self" subconsciously

The driving analogy in life can be quite powerful in increasing our motivation for spiritual growth and self-development. "Self" is both a singular and plural concept, at the same time. It is singular in its expression, but plural in its nature. In other words, we are one, but many at the same time. "Self" encompasses different entities that form our identity, including the body, mind and spirit. It also includes our many roles, occupations and hobbies we have in life. As I write these lines, I realise that I am a father, husband, writer, journalist, business owner, church leader all at the same time. All these things each constitute a separate version of my "self', which is harmoniously connected with all other aspects of me, myself and I. This plurality of "self" adds a layer of complexity that makes the driving job more complicated, given that one has to cater for the various needs of these different entities in a harmonious way.

The mechanics of life are quite complex, but just like when we drive a car, we don't need to understand how everything works in the engine or any part of the vehicle, we just need to know how to drive the whole thing, when we seat at the driving seat. If we handle our driving well, we can rest assured that we will be able to travel the journey and eventually reach our destination. But, because people are not sufficiently conscious of what is moving them and how they are driving their own lives, then they end up taking their lives to places they did not want to go.

Our human mind is prone to all sorts of external influences that start even before we are born. Babies start hearing sound and being influenced by their parents' voices and feelings well before they are born. The environmental stimuli activate things in the baby's mind, but the baby is not conscious enough to really know and understand what exactly is happening. In the same way, unless we guard our mind well and develop our spiritual consciousness well enough, we run the risk of letting ourselves run by various things that play at the subconscious level of our mind and affect our character in ways that we may not even suspect. Whatever we hear, see or experience, consciously or unconsciously impacts our mind and the accumulation of all those things that we expose ourselves to ultimately drives us. Our subconscious mind drives us most of the time when we are awake and it is in full control when sleeping. Most of us are mostly controlled by our subconscious mind. However, the biggest tasks for us Christians is to ensure our spirit dominates and frames both or conscious and subconscious mind (especially).

Our minds are available both to God and to the Devil, besides being available to our own self. This means there are three drivers who have access to our mind and can control it or influence it in some major ways. The level of control we have on our mind is limited, because there are some aspects of the mind that we don't fully understand and can never fully control. This is why the Bible speaks of "renewing the mind", which is simply another way of saying reprogramming our subconscious and equipping it to better serve our conscious mind. We need to keep a high level of consciousness at all time in order to live purposefully. People who are focussed on achieving goals often end up being successful simply because their conscious mind is working in harmony with their subconscious mind to help them make things happen. Setting up goals is a way to tell the subconscious mind to provide the conscious mind with the energy and other resources that are needed to deal with whatever challenges arises along the way. When one is focused at a conscious level, that focus seats well with the subconscious programming. When you lose focus, you lose the ability to recognise, embrace, exploit and make the most of opportunities coming your way.

The universe is full of opportunities for everyone and God sends messages to us constantly and consistently to connect us to opportunities we need, but we can only see and get these messages, if both our subconscious and our conscious mind are tuned to the right frequency to correctly interpret what is going on. Most of the time we are distracted by the many things we have to deal with in our lives every day, along with other noise in the environment. When we are focused on the things of God, we guard our mind against both our own selfish desires, as well as the suggestions and interferences of our immediate environment. We are better prepared to avoid the distractions being cunningly suggested by the Devil who is seeking to divert us from our divine path. If we train ourselves well we can program our subconscious mind appropriately, so that we can quickly weed out any unhelpful thought and emotion and use the massive power of the subconscious mind to propel and drive us to our Destiny, almost automatically or instinctively. When spirituality is well engraved in our subconscious mind, it naturally creates a thrust to enable us to keep moving towards our spiritual vision and goals.

Scientific research informs us that our subconscious mind can process up to 20 million bits of information per second, while our conscious mind only does about 40 bits per second. The extraordinary power of the subconscious mind is available to all of us, as long as we know how to access and use it appropriately. Prayer is the only activity that activates all levels of our consciousness at the same time. Prayer starts as a conscious level activity (happening in the prefrontal cortex), but it quickly connects with our subconscious mind, from which it draws words, feelings, spiritual imagery, energy and power. Additionally, as we pray, we connect with a super consciousness (God) to whom we are directing our supplications. Everything we need is already within us, but it must be activated to be used and become useful. Prayer opens all that we have within and connects our "self" to our spiritual source where we can draw everything that is needed for our growth.

Many Christians would be tempted to say that God drives us. However, this is not really correct, because it will mean that God is driving us like a man drives a car or operates a machine. God designed things in such a way that He does not have to drive us like machines. We have a part to play in the movement and the direction of our lives. God certainly designed us and embedded His will and purpose in us, but He leaves many things to us to do so that we are not controlled like robots. He influences things in and around us, but generally, it is us who decide whether to move or stop, go left or right. At every moment of our conscious life, we are driving ourselves and God is more like a quiet and smooth GPS voice that is talking to us and gently telling us to keep going, advising us to turn left or right or keep going straight. We can only hear His voice if we are focused enough and this is why for a Christian who is focused on Destiny Living, prayer is very important.

So, to the question "what is driving you?", the answer is simple: there is a lot in you that is driving you. Some of it is part of your conscious mind and you understand and control it most of the time. However, a whole lot of things in you is part of your subconscious mind, which you don't understand. Last, but not least, some of what drives you is from your spirit and its interactions with God, the super consciousness, who is making this world go around. Most of the time the interactions between the spirit, the conscious mind, the subconscious mind and our thoughts and feelings go unnoticed, at the conscious level of our mind. Unless you train and program yourself to recognise these things, you have no idea of how they affect your life and how they drive you on a daily basis.

Key steps to help you drive your life Divinely

Driving your life is like driving your car. When you drive a car, you need to do several things using different parts of your body to control the vehicle. You use your hands, your feet, your head and your mind to control the mechanics and the movement the car generates. As you do so, you also need to consider the condition of the road you are travelling, at the same time as you interact with other road users. Most of our driving is done subconsciously, simply because we have learned to repeat the same things over and over for years and no longer think of the process in a conscious way. There are a lot of great lessons to learn from driving a car, which can inform us on how to best run our lives and help ourselves move forward towards our Destiny. Here are some useful analogies for you to consider:

1 Learn first
No one was born a driver, we all have to learn to drive. It is the same in life, no one was born knowing how to live, we all had to learn to speak, to walk, to think and do many things. Learn and practice every day. The more you practice driving the better driver you become.

2 Have a clear destination in mind
When you get into the car, you must have a destination in mind, which is the point where you want the car to take you to. The car has no destination of its own. It is the same in life, you need to have a destination you want to take your life and then steer your "self" to that place.

3 Obey laws and signs on the road
To drive well, obey the car manufacturer's instructions, such as using the right fuel type and pushing the right buttons inside the car. You also need to obey government laws and road signs otherwise you are exposing yourself to trouble, including a fatal accident. It is the same in life, if you disobey your manufacturer's (God) laws, the government laws (give Caesar what is his) and all the signs that life is showing you as you move around, you are calling for trouble and if won't be long before you are immobilised in some way.

4 Stay focused all the time
Being distracted while driving can be lethal and not just for you alone. It is also the same in life, losing focus can kill you and kill

other people's dreams, whose destiny is linked to yours. Stay focused on your vision, life goals and the journey to your destination.

5 Look, front, back, left and right
When driving you look front, back, left and right, but mostly look in front of you. If you look back too long you will eventually crash. Only look left or right if you want to turn. It is the same in life, stay focused on the future ahead of you, not the past behind you. A glance in the past can be helpful, but don't make it too long or it could hurt you a lot.

6 Control your speed
Driving too slow or too fast will get you into trouble on the road, eventually. The safest speed is not the speed limit, but the speed that will enable you to safely stop or turn without crashing. In life things work the same, you need to know when to move fast and when to slow down and how much distance to keep between you and other people who are sharing the journey with you.

7 Signal before turning
Safe driving requires that you signal before you change lane or turn. This is needed as you must let your significant others know your intention and warn them in a timely manner to avoid a crash. Your safety on the road doesn't just depend on what you do, it also depends on what others around you do. In life it is the same, you are on a journey of life with friends, companions or partner(s). Keep your lane and let others drive on theirs. Warn important people in your life if you want to change direction, it will help them and you not hold each other up and not crash into each other, because you will both be affected and may not reach your respective destinations.

8 Always have a spare tyre in your car
No driver is able to predict when they will need a spare tyre next, therefore just keep one with you permanently. In life it is the same, you need to be prepared for things that will surely happen and stop you from moving temporarily. You need to have one or two spare motivational tyre(s) to keep you going when you need them.

Besides all the above points, it is important to know that you actually have no control whether you will reach your destination, because the manufacturer of the vehicle (God who created you and your body) can disable it remotely at any time He wishes to and when He does so, you simply die. Death can find you anytime, ending your journey abruptly. So, the most important thing in the journey is to stay focus, maintain the right direction and enjoy the ride. The rest depends on God. True Christianity is manifested through the way we conduct ourselves in life. We need to always be aware of the chief motivation that is driving us in doing what we do. If we have wrong motivation or no motivation at all to do anything in life that resembles the life of Christ Jesus, then we need to be reprogrammed so that we can generate enough motivation within us to drive ourselves to our Destiny with the help of God. That reprogramming is mostly our responsibility and God is always ready to lead us if we ask Him and we open ourselves to His leadership with sufficient focus and commitment.

CHAPTER TEN

Keyword 10

Destination

> **KEY IDEAS**
> - Your life journey is taking you some place, the question is where?
> - Set yourself a divinely-inspired destination and deploy yourself fully to reach it
> - Trials and tribulations in life are training programs necessary for your journey
> - The journey to your destiny is more important than the destination itself.

Destination Matterville

THE DICTIONARY DEFINITION OF DESTINATION IS "THE PLACE SET FOR the end of a journey, to which something is sent, place or point aimed at" (Webster). Destination is also defined as "the purpose for which anything is destined, predetermined end, object or use, ultimate design".

There is no doubt that life is a journey, a journey taking us somewhere. It starts with the cradle and ends with the coffin. God gave us two solid feet so that we can move around in life.

Destination

Movement makes life interesting, meaningful and enjoyable. It allows us to experience new things, see new horizons and initiate new interactions with other occupants of the world, as we are led by Him in the "Garden of life". In that garden, He has set the ultimate destination for us and that destination is our Destiny.

Every journey is a movement towards some final point, which we call destination. The destination of our life is either a default destination or a divine one. A default destination is like the destination of a piece of wood that is thrown into a river. It will end up somewhere based on the current of the river and the direction of the wind. Spiritually, the destination of your life is ultimately what your destiny is. In fact, the word destiny comes from the word destination. This word has its roots in Latin, from the word "de-stinare", which means make firm, make something "matter" (from nothingness into something firm or tangible). For us Christians, the job we have in life is to convert the vision of God into something tangible that can be seen and experienced both from within ourselves, as well as through what we can produce and deliver to humanity as the fruits of our faith and our relationship with God.

When thinking of our destiny, we need to think how we want our life to matter in the end, what real value do we want it to bring to humanity. We learn from the Bible that our life is a gift, a gift from God. Our source and our origin are spiritual and we are actually spiritual beings with a physical body and not the other way around. We are given life as an opportunity to experience physicality and impact the physical world and bring value to our generation. This means, despite our very tangible biological structure (the body), we are fundamentally spiritual beings on a mission into planet earth. We have a body because it is the suit that we need to put on so that we can operate on this planet, just like astronauts have to wear special suits when they land on the moon. We are not the suit (body), but what sustains the suit (the spirit). When Astronauts go to the moon, they don't go there for themselves, they are sent by Mission Control to explore and study a number of things that will benefit science and humanity. In the same way, from a Christian perspective, we come to earth sent by a spiritual Mission Control (God) for a mission that is important for the one who sends us and for the human family. We are given a body to enable us to function and get things done, in line with the will of the one who sent us.

In the eyes of God, your life is more about others than it is about you as an individual. Even Jesus, the only begotten son of God came to earth, not really for Himself, but for the sake of the one who sent Him and for humanity. Every Christian is a gift from God to humanity. We are called to bring something to the world. Just like a tree is called to produce fruits, not for its own sake, but for others. No tree eats its own fruits. You are a gift for your generation, as long as you know your true identity and your mission in life, as designed and pre-destined by the Almighty. God has literally packaged you as a gift to your generation. He gave you life for a purpose that is beyond your own personal plans and benefits. You are expected to deliver something useful to humanity, therefore you must always remember what difference you are expected to make in your family, community, country and the whole world. This is why, as a Christian, you must constantly think of destiny as a way to make life "matter" for something. Thinking of destiny is thinking of what you want to leave as a legacy, at the end of it all. It is about the tangible value you see yourself bringing to your society and the entire world. How do you to want "matter" positively? If destiny was

Destination

a city, it would be called "Matterville", the city for those who want their lives to matter in a divine kind of way.

Once we know and understand our mission and we focus enough on delivering it, as God wants us to, we put ourselves at a place from which we can add a lot of value to humanity, and do so even after we have perished. Jesus lived more than 2000 years ago, but He is still impacting peoples' lives today. Martin Luther King Junior died several decades ago in America, but he is still impacting the national consciousness of the USA and inspiring people all around the world. You can do things in your life that may not be as great as Jesus or Martin Luther King Junior, but still very useful to God and to the human family.

In order to reach your destination as inspired by God, you need to ensure first that you are moving and doing so in the right direction and at the right speed. You cannot stand still. The Devil will always be busy trying to pull you back towards a different direction from the one set by God for your life. He will try to destroy you spiritually so that you get diverted to a different direction and miss your destiny. Because the world is dominated by the devil, the natural flow of life is unfortunately always taking people downstream. The only way to avoid drifting downstream (like a dead leaf on a river) is to use some energy to create a thrust and move upstream towards God. People of God don't go with the flow of life, because God lives upstream and we need to do all we can to move towards Him. If you don't use power within you to move upstream, you automatically drift with the current, your spirituality goes down, you die and end up with a default and empty destiny. Only "power" can enable you to move in God's direction, towards "matterville". Hence, you need an engine to create the necessary thrust to sustain the movement towards our destination. You must have some spiritual thrust within you to overpower the natural flow of life and control your movement towards your destination. That engine is the faith that God gives you and you must use it to move places as directed by God.

Spiritual thrust, vision and destiny

The majority of people on earth go with the flow of life and end up being controlled by the circumstances they encounter in their life. People get conditioned from very early age to follow a certain path, a particular template of life that is socially and culturally constructed and regarded as "normal life". Although many Christians know in their mind that circumstances are not to decide the direction of their lives, but the cost to live by faith and for one's divine destiny is often very high and the mechanics of it too demanding. Therefore, people don't always want to pay the price for their faith and conviction. Many simply stay at a level where they pay lip service to God and they don't really go deep enough to live their faith, as expected by God. Unfortunately, today's church leadership is not helping Christians to grow to maturity and be in control of their God-given destiny on earth. The church leadership today cares more about the number of people coming to church and what is needed to accommodate them, rather than helping and supporting people individually and closely to grow spiritually, to focus on their Destiny and work to deliver it on earth.

We need to have a clear sense of direction in life and that comes with a number of things. First, we need the light of the Word of God, which gives us a spiritual vision that we can focus on. Secondly, we need to stay connected with God, interact with

Destination

Him constantly so that we receive instructions, wisdom, understanding, revelations and power that will enable us to stay the course. Thirdly, we need commitment, discipline and determination to run the race, persevere and reach the mountain top. Only these things will help us keep moving in the right direction as we meander through the streets, corners and roundabouts of life. When we are with God, even though the navigation of life may not be easy, but the journey will always be fulfilling and the end victorious.

The beginning of our "Destiny journey" starts with a spiritual vision. Vision is very important in life and it is probably the thing that makes us significantly different from animals. Animals are driven by natural instincts that are mostly limited to the desire for food, shelter, sex and social norms. They don't have the capacity to picture themselves as having a particular mission or vision in life. Humans have more than instinct. We can picture ourselves in the future and work hard to make that future materialise. We can dream of becoming one thing or another and work to achieve that vision. If a man lacks vision in life, he is not much different from the permanent inhabitants of his local zoo. Vision is not light alone, it is a product of light and attention put together. You have a vision when you can see something and understand what it is or connect with it somehow. Light is required for clear vision, but light is not vision in itself. The first thing that God created in the book of Genesis was light and immediately after that, the Bible says "God saw that the light was good". This shows God's attention being brought to the light, Him noticing it and observing that it was "good". Jesus also said

"I am the light of the world. Whoever follows me will not walk

in darkness but will have the light of life".

(John 8:12)

Whenever the Bible talks about the light, it connects it to some action or attention.

We need the light of God to see His plans for us. Without light there is no vision and without vision people perish. If you cannot see yourself becoming somebody, you probably won't become anything, but if you can picture yourself as someone important in any field, then half of the job is done, because you have something you can work on. It is not given to everyone to have a clear vision of his or her destiny. Many times, we may need other people to tell or show us who we truly are. This is because your mind may be full of darkness and your spirit may be blind or dead (remember Jesus' words: let the dead bury their dead), hence why it is very important to have good mentors, coaches and role models in every society to inspire others. Both poverty and wealth get passed down generations because of what children see in their family and their immediate social-cultural environment, as they grow up. If you can see the true You, you can believe in You and if you can believe, then you can become.

See, Believe, Work and Become

The formula for your destiny goes like this: See, Believe, Work and Become. It is important to note that seeing doesn't need to be done with physical eyes only, it can be done with spiritual eyes, as well. Spiritual images or visions are often much stronger than the physical ones, because you can take a spiritual vision everywhere you go and you can see it even in darkness or with

Destination

your eyes closed. But for a physical image, you are often limited by light and distance and you need to be paying attention.

Attention, is the second indispensable element for vision. Something can be staring at you in your face, but you may not see it if your attention is somewhere else. Attention happens when sight or vision connects with meaning or purpose. You may have sight or vision, but if what you see doesn't register with anything meaningful, then you cannot see it.

When you think of your destiny, what do you see? If you can picture your destiny, half of the job is done. The other half is to work hard and make it happen. Your Destiny is about being or becoming, not having or possessing things. Jesus Christ is in the business of spiritual transformation of people, not in the business of distributing material goods to people. However, when you find your true identity and you connect to God's vision, abundance ultimately will follow, because you receive all the provision that is connected to the vision, as designed by God. The gift you have in you, if developed appropriately, will bring you people and opportunities, because, just like a fruit tree with full of ripe fruits, you will attract all types of entities (animals, fruits, humans) coming to get the fruits and when they show up, they will leave something useful for you. This is why Jesus says *"seek first the Kingdom of God and everything else will be given to you"*. God is in the "Being" business, not in the "Having" business. He deposited a gift in you so that you can be what He wants you to be. Being is becoming, which is linked to transformation and work. When you focus on being or becoming, you start building a vision and the vision leads you to your Destiny.

We all have a vision of God in us, but we need His light to see it and be able to make sense of it and strive to accomplish it. Without light we are unable to see the true value of tings. Even the most precious things like gold and diamond are useless in the darkness. There is no life without light. The light of your vision is deemed with sin and it gets brighter with God. Light makes it easy to move to a desired direction, without hindrance. However, reaching your destiny requires more than the light or the vision, you need tools to make the journey easier and more fulfilling. Let us examine some of these resources.

Tools, resources and equipment for your Destiny

Once you have a clear vision about where you must go, you need to generate the movement to get there. God has given us all everything we need to move in life, both literally and figuratively. Physically, God gave us a body that is designed to generate and sustain movement towards different directions. We can move our body forward, backward, left, right, higher or lower. All we need is some energy, intention and motivation. Spiritually, once the spirit has captured the vision, it can command the mind to work towards a desired direction. When spiritual vision is clear and the mind is connected to it, you need to create power or thrust to move towards that vision, otherwise the vision will remain a simple dream. You need an engine to create the thrust and fuel to keep the engine running. Naturally, God has packaged all of us with all the (intangible) resources we need to accomplish of our Destiny. Those tools include:

1 Consciousness
If you are reading this book, it is evident that you have a working consciousness that can make sense of the letters and characters that are put together and arranged in meaningful ways through

the lines on each page. Beyond that, you are also capable of understanding that you exist, you are part of an intelligible ensemble with other humans, animals, plants. You may also be aware that you are part of a plan and you are one element of a much larger whole that the human mind is incapable of fully understanding. The same consciousness also informs you that there is more to life than what is directly observable with your five senses. Last, but not least, your consciousness is capable of tuning to the spiritual realm where God, the maker of all things exists and this is probably why you were interested in reading this book in the first place. Human consciousness is not one thing. It is an outcome of the workings of our biological structures combined with our mental, emotional and spiritual faculties. It is the first and most powerful tool we have for our Destiny accomplishment. It provides awareness, awakening, meaning and purpose to help us make sense of who we are, what is reality, what is life and what we want to do with it. It is consciousness that enables us to see the light, capture the vision and keep a focus moving forward to where God expects us to be. While all human beings have consciousness, not all of us have a spiritual consciousness. Many people are spiritually dead and this is why Jesus had to come to give life, to resuscitate our spiritual consciousness and help us migrate back to our original territory, the Kingdom of God.

2 Gifts, Skills and talents

Besides consciousness, God has given us various gifts, skills and talents. Consider your life as a delivery vehicle to enable God to transport and distribute gifts to your generation. You have been given a mission to deliver your "Self" to humanity and create value for the human family. Jesus' life was about delivering His "self" (or himself) to humanity by sacrificing His human life on the cross. He had to drop the suit that brought Him to earth and that suit needed to be cut opened to deliver His blood on planet earth. That blood needed to penetrate the earth and to deliver His power and salvation under the earth. The blood was also the divine ink with which God was signing a new covenant with humanity. Last, but not least, the blood was flowing on earth to deliver a new bloodline for the second Adam whose job was to bring about the restoration of humanity, after the first Adam wrecked things.

As a born-again Christian, you are part of a new bloodline. Like Jesus, you too are expected to deliver the gifts that God has placed in you. But the delivery of the gifts you are carrying is only possible if the "self" in "You" is appropriately "led" or "guided" by God. You cannot rely on your own strengths, you need God to recognise what has been deposited in you from a spiritual standpoint and then move around and move things around to execute that delivery.

Imagine you were an engineer and have created a robot to deliver mail in your neighbourhood. You would want the robot to be skilled enough to move around the area safely, recognise each house individually, be able to walk to the mail box and drop the mail or get to the front door of the house, knock and hand over the mail to the occupants. You may even want to equip the robot to be able to have a meaningful conversation with the receivers, if they are present, connect with them emotionally and offer something of value while they are there. Last, but not least, you would want the robot to be able to successfully address any challenges it may encounter along the way as it delivers mail.

This is similar to our relationship with God. Although God did not create us as robots, the above analogy provides a useful insight. We not only have consciousness to comprehend and manage life as independent entities, but we also have a lot of skills, talents and gifts, which we must put to good use in order to deliver something of value on earth from our creator's perspective, at the same time as we impact our fellow humans in a positive way.

In today's world, Christians don't just need spiritual gifts like wisdom, understanding, counsel, fortitude, knowledge, piety, and fear of the Lord. They also need to develop skills such as leadership, communication and business management. Such skills are critical for the management of life in this generation. Serious deficiency in these areas can cripple us in many ways and render us incapable or less efficient in the management of the "business of life" that we are all involved in. I once interviewed a church leader who said that he manages his life using the concept of 4Fs: Faith, Family, Finance and Fitness. He added that he had built a routine that ensures he invests time and energy for every one of these areas every day in his life and this has worked very well for him. Such a life strategy is quite useful given the growing complexities of life, especially in first world countries. You cannot just rely on prayer, studying the Bible and thinking that somehow God will make a way. You need a plan and a strategy. Set one up and bring it to God and let Him lead you.

Gifts, skills and talents are all various forms of one simple thing that we know as "energy". It is important to understand that at the centre of all reality, both physical and spiritual, lies the key concept of "energy". Life is all about "energy" and our job in life is nothing more than management all the different forms of energy within and around us. We need to strategically manage our spiritual, intellectual and physical energy and put them to use to achieve a particular vision that leaves a legacy. God is energy (spirit), so is love, the Word of God, the spirit and power of God, as well as our own spirit, just to name a few things. We need skills to manage the spiritual energy within us and everything related to it. We all have some sort of "spiritual economics" to take care of in our lives, which is the trading or exchange of energy between self and all other entities in the universe and how that exchange can be used to enhance our fruitfulness in key areas of our life (Love, work, creativity etc...).

At any moment of awareness in our life we are always processing and trading energy biologically, intellectually, emotionally and spiritually. We trade energy with other humans, with God, the devil, nature and other spiritual entities in the universe as set by God. We may not always be aware of things, but energy is always in motion; it is moving in us, with us, out of us, into us and through us. The more skills we acquire or develop in managing energy the easier it gets to progress towards our God-given destination. Your gifts, skills and talents are nothing but the way you process and manipulate energy within yourself when dealing with particular situations or circumstances. God expects you to develop and strengthen everything He placed in you to accomplish His mission on planet Earth.

As Christians, we also need to understand the concept of "spiritual primacy", meaning that we must always put the spiritual before the physical. The supernatural before the natural. Everything comes from the spiritual before manifesting in the natural. Whatever you plan, whatever you want to do, start from the spiritual. Take your plans to God and focus on managing all forms of energy in your life from a spiritual perspective. This doesn't mean that you need spiritualise everything, it simply means you must filter all your major activities with a spiritual prism that is informed by the Word of God.

3 The Physical Body

The human body is an incredible divinely-engineered vessel that God has given us, as spiritual beings, to enable us to discharge His mission on earth. It is an incredible tool for the delivery of our earthly destiny. The Bible says our body is the temple of the Holy Spirit. God needs our body to impact the physical world. He wants us to take care of it, not just for our own sake, but also for His sake, because He needs it to do things on earth. We must ensure our body is maintained well and is always ready to perform the best for the distribution of God's grace on earth, which is our mission. There is a French saying: "Un espirt saint dans un corp saint", meaning that we need a healthy body for a healthy spirit. Although we need to tame our physical body and subject it to the desires of our spirit, we ought to give enough respect, care and consideration to the wonderful vessel that our body is for the work of God. Sometimes, people become too spiritual and enjoy torturing their body in the name of some higher spiritual consciousness or experience. The truth is that without a body the spirit is illegal on earth and unable to function properly. A sick body also blocks the flow of spiritual energy and becomes a handicap for the accomplishment of God's Destiny. This is partly why Jesus was healing people, because, besides demonstrating His divinely miraculous powers to the multitudes, He was conveying a message that people of God need a healthy body to live out their Destiny. We must ensure we don't poison our body with what we consume every day. Unhealthy drinks, food, drugs and substances don't just harm the body, they block the flow of spiritual energy within us. Keeping healthy and fit is also part of our spiritual responsibility.

Connecting the dots

Our Destiny is a destination. We need to keep moving to it, day after day, until the end of our time on earth. Spiritually, whilst the destination is important, God is more interested in the journey than the final destination itself. He knows the destination already, but He enjoys the interactions and the overall experience that is generated as we move about. He likes to see us growing and overcoming the tests, trials, tribulations and temptations that we encounter in life.

We need to know that we may not see the "promise land", hence we need to focus just as much on the journey to it as we focus on our vision of what it is. We actually do not have any guarantee that we will always reach the destination. Moses was chosen by God to lead the Israelites to the promised land, but he did not reach the destination himself. The Israelites messed things up and God led them to go around and around through the desert for 40 years, because He wanted to achieve what could be described as "spiritual filtration", removing the spiritual impurities out of the Israelites so that the promise land would be occupied with the right people, given that many were infected by spiritual filth from Egypt and throughout the voyage in the desert.

The best thing we can offer God is to increase our interactions with Him and our reliance on His leadership, as we put together all that He has placed in us for His mission. He stands ready to help us attend to the mechanics of the journey to ensure we don't break down permanently or encounter a fatal accident along the way. To reach our destination with God we must ensure that we have clarity of vision for what He wants us to become and the goals he expects us to achieve. With a clear vision from Him we can plan and take steps to propel us to our destiny using a divine thrust. That thrust will be generated by harnessing the spiritual energy within us. The thrust needs to be controlled in order to build and sustain the right speed for the journey. We must control the "self" within us as a divine vessel for the transformation of the world. We must submit that "self" to Christ so that he can help us to dominate the "unholy" ideas, emotions and desires that may derail us and jeopardise our journey. When we are in Christ and He is in us, we can navigate the world with confidence, staying the course and let Him lead us to the destination.

CHAPTER ELEVEN

Keyword 11

Determination

> **KEY POINTS**
> - The road to Destiny is rocky, but with determination everything is possible
> - De-termination means not terminating, not quitting. You must stay the course until the end
> - Move towards your destiny using God's navigation made available through the scriptures
> - Keep moving. If you fall, rise up and move again and again, until the end

DETERMINATION IS THE ABILITY TO REMAIN FIRM, FOCUSSED AND driven to achieve a particular purpose. It requires not just faith, knowledge and understanding, but courage, confidence, resilience and stamina. Many people want to succeed in life, but only a few people can stay determined enough through consistent action combined with healthy habits and perseverance of the spirit to see their plans come to past. Strong determination is often a product of the spirit and not just the mind, because it is easy to find rational reasons to quit when things don't work. Many times, things of value don't come easily, they come with

Determination

pain and suffering and both the body and the mind naturally wants to avoid such things. Only the spirit can stay put and keep going in the face of pain and suffering. If the spirit is strong, it can help resist the natural inclination that we all have to enjoy our comfort zone and avoid any pain, discomfort or uncertainty in life.

God is the Creator of the world and we humans are the creators of the world's reality and the history of humanity. We not only create our own reality as subjective beings in our own minds, we also contribute to creating the social reality in our communities, nations and countries. The world is what it is because of what the human beings did in the past and what they are creating presently. What every human being does in his or her personal life (both in their mind and deeds) influences other people positively or negatively. Everything we do affect the spiritual field which is immaterial and transcends time and space. This is why Martin Luther King said *"injustice anywhere is a threat to justice everywhere"*. If we are determined to spread good rather than evil, we don't just affect our own life positively in doing so, we influence the whole world as well. It is the same if we chose evil.

Determination has to do with a person's decision to continue a course of action, regardless of the resistance, uncertainty or difficulty they may encounter on the way. The delivery of our destiny is about making consistent decisions and choices that start from the spiritual, but have consequences in the "the real world". The real world has two aspects to it, the "reality out there" and "the reality within". The first one is often referred to as objective reality and the latter one as subjective reality. Focusing on our Destiny is a way to participate in the realisation of God's plans, to create a reality (out there) on earth from the reality within. That reality within must be aligned with God's will and purpose. On this planet, besides natural phenomenon that cannot be controlled by mankind, God can only work through physical conduits or agents such as us human beings in order to impact humanity in any meaningful way. He can only change the physical reality through us humans, and this explains why Jesus had to come on earth, why God had to become man to bring a new reality on earth and create a new breed of humans that He wants to call His "children". Because not all human beings are children of God. We are all God's creatures, but only those who receive Jesus are God's children. The Bible says

"But to all who did receive Him, to those who believed in His name, He gave the right to become children of God". Children born not of blood, nor of the desire or will of man, but born of God."

(John 1:12)

The work of transformation or restoration of the human family is at the centre of the destiny of every Christian. It is not an easy job. It is tough and even Jesus experienced difficulties, challenges and issues in His ministry as He delivered His destiny on earth. It is God's law that every "action" on earth will call for a "reaction", which can be positive or negative. This means we can expect that resistance (or reaction) will always be present when we act to deliver our destiny mission. In other words, the devil will always be present to try to derail us. However, we have assurance from God that He will never forsake us and that He has won the victory already and has made us more than conquerors. This must give us confidence that although we will face many battles of life that we cannot avoid, in the end we shall overcome. Our confidence must come from God's promise and from the depth of our character as children of the Almighty. Hence, we must not quit, we must be determined to go till the end

Determined to build a godly character from inside

All of us Christians are God's vessels pre-destined to partner with Him as agents of restoration and workers for the expansion of His Kingdom on earth. We are all called to create and propagate the "Kingdom reality" on earth. This is done when we promote the vision, laws, wisdom and culture, of the Kingdom of God here on earth to help transform this devil-dominated world. Creating a kingdom reality requires that we are first reconnected to God on a personal level, so that we can access a little bit of His reality and power and be able to communicate and work with Him in order to transfer that reality unto the world. We need to access "vertical inspiration" in order to exercise "lateral impartation". It means receiving inspiration from above (vertical connection with God) and delivering value to our fellow humans (lateral impact) on planet earth. God expects us to pull His 'supernatural' plans and desires from the spiritual realm into the physical one. Doing this will require a lot of work and to sustain that work all of us Christians will need and plenty of energy, commitment, persistence and determination. Without determination and perseverance, it is not possible to achieve much in any endeavour. The Bible says in James 1:12:

> "Blessed is the one who perseveres under trial because, having stood the test, that person will receive the crown of life that the Lord has promised to those who love Him".

Focus on Destiny

We must be focused at developing a divine character as the structure upon which we build everything else in our destiny-focused life. Building character is shaping our internal energy to focus on the values we hold dear and framing our habits, thoughts and feelings to serve those values. When we have a divine character, it means we are highly energised to communicate with God and reflect his nature through what we say, do, value and focus on.

As described in the previous chapter, everything in life is about managing various forms of energy inside and outside of us, transforming and transferring energy from one form into another. "Thinking" and "feeling" are the two things we do the most in life and they are all about processing energy within us. Love, happiness, joy and peace are all different forms of energy that we experience in life from within. If we pay sufficient attention to our thoughts and feelings and focus on improving them, we have the keys for success in life. For example, it is very easy to have some sort of idea or plan in mind about any goal you may want to achieve, but transferring that plan into reality can be very challenging. It will require a lot of thinking, which will ultimately affect your feelings and vice versa. Together, the thoughts and feelings you experience will affect the quality of your plans and the work that you need to do to achieve your vision. If a man can find ways to train his thoughts and feelings to always support his work, that man will surely succeed in his vision and plans.

If God Himself could not get His own plan to work perfectly in the Garden of Eden, how much more difficult is it for us human beings to be successful with our own plans? Nothing of value comes easy in real the world, because it takes energy to transform energy. The road to our destiny is full of hurdles, some low and others quite high, but they are all usefully as ways in which God trains and tests us for the sake of improving our abilities to process spiritual energy into physical reality until we win the race. When we interact with God, He is always training our character to make it strong and help us manage all the challenges that are linked to the accomplishment of our Destiny. Character is the key for personal change and it fuels a man's journey for the transformation of the community.

Between God's tests Devil's temptations

Destiny work is particularly robust because, spiritually speaking, the Devil and his agents are permanently busy tempting us and trying to divert us from our mission. The more we focus on the accomplishment of our Destiny, the more active the Devil becomes in trying to divert us from it. He uses many tools, tricks and traps to try to get his way. He even tried to divert our Lord Jesus himself from His purpose, offering Him food, power, and dominion over the earth. When he did so, he tested Jesus' knowledge and understanding of His own Word and he ultimately failed because everything was a scam and Jesus could see through it.

While the Devil tempts us, as a means to divert us from our Destiny, God tests and trains us to refine and strengthen our character and our ability to trust in Him, do His will, obey His commands and accomplish His purpose on earth. He tests us to see if we can remain faithful despite the circumstances of our lives. As a result of these things, we as Christians are constantly sandwiched between the devil's temptations, on the one hand and God's training and testing, on the other. This is why it is such a tough life for the true disciples of Christ. However, we have assurance from God that we shall overcome the world, if we remain faithful to Him. As much as it is tough to live our Christianity as soldiers of Christ, in this fallen world, it is also amazingly fulfilling to do so.

As long as we remain alive, the tests, trials and tribulations will not cease. The temptation of Jesus by the devil, as described in the Bible, can also be regarded, in a way, as a test from the Father for Jesus who can carrying the Christ in Him. The Bible says, Jesus was "led by the spirit" to be tempted by the devil. This suggests that God wanted that temptation to take place. While Christ could not be tempted, but Jesus (as a man) could not escape temptation from the king of this world, the devil. The test was for the "man" Jesus to see if He would uphold the "Christ" in him. "Christ" needed "Jesus" as a carrier, a human vehicle to deliver His mission on earth, as the "Divine Messiah", so that He could accomplish His father's mission to save humanity. If Jesus had obeyed the devil, He would have lost His ability to sustain the Christ in Him. The man, Jesus probably would have died without the ability to resurrect and Christianity and the plans of God for the restoration of humanity would have failed.

Through the devils' temptation of Jesus as recounted in the Bible, we must understand that our spirit, which is the divine part of our identity cannot escape the testing of God and the temptations of the devil, because these are the ways in we strengthen and reinforce our human capacity to sustain the Divine (spirit) in us. Our mind will always remain the battlefield where the eternal battle of good versus evil will take place. That battle is part of the process through which we will refine our character and achieve self-affirmation. As long as we remain connected to Jesus, the spirit will always be willing to take elevation and obey

God, but the body will often want to remain "grounded" on earth, pulling us down with the gravity of sin. For us to overcome the gravitational force of sin, we need to vibrate our spiritual energy intensely enough so that we can create a force that pull us upward towards God. We need some sort of "spiritual levitational force" that is constantly holding and pulling us upward. This is where determination becomes necessary to facilitate and enable elevation towards God. When there is enough determination, the spiritual vibration intensifies and we can gather enough energy to lift off and head skywards. But unlike Jesus who was perfect and passed every test during His journey on earth, most of us as mere humans are set to experience failure and imperfections from time to time throughout our lives. This is part of the plans of God and we cannot escape it. This is why we must be determined to keep running the race, no matter how many times we may fall.

Determination and the management of desires

Determination is something that is needed when someone decides to get into action with the aim of achieving a particular goal, purpose or vision. But how do you develop enough determination to achieve your God-given Destiny? The answer to this question becomes easier when you understand the overall picture about Destiny. Our Destiny is part of divine creation and restoration. God did not finish creation on earth. He created everything that was needed to set the physical world into motion. He created the earth and put everything in place to sustain life in it, before creating man and putting him in charge of creation. God expects mankind to complete the creation work by using all the faculties

He deposited in Him. Those faculties are meant to enable us to put things together and add value to what exists (nature), to our own life and to the lives of others around us. God gave man the ability to continue creation and He invested His divine "capacity" into Him for that purpose. All human beings have the capacity to create, just like God. The only difference is that God started from "nothingness" and brought things into existence using His Word, but we humans need to start from Gods creation (nature) to transform and re-arrange things in new ways that add value to life on this planet. Our capacity to create can be used both negatively and positively and it is the character in us that will lead us to focus on the positive aspect of things.

Dr Myles Munroe once said: "God knew that man would need a table and He hid it in the trees". Man had to use his intelligence and skills to cut down the tree, make wood out of it and create a chair from the wood. In the same way, God knew that man would need bread and He hid it in the bush. Man had to grow wheat, harvest it, process it and mix it with yeast and water and then use fire to create bread. Both the process of getting a table out of trees or getting bread out of a mixture of wheat, yeast, water and fire have been made possible through a determined use of our divine creative ability. Unlike animals, we are able to conceptualise the table, to study things, to create sophisticated tools to cut down the tree and get the wood out of it, to cut and shape the wood accordingly, to create and use nails, ropes and hammer, to learn carpentry and to assemble the table together. The process to get all these things happen in a harmonious and creative way takes place in a way that God does not control, not because He can't, but because He won't. He wants us to do this bit by ourselves. He did His job by creating nature and sustaining it and then gave us creative skills and abilities. He expects us to do the rest and manufacture new things and create new experiences and new realities. As long as we are determined to create, we can do so. We have the "spiritual licence" from the Father, besides the cognitive faculties.

With determination, we can combine our various faculties to produce all sorts of things that make our lives better in different ways. Once we understand that we are called to continue creation from where God left, we also need to understand that we will need determination and commitment to create anything of value. We don't always have to create physical things, we can create intangible things such as building a social environment, a system or an interaction field that enables people to discover their true identity, to feel valued, to develop their God-given gifts and pursue their Divine Mission on earth. This is done through the manifestation of love, care and attention to the various needs of mankind, especially those who are unable to help themselves. We are the tools that God uses to distribute His grace in tangible ways to the human family. This is why the Bible says in James 1:27

> *"Religion that God our Father accepts as pure and faultless is this: to look after orphans and widows in their distress and to keep oneself from being polluted by the world".*

Determination is crucial in delivering our destiny on earth, because we need to work to transform the energy we get from our faith (in God), into palpable things and lived experiences that bring the love of God to the human family. For some people, destiny may be linked to hard labour that produces no immediate results for a long time. It may take years for them to even just discover their true identity and understand their destiny mission. It may even take longer for them to do the work involved. Noah took approximately 75 years to build the ark before moving to the next stage of getting the animals to board it. He was mocked and humiliated many times while doing the work, but he remained determined to achieve his mission. Even Jesus took 30 years, before starting the active and practical aspect of His ministry. He only worked actively for 3 years, which means he took 90% of his life time to get ready and only 10% to get busy and deliver the work. Both Noah and Jesus needed determination to progress and accomplish their work on earth. They both had a strong desire to see their God-given mission through, despite the difficulty, humiliation, trials and tribulations that they encounter.

Seven ways to build and develop determination for your destiny mission

There are many ways we can build and develop determination in our lives. Some of the steps we can take include:

1 Have a clear vision of what you want to achieve in life

You cannot be determined to achieve something if you are not clear about what it is that you want to do, and what it will look like at the end of the day. When you are clear about your God-given Mission and understand how that Mission is expected to impact you and your community, the courage and determination to do it comes more easily. For us Christians, the clarity of the vision starts with our own identity in Christ and God's purpose in our lives. Jesus knew that He was the Messiah and His destiny was to become a Saviour of humanity. He knew very well His chief purpose in life, which was linked to the message he had to deliver to humanity (the gospel), as well as carrying the cross for the atonement of the sins of the world. He was aware He had a job to do on earth, a mission to accomplish before returning to the Father. He prepared Himself for it and delivered it accordingly. However, unlike Jesus, Apostle Paul did not know his true destiny until when he was "spiritually arrested" by Jesus and assigned his apostolic mission. He spent many years as a Pharisee who was very active in killing and persecuting Christians. He did not know this critical role in preaching the good news to the gentiles. The strength of God's impartation in his life provided him with a great amount of determination to accomplish his life mission.

Determination is often a product of the spirit, but it needs a good mind to remain healthy and strong. It is connected to vision, identity and purpose. Do you know what your identity is in God? Do you know your Destiny? Do you know your purpose in life? Can you express these things clearly and concisely? Have you got your life goals written down somewhere where you can see them every day? What role do you plan in the Kingdom of God one earth? Are you a leader, a teacher, a carer, a healer, a singer, a prophet, an evangelist, a preacher, a communicator, a businessperson? What is your way of adding value to the vision of God and His people on earth? Are you clear in your mind about what your divine mission is in your life? The higher the clarity in your mind about any of these things, the easier it is to be and remain determined to deliver your destiny one earth.

2 Seek good leadership and mentorship
When you embark in any serious long-term endeavour, you do need leadership and guidance. This is why it is crucial to have good leadership and a good mentor in life. Even Jesus was

mentored by John the Baptist. God is our Heavenly leader and He can guide us through His Word and through His spirit, if we allow Him to. God can work with us to help us develop our own self-leadership abilities. But besides God, we do need spiritual leadership, coaching and mentorship from gifted individuals in our network. The best leadership we need is the type of leadership that Jesus provided to His 12 disciples, which was vision-focused, intimate and devoted to the work of God. It was a type of leadership that was centred on spiritual growth and the discharging of one's Destiny Mission. It included both teaching, preaching, field work and mentorship. This type of leadership is what most pastors in churches and ministries should be busy providing to their congregants. Church leaders today are letting believers down by not investing enough time to lead, coach and mentor their flock appropriately and help them focus on and achieve their God-given Destiny. Every pastor (or minister of God) in every church pastor should a "Destiny Coach" for their congregants and not just "a church overseer" (a manager of church affairs).

3 Develop a new vocabulary for your Destiny Mission

Language is important in shaping consciousness. The words we use and names we give to things affect how we conceive of things and how we interact with people. It is important to look at the names and words that we use to frame our spiritual transactions. There is a reason why God asked Adam to name animals as part of his first task in the management of creation. There is also a reason why God asked many Biblical characters to change their names when they met God. Names and language are critical aspects that need to be attended to when managing things and new relationships.

Determination

The vocabulary we have inherited from ancient biblical language such as pastors, sheep, shepherd, spiritual father and many other similar terms may no longer connect well with today's societal realities and norms. The times have changed and the challenges of life today are very different from the challenges that people were faced within ancient Israel. Therefore, a new set of vocabulary that is connected to the imagery of every day's life in the 21st century is needed, if we want to connect to today's generation in profound ways.

Imagine if your pastor at your local church was called a "destiny coach" and he understood his work as not just being a preacher of the Gospel, but a personal trainer (spiritually), a leader, a mentor, a guide, a motivator and a supporter to help you and the rest of the congregants to grow your faith and deliver your God-given destiny on earth. Do you think this is likely to encourage a new type of spiritual leadership between the church members and their pastor? The answer to this question is definitely positive. A destiny coach conveys a different set of meanings from a pastor or shepherd and such a change of name will not compromise the Word of God either.

The names and titles that we give ourselves or that we are given in life, not only frame our consciousness and shape our actions, beliefs and behaviours, they also affect the way others relate to us and what expectations they have when interacting with us. In the Bible, when people change their names after encountering God, it was meant to mark the transformation from the old person into a new one. When God gave Adam to name animals in the garden, it was more than simply about labelling things, it was a way to create order and format his consciousness. God Himself separated and named things as He created them, before Adam was created. He did so as part of creating order out of chaos and formatting nature to prepare the ground for man's consciousness.

The vocabulary we use in our everyday life and the manner we speak affect our consciousness and impact the way we understand things, relate to them and behave outwardly. For this reason, if you want to build determination for your vision, you need to develop a new vocabulary and name things that are important in your environment with new labels. Many businesses, including the military and other large organisations with important strategic gaols often develop their own vocabulary to shape behaviours and expectations. Social scientists and politicians coin new words as they seek to change people's minds and understanding about things. The nomenclature battle is well real in the world. If you are determined for your destiny deployment you must adopt a new personal language/vocabulary for your spiritual life, coin new words and relabel things in ways that that keeps your focus where it is supposed to be so that you can keep you moving to your destination.

4 Grow your knowledge

Vision and knowledge are important in achieving one's Destiny; they go together. "Without vision my people perish", God says in Proverb 29:18 and "My people perish because of lack of knowledge". He declares in Hosea 4:6. Vision is a picture of the reality of a thing, but knowledge is an understanding of what that thing is, its nature, its features and how it is supposed to work or simply exist. When someone has a clear vision of their mission along with the knowledge and understanding of what they are expected to do to turn that vision into reality, then they are more likely to be determined to do the job. Christians must know the scriptures well to access God's mind and His will for humanity.

The knowledge will help to arm them with a godly vision and when that is done they can take steps to acquire and develop plans and strategies to implement the vision in question. This explains the importance of good education, both spiritual and secular. The primary purpose of education should not be about teaching people new facts or concepts, but it should be more about teaching them how to seek relevant knowledge for their own vision, as well as how to create and develop new knowledge they need to have in order for them to accomplish their vision in life. In other words, education should teach people how to learn and how to create new knowledge from their own experience and observations.

5 Be strategic

Knowing your life mission is just the beginning of things, you need to have a plan for the work you are expected to do so that you can accomplish that mission. Only God can create things using His "Word" alone. For us human beings, we need to make plans and do work. We need to sweat to make things happen, because when Adam was chased from the Garden of Eden, he was told he needed to sweat in order to eat (Gen 3:19). Anyone who is serious about achieving anything worthwhile sets up a plan for it. Even Jesus had a plan for His work. He started recruiting disciples and took time to put His team together. He told His disciples not to talk about Him being Messiah for a while until it was the right time to do so. When He started His ministry, He took time to pray and fast on a regular basis, He moved to different cities to speak to various communities. All of these things were part of a plan that guided His work.

When you know you have power in this world, you must be strategic. In fact, strategy can create power where power does not exist. This is why you hear the term "strategic plan" a lot of times when dealing with people of power or people with big responsibilities. The Bible also says that God told Jeremiah *"I know the plans He has for you"* (Jeremiah 29:19).

If God has plans for your life, you must do all you can to find out what those divine plans are and then set your own plan to implement the plans of God in your life, because God can only implement them with your cooperation. If you are not clear about God's plans in your life, dig deep in your spirit and in your heart, ask God to reveal His will and purpose for your life and write down What God is telling you. You will need to pray, meditate, fast and listen to the quiet voice of God talking to you and then start drafting a plan using the ideas, dreams, inspirations and revelations from God and ask Him to lead you in refining them and He will surely do so. God has already finished Creation and this includes the plans for your life. Everything you need to know from Him has been released already and it is up to you to tune yourself to His frequency and download the "data" in our consciousness and start the process of transferring it from the intangible realm into the tangible reality.

6 Dealing with failure and opposition

As we set ourselves to accomplish our Destiny on earth, we need to know that there is no alternative to work. We need to work, work hard, work smart, work with others and work always. By work, we don't simply mean deeds to show holiness, because we have already received holiness by grace, but it is work understood as life mission. As we get into action into action for our Destiny, it is inevitable that some of our efforts will not succeed. Failure is a part of the human experience and it is often part of every success story. It is important for us to understand the concept of failure in a godly manner and learn to handle it well, so that we don't get discouraged and don't quit prematurely when things start getting tough. We must learn to fail forward, meaning that we have to get up each time we fail and continue the journey until we succeed. We cannot let ourselves be discouraged easily. We may fail and even be humiliated in many ways and on many occasions, but we are soldiers of Christ, we have a cross to carry and we don't quit until the commander gives the order to do so. We learn from the Psalmist who says that *"even though I walk through the valley of the shadow of death I shall not fear no evil, for You are with me"* (Psalms 23.:4). Walk through the shadow of death with confidence. It is only a shadow, not the real thing, because death does not exist for true Christians.

Besides failure, we must also learn how to deal with opposition, because we are called to create things in an environment where other individuals in the natural world will be exercising their own free will to choose and do evil. Evil is always part of the equation and it cannot be removed or ignored. Such people may want to fight or oppose us, because they want us to fail or they perceive us a threat for their own interest. It is also evident from the Bible that the Devil has a grip on this world, and he will not want us to succeed. Jesus faced a lot of opposition when He was on earth and a lot of it came from the so-called people of God, the religious leaders (Pharisees, Sadducees and others). The mystery here is that the opposition from these groups, which was a bad thing, eventually led to Jesus' demise on the cross, but the death was necessary for the glorification of Jesus, as the resurrected one. Death was also necessary for the establishment of the church. This shows us how God turns our opposition into success. It also explains why Jesus asked us to love and pray for our enemies, because our enemies have a role to play in our destiny. Their negative attitudes and behaviours towards us bring troubles, trials and tribulations in our lives, which ultimately help us to become stronger once we overcome them. As the saying goes: "whatever doesn't kill you makes you stronger". Our enemies may want to kill us for our work, not knowing that we have the power of resurrection within us. Keeping our enemies in our mind creates awareness as a force for motivation to keep us going and show what we are made of.

Western democracies have captured this notion of opposition very well by including it in their governance system. The "political opposition" enables the government of the day to watch itself and behave appropriately to avoid the criticism of the opposition, which is focused at exposing their incompetence or weaknesses. The presence of opposition helps to motivate the government to do better and the people of the country are often better for it, compared to other political systems where there is no formal and organised opposition to the government of day. Your enemies are the opposition for your self-government, both spiritually and intellectually. Let them do their job and pray for them that they keep you awake and active.

7 Don't be too comfortable

A lot of people wonder why everything in life seems so tough and difficult, especially when you want to live in righteousness. We forget that Christians are "foreigners" in this world that is dominated by the Devil and, because of this, we will always face challenges and we are not meant to be too comfortable because we are on a mission. The world is infected by sin and the Devil will always be active trying to infect us and make us useless for the work God. Destiny Living is a life that will be constantly challenged. As a Christian, when you become too comfortable in life, it could be a sign that something is wrong.

Determination

All great champions in all types of sports understand that it is not a good idea to be too comfortable and they intentionally challenge themselves constantly at different levels, as a means to strengthen themselves. When Myke Tyson was at the height of his boxing career, he once declared in an interview that he was getting out of bed at 3AM to start running and training for up to 5 hours uninterrupted. When asked why he did that, he responded by saying that he imposed himself that sort of training regime because he knew that none of his opponents would be doing the same and that gave him confidence in his mind, which helped him win more fights. Most champion sportspersons, when they lose a fight and are humiliated by an opponent, rather than being discouraged by the loss, they use it as a motivational tool for growth and improvement so that they can do more to beat the opponent the next time around.

8 Expect betrayal

We are God's champions on earth, we must learn to deal with failure, opposition, humiliation and betrayal. Jesus was betrayed by one of His disciples and you can always bet one day people that you trust will betray you. When this happens, instead of dwelling on your hurt (because it will hurt), learn the lesson that you need to learn and keep on moving forward with a focus on your destiny. Many people will come to your life to teach you lessons and the best lessons humans learn are those that are emotionally charged, especially those that hurt the most. Don't let the hurt lead you to hate people, rather let it motivate you to better choose people you associate with as you move on with your destiny mission. You cannot achieve your Destiny on your own, you need to work with people and some of those people will help you and others will hurt you.

FOCUS ON DESTINY

Spiritual motivation and destiny living

When we speak of determination in relation to destiny living, we are ultimately talking about strong and consistent spiritual motivation to achieve our purpose on earth. On the surface it may look like determination is a product of a mindset, but it is actually an outcome of both spiritual and mental processes being geared towards the achievement of a goal. Developing and nurturing determination in one's mind requires a lot of effort and discipline, but without it is difficult to achieve anything of value with God. God may give us a great vision in life, but we need determination to make that vision come to past. God doesn't give us determination; it must come from within ourselves. God touches our spirit and our spirit influences our mind to build and develop determination. One of the best ways to ensure we remain spiritually determined to live out our destiny is to develop a kingdom mindset. Renewing your mind and developing a kingdom mindset will enable the spiritual impartation from God to settle within you and be utilised appropriately to provide power and fuel for your destiny journey.

Spiritual motivation is probably the strongest form of motivation and determination. Wherever the spirit leads, the mind follows, just like the body follows where the mind goes. Therefore, both God and Satan target man's spirit in order to use him for their respective work on earth. When spiritual motivation is high, people are so motivated to the point of sacrificing their lives for what they believe in. This is because quite often people view themselves, in such circumstances, as mere instruments for a bigger cause for which they are happy to offer their lives. The case of Islamic fundamentalism and suicide bombers blowing themselves up while shouting and praising the name "Allah" is one good illustration of the power of spiritual motivation. Killing people is obviously not a good thing, but one can see the power and strength of spiritual motivation, even in such despicable acts of violence. When spiritual motivation is very high, whether it is good or bad, determination follows, and people can go very far in their actions to express their beliefs and convictions.

Jesus brought us salvation and inside the "salvation box" there is eternal life (in Heaven) and purposeful life (on earth). The gospel of salvation that many congregations tend focus on is important, but it will remain crippled if it is not completed by the destiny gospel or the gospel of purposeful living. Jesus can come in your life in a matter of a second, but sustaining Him in your heart and serving His purpose in your life is a matter of a lifetime commitment and an unrelenting determination. Our focus, once we have received Jesus as Lord and saviour, is to deliver our destiny on earth through purposeful living. The more we are determined to do this, the more God will enlighten, empower and equip us so that we fulfil His mission on this planet. He knows that we are working for Him and will do everything to get His work done through us.

In this day and age, we hear a lot about "success" in life. Often the word success is used in its capitalistic connotation and linked with financial abundance. This is the motivational mantra that has dominated the self-help industry and still defines the whole positive thinking narrative in most western countries. But for us Christians the main motivation in our life should not be about being successful, as the world understands the word success. Rather, it is about living our God-ordained Destiny, letting ourselves be transformed by God and using the power of that transformation to become change agents with a divine agenda. Success in the world is not the same as success in

Christ. Jesus did not use the word success in the Bible, but He used the word "great" (greatness). For Him greatness is found in the service to others, in helping our fellow human beings. In Matthew 20:26, Jesus says: "it shall not be this way among you. Instead, whomever wants to become great among you must be your servant". This shows a different mindset at play, the Christ mindset or Kingdom mindset, which is different from the world's mindset. Set your mind in Christ and He will help instil determination into it.

Developing our relationship with God and conditioning ourselves for His work through regular prayer, meditation and the study of the scriptures can also help us to increase our motivation and determination for His work. Ultimately, God assesses success not in human terms, but He looks at the "spiritual fruitfulness" of our lives. That fruitfulness is only possible through our relationship with Him and how we contribute to His Kingdom on earth. We can only be fruitful if we are able to grow to maturity and spiritual growth will come from our determination to seek God's presence, purpose and provision in our lives. We must ensure that we are always submerged in divine environment where spiritual growth is encouraged and enabled thru the relationship we build with everything and everyone divine.

Another common saying in our societies today is that "all humans are products of their environment". What is actually meant by this is that we are all products of our relationships, which condition us in particular ways. Our relationship with people, our relationship with nature, with our culture and its spiritual aspects, all of these things are influencing factors that ultimately make us who we are. The right spiritual environment gives us what a good natural environment gives to a plant: it enables the seed in us to germinate, shoot above ground for self-affirmation and develop strong roots to support its maturity. Therefore, it is very important for Christians to belong to a good church that is able to provide the right environment for spiritual growth. The activities we do at church can be very helpful in raising our determination for destiny living. The prayer, praise and worship, preaching, teaching, charity and fellowship, if all done correctly are very powerful tools for spiritual fruitfulness. These tools help to program and re-program our mind and connect us with the Divine in powerful ways and not just on a philosophical level, but at a deeply spiritual level, as well. A good church environment that focuses on spiritual growth rather than religious rituals and obligations is particularly important for God's plans to manifest on earth. Our churches need not to be spiritual massage parlours where people are made to feel good, they need to be training grounds for soldiers of Christ, where people are challenged in various ways to be better servants.

The determination to deploy and deliver your destiny will also come from the network of people that are able to build you up and support your work. Even Jesus built a network to support His work by recruiting a dozen disciples. He was always with people, both the crowd and the crew. The crew (his disciples) was needed as a deployment team. He formed the best leadership team in the history of humanity. Only 12 people (later reduced to 11) who have managed to spread the Gospel and transform the world dramatically. Since Jesus showed up in the world, Christianity has been one of the most powerful civilising forces in the history of humanity, despite abuses by some individuals and groups in the course of history. Jesus came to change the world and although He had the power to do everything by Himself, in His divine capacity, He chose to work with people. This shows us that even for God (in the flesh), He needed to build a network of people to get His work done. What He did can be referred to as "Destiny Networking". It is about building connection with the right people who can inspire, motivate and support you for your work, at the same time as you also bring value to their own lives and work. Being part of a supporting team can be extremely useful in increasing your determination to deliver your destiny on earth.

In the end, determination for the work of God in our lives is developed through many things, including a high spiritual motivation and enlightenment, a Kingdom-focused mindset, a strong and intimate relationship with God and our willingness to surround ourselves with the right people for the purpose of accomplishing our mission on earth. As a Christian, your determination should not be directed simply at living holy, being saved and going to Heaven, even though this is important, but it must be more about on transforming the world with your Gospel-inspired lifestyle, your focus on living your destiny and using all the gift(s) and resources that God has deposited in you to impact the world.

CHAPTER 12

Keyword 12

Deployment

> **KEY POINTS**
> - It is not enough to have gifts, you must deploy them and use them appropriately
> - The gifts in you are not for you, but for the world. A tree does not eat its own fruits
> - You are part of an army of God, deployed as part of the ground force, while God provides air power to help you accomplish your mission on earth
> - Let death find you busy in your deployment, there is no retiring from your Destiny mission

Destiny deployment

DR MYLES MUNROE ONCE SAID THAT "YOUR DESTINY IS ORDAINED in Heaven, but it is not guaranteed on earth". He went on to explain that God has ordained our Destiny in the spiritual realm, and He expects it to be realised on earth, but the accomplishment of that Destiny in the physical world depends on man fully cooperating with God. The key message about Destiny is that God has an agenda for every one of us and He has given us everything we need in order to fulfil it. The fulfilment of that destiny will require that we exercise our will, our faith, our spiritual, intellectual, emotional and physical abilities to connect to God and work with Him to complete our mission on planet earth.

Destiny is ultimately about work; it is a life mission in the name of God. It is centred on discharging our duty as children of God, as ambassadors of Christ and partners of the divine restoration of the earth. Our father invested in us by equipping us with gifts, skills, talents and resources. He has also given us faith to ensure we know Him, believe and trust in Him, as well as interact with Him in meaningful ways.

The first thing in our Christian life is receiving Jesus as Lord and Saviour. Once this is done, you become a new person, the old one is gone. The spiritual transformation that takes place as we meet Jesus generally comes with a new "burden" in our heart. That burden often drives people to speak of Jesus and what He has done for them. That same burden drives believers to want to do something for Jesus. Some will want to preach and evangelise, others may want to start a charity or embrace any particular cause where they can show the love of Jesus in their lives.

The spiritual transformation that we go through when we meet Jesus can be dramatic in some cases and a silent experience in others, but it is always powerful. Whether you are on the dramatic side or the quiet side of things, the question that everyone must ask themselves is: "what is the purpose of my faith in Christ, what is my faith for?" The answer to this question will vary according to various Christian doctrines and individual endowment, but if you look at things closely, there are essentially two main benefits we get from our faith in Jesus Chris: Salvation (1) and Destiny (2). Salvation is about living with God in eternity and Destiny is about living for God on earth. The gospel is not just about giving us a passport to Heaven, it gives us a blueprint for our destiny on earth. Both of these things are very important, but a life that has not achieved its Destiny on earth is a wasted life, in the eyes of God. Those who waste their lives here on earth run the risk of meeting Jesus in Heaven on Judgement day and being told "I never knew you".

The essence of this book is not about evangelisation in the sense that it is not focusing on bringing people to Christ, even though this is not excluded. The focus here is to help Christians grow and accelerate their journey to spiritual maturity and get busy with their Destiny mission. Our focus is on providing new insights to help believers become true disciplines of Christ and agents of the Kingdom of God on earth. Believers must grow and become true disciples of Christ by focusing on the work that God has given them life for.

Being a disciple of Christ means showing leadership in whatever area God has called you for and working for Him to progress His agenda on earth. This is the ultimate purpose of the Christian faith. It is not just about singing, dancing and shouting "Lord! Lord! Lord!" on Sunday morning at church. Many Christians are not sufficiently focused on accomplishing their Destiny here below. A great number of them live their faith as some type of obligation to worship and obey God, because God is God and He requires obedience and deserves reverence. Some Christians understand that Jesus Christ is the Lord and He wants us to live a holy life. However, so many believers are yet to understand that faith in Jesus must be exercised in the framework of "Destiny Living" or "Destiny Mission". This means we must live our faith by dedicating ourselves to the implementation of the divine assignment that we all have. A lot of Christians remain "cultural Christians" and practice their faith simply by attending church service on Sunday, singing hymns, praying when they can, giving offerings and trying to be as holy as possible.

The world is a battlefield and you have been deployed to serve

Deployment is a word that is often used by the military to describe the act of sending troops into duty, at a particular location, often away from home. Deployment is also used to refer to the act of assigning soldiers at various locations (often on foreign land), for a given mission, which may be part of an armed conflict (war) or a peaceful mission (such as a peace contingent). The Bible uses military imagery and metaphors in many passages to convey the idea of Christianity being like a militaristic mission and Christians being deployed on earth for various assignments that are part of the bigger mission of colonising the earth for the Kingdom of God.

In Timothy 2:3-4, Apostle Paul says: "share in suffering as a good soldier of Christ Jesus. No soldier gets entangled in Civilian Pursuits, since his aim is to please the one who enlisted him". This passage reminds us that part of our identity in Christ is that of a soldier. In fact, many of us are a type of "one-man army", just like we speak of a one-man band. We may view ourselves as individual beings, but there is more in us than just one thing or one identity. We are many things in one, our identity is always plural. We are many things packaged into one body. We exist in 3 dimensions: mind, body and spirit. Most of us have to juggle with different identities in our lives. As the author of this book, I realise when writing these lines, that I am a husband, a father, a brother, a business operator, a broadcaster, a community leader, a boss, a church leader and the list can go on. I do so many things in my life. Each of these descriptions is an identity of its own and all of them together describe me as a person with a unique and single identity. While not everyone may do as many things as I do, most people juggle with different aspects of their identity too. We are all people with multiple skills and resources. We are good at more than one thing and can do a lot of things in a way that military troops do when they are deployed on the ground for a mission or for war. Each one of us is some kind of mini commando (both singular and plural) in the eyes God and with the Holy Spirit guiding and supporting us, we can win many battles for God.

Even though the Bible says that the battle is not ours, that applies only for the spiritual part of the battle. Jesus has fought and won the spiritual battle for the redemption of humanity and He has given us spiritual authority over the king of this world. However, there is a battle that God has left for us, the "transformation battle". We have to use our will, energy and focus to seek God, renew our mind, resist the devil and dominate the flesh in us. We also have to do something for the transformation of the world. God can help us fight these battles, but He let us fight these battles so that we can get changed and strengthened in the process.

Know and develop your weapons for deployment

God expects us to deploy everything He deposited in us even before we were born. He wants us to bring out everything He has placed in us for the battles of our life. Apostle Paul speaks of the Armor of God to take a stand against the devil. God expects us to make a good use of all the resources He has invested in us to accomplish His assignment on earth. It is important to do our own personal assets/weapons inventory.

Ephesians 6:10-18 says:

> Therefore, put on the full armor of God, so that when the day of evil comes, you may be able to stand your ground, and after you have done everything, to stand. Stand firm then, with the belt of truth buckled around your waist, with the breastplate of righteousness in place, and with your feet fitted with the readiness that comes from the gospel of peace. In addition to all this, take up the shield of faith, with which you can extinguish all the flaming arrows of the evil one. Take the helmet of salvation and the sword of the Spirit, which is the word of God.

Besides the conventional weapons of faith as described above, we all have our own specific weapons that come with the gifts that place in us. We need time to dig deep in our heart, mind, spirit and soul and identify everything that we have been entrusted with by God and, in line with our vision from God. Once we are clear on what we have, we can then develop and use these things to deliver the Mission for which God gave us life.

Any Christian who is serious about living their Destiny needs to know what they have inside of them. Some believers need outside help from their church leaders to identify their spiritual weapons and assets. However, often it is just a matter of spending time with God and doing introspection, prayer and meditation. The tendency for many people is to discount what they have, doubt their ability and neglect their potential. The Bible is full of examples of people who did not think they could be useful to God. Moses thought he wasn't fit for the mission that God gave to him. Gideon shied away from God's call and there are many other Biblical figures in the same category. Not many people are good at assessing themselves and being aware of the treasures they hold inside of them. This is why our destiny is tied to each other because some people's work in the Kingdom of God is about helping others to pay attention to and notice what is inside of them and encourage them to discover, develop and deploy their true identity in Christ. Sometimes people may even be very clear about their talents, gifts and skills, but they are too afraid to start anything on their own. They lack confidence, or they procrastinate a lot. This is where good leadership and good education in the society is so crucial. The church of Christ must do more to encourage good teachings in this area and imbed "destiny education" in every aspect of the ministry. The quality of leadership should not be judged simply by the number of people following the leader. Great leadership is about enabling people to discover their own leadership qualities and actively use them, more than it is about leading followers to any particular vision or destination.

Deployment versus Employment

Destiny deployment is about putting into use the gifts, skills, talents, energy, focus and all other resources that one has for the sole purpose of discharging their God-ordained Destiny on earth. Often, we say that life is a battle. The primary definition of a battle is "a sustained fight between large organised armed forces". When a nation is involved in a war, it deploys its troops to fight. Mighty armies deploy troops with lot of equipment and all the technologies they have to support them on the ground. The church of Christ (the body of Christ) is the nation of God on earth and it is at war with the enemy who controls the earth temporarily. The more believers and disciples of Christ we have deployed on the ground, the better for the Kingdom of God. Hence, the need to deploy ourselves for the mission we have. This is what Jesus meant by saying in Matthew 9:35-38

> "The harvest is plentiful but the workers are few. 38 Ask the Lord of the harvest, therefore, to send out workers into his harvest field."

We need to be active and use everything we have for the assignment that we each have, as we get deployed in the field of God.

Practically speaking, deploying ourselves for God means spending most of our time working on our mission, supporting fellow (Christian) fighters or preparing ourselves for particular assignments from God. This is in contrast to being employed and spending most of our time earning income to pay bills and accumulate material goods. When we are in active deployment it means we are living a life that is based on the vision of God in us and not just being concerned about things that most people in the world are focused on such as career development and other similar things. Destiny deployment is living like Jesus, totally focused on doing the will of the Father, even if this may mean that we may not be able to own a house, a car, nice clothes and any other material possessions. You are "deployed" when you work for God's vision in your life to be materialised and you do not worry too much about financial security and or running the rat race. The funny thing is that those who are truly and fully "deployed" for Christ often end up leading a more fulfilled and happier life than those who are simply "employed" in a job or career context or those doing business for sake of building wealth.

Some Christians understand their calling and the need to shift from employment to deployment, but it is often the transition from these two modes of living that they are afraid of. Shifting from employment to deployment means stop working as an employee and abandoning the security of the pay check, no matter how small it may be, and going into self-employment. When you shift into self-employment it often takes a while to start earning good income and there is a level of uncertainty that makes people uncomfortable and they shy away from taking the step to cross to the other side. But we must all remember; what benefit is there for someone to have a successful career and miss his/her destiny? As Jesus said in Mark 8:36:

> *"For what shall it profit a man, if he shall gain the whole world, but lose his soul?"*
>
> Mark 8:36"

Time and Destiny Deployment

Time is an important element in life. We are not on earth eternally. As soon as we enter physicality, the clock starts ticking and it does not stop. Most people in the world spend the majority of time working as employees in an organisation, running a business or simply trying to survive in difficult economic settings. In first world countries, a large majority of people spend about ten to twelve hours of every weekday at work, including commuting to and from work. More than 80% of the workforce in most countries is motivated by the desire to make money to pay bills and acquire material goods. As we work, most of us are employed to help achieve someone else's vision, goals or dreams. While employment is a great thing for a healthy economy, it is often very toxic for the individual soul, spiritually speaking. In many cases, employment negatively affects our personal ability to have a high spiritual focus. Therefore, As Christians we must regard employment as a temporary training opportunity to help prepare for our destiny deployment, even if it may take years before we are able to launch ourselves into what God has called us to do with our lives.

With deployment we employ ourselves, not for the sake of making money, but achieving our Destiny on earth and adding value to the Kingdom of God. When we are employed in the world, we have a Master (boss) to please and we focus on the financial gain (money) that we get from him or her, even if they may make our life miserable for months or years. When we do this, it is very difficult to be engaged in our own personal and spiritual deployment. Often it is difficult to discharge one's Destiny within the context of a regular employment, even though this is not impossible. In normal employment settings, everything we do is dictated by the will and policies of the employer and we are left with very little freedom, to let our spirit and our hearts lead us in the everyday exercise of will and freedom in the context of our occupation.

However, it is important to stress that employment is not without its benefits and usefulness. We are not suggesting in this book that Christians should not seek employment at all. We all must start from somewhere and employment is a great way for anyone (especially young people) to learn the value of work and the business of managing work-related activities. Employment helps people develop skills such as teamwork, goalsetting, prioritising, time management and many other things. It provides us with financial benefits to give us a foundation from which we can build our destiny deployment. Most of us will start our active life by being employed in some type of occupation. Even Jesus was a carpenter and Apostle Paul was a tent builder. The problem arises when we forget to take the next step from employment, and we become very comfortable and settle into our jobs for the money, security and prestige (sometimes) that we get from it.

Many Christians are not focused on deployment, not always because of the financial and materialistic benefits of employment and the fear of stepping into the unknown, but because they do not have a clear idea of their God-given Destiny. They also lack proper guidance to help them make progress in this area. For some it may be ignorance and laziness and for others it is fear or lack of proper Christian education. They may not have been sufficiently exposed to the right teachings within their congregation in relation to Destiny Living and they remain in the framework of "cultural Christianity". Many people are Christians simply because they were born Christians and have grown up in the church and they continue to practice Christianity as a consequence of cultural or societal conditioning. There is also another group of Christians who go a little deeper than cultural Christianity, but they are only fed the Gospel of Salvation and focus on living a holy life on earth. They are not taught much about purposeful living. Like the majority of people on earth, many Christians may claim to have Jesus in their lives, but they still do not know why they exist and what God created them for. They have no clue to what their lives are all about, at an individual level. They go to church every Sunday, they read the Bible, they try to help at their local church, and they do some good deeds, but still have no clear idea about what their chief purpose in life is, hence they are not busy with their destiny mission.

The Bible clearly says that God created all of us with a Destiny. He foreknew, predestined, called, justified and glorified all Christians.

> *"For God knew his people in advance, and he chose them to become like his Son, so that his Son would be the firstborn among many brothers and sisters."*
>
> Romans 8:29, <u>NLT</u>:

As mentioned in earlier chapters of this book, part of our Destiny needs to be discovered through our interactions with God and the other part is to be created, i.e. designed, developed and implemented on earth (from what God shows us), through the investment of work, time and energy in the mission that God gives us. Christians who are not deployed for their Destiny work are handicapped in their faith, to say the least. They have faith, but they are missing the "action" part and one day they may discover that their faith has been dead all along.

3Ws of Destiny Deployment

Here on earth, God's plans depend on the cooperation of man to be physically implemented. Imagine sending a (somewhat intelligent and independent) robot to Mars and the robot gets there and it refuses to work. Mission control would be extremely disappointed because of the investment made to manufacture it, put it in a space ship and launch it. The robot would be packed with expensive and sophisticated tools, but no matter how sophisticated that robot may be, if it cannot meaningfully communicate with Mission Control, it would be useless. In the same way, the participation of man in the plans of God is crucial. Faith is the "communication software" that allows God to communicate with man, but that communication should not be limited to simply acknowledging and praising "Mission Control", it needs to enable all the features that the machine is packed with to work so that the mission it was sent on the planet for can be accomplished. This analogy enables us to understand our relationship with God, even though we are not robots.

The will of God and the will of Man

Man's participation in the plans of God happen through three things: will, wisdom and work. I like calling this the 3Ws of Destiny Deployment. The will of God and the will of man must meet for destiny deployment to kick in. Will is a faculty that combines intention, desire and intelligence. There is a reason why Jesus asked us to pray to the father and say "Your will be done on earth as it is heaven". Jesus wanted us to pray about this because we have a role to play in bringing the will of the father from Heaven to planet earth. The road to 'Destiny Deployment" is a rocky one, full of meanders and hurdles. God has designed it so because it is only through the challenges and difficulties that we can demonstrate our ability to use our independent "will" and freely choose to embrace Him and dedicate ourselves to doing His will in our lives. One thing is clear from the Bible: if we commit ourselves to God wholeheartedly, if we take the right steps to gain the right knowledge, to focus and commit ourselves for the achievement of our (co-) mission (with God), we will get to the destination that God has for us. God sent us on earth with everything we need, and He established a permanent communication centre inside our heart so that we do not have to struggle to find out His will for our lives. We must all learn to listen to our hearts.

It is also important to know that God has a global will for the human family and a specific will for every individual believer. When the scriptures talk of the will of God, it is not just about what God wants for all humans, it is also about God's purpose, plans and provision for everyone of us. This is why every Christian must ask God to reveal to him or her what His will is for their individual life and help them invest all that is required to serving Him in accordance with that will. We all need to learn to listen to God's directions and instructions to ensure that we are constantly downloading the spiritual "feed" that is needed to help us run our spiritual software, which makes our "Destiny Machine" work effectively. When the spiritual data transmission is interrupted or terminated, the Will of God is no longer clear, and the machine eventually stops or get bogged and cannot produce the goods. It must be noted that saying that God's will for humanity in general or for every individual Christian depends on our cooperation here on earth does not mean we are limiting God in some ways. It is simply a principle that God himself established through creation by giving man freedom of thoughts and action, as well as dominion over the physical world.

Wisdom of God and Wisdom of Man

The Bible does not speak much about intelligence, but it talks a lot about wisdom. In the eyes of God wisdom is much better than intelligence. Wisdom is about applied intelligence where the actions and behaviours are as ecological as possible in the environment in which they are applied. Wisdom is achieved when information, knowledge and experience are put together to achieve any goal with the least amount of harm and conflicts for all who may be affected by that decision, both in the present and in the future. In the biblical context, wisdom also includes righteousness, besides everything else as described above. Wisdom is always better than knowledge, in the same way knowledge is always better than simple information. You can be informed of something without really knowing what it is and in that case the information is almost useless and it can even be dangerous.

In the eyes of God, having the right information about anything is not enough; being knowledgeable about something is not enough; being righteous or ethical is not enough and having experience in one field or another is not enough. All of these things need to be put into use together for the pursuit of His vision and purpose through the mind of man. If God's vision in our life is clear enough and we are obedient and focused enough, then all the provision for it will be available and accessible to us. God does not give a vision without provision, but provision doesn't come free. Vision is free, but provision requires some efforts from man to at least stay connected to God, to pray and seek His leadership and follow His instructions step by step. When God gives us a vision to accomplish something, He has already deposited in us all the right ingredients for us to be able to achieve His purpose. What remains is just our awareness of that vision, our obedience and willingness to let ourselves be led and moulded by Him through the journey towards the final accomplishment. The secret for a successful journey with God is focus and work, put together with wisdom.

Focus on Destiny

The best provision that we get from God, besides His Word (Jesus) and His Spirit (the Holy Ghost), is His wisdom. This is why the wisest man who has ever lived did not ask God for money, power or fame, but he asked God to give him Wisdom. The Holy Spirit wasn't permanently available to mankind before Jesus Christ. Therefore, the most powerful and precious thing that God could give any human being was His wisdom, which could guide him in a permanent fashion, in the absence of the Holy Spirit. The word of God is linked to His Will and Wisdom. But the Wisdom of God cannot always be understood by our human mind and may at times look like total foolishness. No one can know the ways of God in full. There is a part of God that will always stay mysterious to us humans, otherwise He can't be God anymore, if our human mind can fully conceive of Him and understand all His ways.

When God took the Israelites, through the leadership of Moses, back to the Promised Land, He already had a land available for them to occupy. He divided the seas to let them through and escape the wrath of the Egyptian King and his army. He could have miraculously shortened their journey to reach the land within just a few days or weeks. However, He deliberately made the journey much longer than it what was. He did so, because the Israelites needed a long journey of transformation before being allowed to re-capture and re-occupy the Promised Land. While the Israelites were focusing on the Land, God was focusing on the transformation of their hearts, spirits, minds, and souls.

In today's overly rational and scientifically conditioned framework of thinking, we would all be wondering what the logic of God was, leading a whole population through the desert for 40 years, for a journey that should have taken only weeks.

For many of us, the whole logic for that journey would simply not make any sense. But the wisdom of God is not wisdom of men and we must learn to trust the ways through which God takes us, even when we don't really understand them. We must also embrace the challenges we encounter as we walk the journey with God. Those challenges are opportunities for growth and transformation, and we must be transformed to fit God's purpose in His bigger scheme of things. The challenges that God puts us through also provide us with opportunities to identify, develop and to deploy all we have been entrusted with by our Creator. If you do not fight, you may not discover that you have great fighting skills. There may be a "Mike Tyson" inside of you that you will only discover the day you are forced to fight to defend yourself or your family.

Work of God and Work of Man

God gave us many clues through His scriptures to tell us that our Destiny is about work. What work? The restoration works. The destiny of every human being who has ever lived on planet earth, including Jesus Christ, is linked to God's work for the restoration of the human kind. In the beginning God "worked" to create Adam. He didn't just "speak" Adam into creation, like He did for everything else He created. He actually worked with His hands to mould clay before breathing life into it. Then after Adam was created, God gave Him work, the work to manage creation, to take care of the garden. That management work involves man being able to administer not just what was placed around him (creation), but also manage himself and manage what he can create using his intelligence and skills. God told

Focus on Destiny

Adam to eat of any fruits in the garden, but not to eat of the Fruit of the Knowledge of Good and Evil. This instruction from God effectively asked Adam to "manage" himself, to manage his desires and know what to eat and what not to eat. The work that God gave to Adam to manage the Garden could not be done if Adam were incapable of managing himself. This is the reason why, besides disobeying God, Adam was chased out of the Garden after he failed to manage his desires despite being given clear instructions. It is not possible to achieve excellence in any management where the manager is unable to manage himself or herself. As a result, whatever you manage well will be blessed by God and become fruitful, whether you believe in God or not, because it is a principle that God already established at the beginning of creation.

The first, Adam was given the work to manage creation. But the second Adam (Jesus) was given the work to restore humanity, after the first Adam had messed things up. This explains why, from the fall of mankind to the arrival of Jesus, the centre of focus in the relationship between God and mankind was about the Law. Adam had violated divine law and wrecked God's plans for creation. The law was broken, man needed to re-learn to obey the law and God wanted to reinforce that as much as possible, but it was not God's plan to have to focus on the law. Now, with the coming of Jesus, the focus turns from the law to the restoration of the relationship between God and humanity. Ever since mankind sinned and was removed from the Garden of Eden, God's agenda has been centred on the restoration of humanity to bring mankind back to Himself. The restoration is focused on the "relationship" because sin had separated man from God and God wants him back. Once the relationship is back between God and mankind, then the management assignment returns.

We must work to manage ourselves in line with God's expectations and we must also manage and care for Creation. There are two things to learn in this regard and if we don't do this we will not serve our purpose on earth. Jesus cursed the fig tree (Mark 11:12-25) to show us anything that does not bear fruit or serve its purpose will die and end up in the fire. It is a fact of nature that any living thing that stops working will die soon after. When the heart stops working it dies and the rest of the body follows. Any organ in our body that stops working leads to death unless there is restoration or an adequate replacement. In fact, what we call death in the natural world is the state in which everything stops working. These insights provide us with a very important clue about our Destiny. We must work, we must bear fruits, and contribute to our own restoration and the restoration of the rest of God's Creation, both people and nature included. If we stop working, we die. Work is not supposed to be a chore, it is meant to be an expression of identity and a journey towards becoming what we are called to be. A job can be painful, boring and inconvenient, because the motivation is to gain money for survival, but when you find work, your work as ordained by God, it becomes a pleasure, no matter how many hours you spend and how demanding it may be.

Another important insight in relation to work is about the relationship between faith and work. The Bible says that faith without action is dead (James 2:14). The word "action" here is not really about performing any particular act. Other translations have changed "action" to "works", which is understandable, we believe that the most profound meaning of this verse is "faith without work is dead", work understood as the work that God has created us for. The wisdom in this passage of the scripture is that without work faith has no value, just like a machine with the best "software" would be useless and considered dead if it does not do the work for which it was created. It is work that keeps the faith active and it is faith that directs and gives meaning to work. They co-exist in a divinely beautiful paradigm

If we think of the human body, the moment anything stops working in our body, we start dying. At every moment of our physical existence, there are billions of harmful bacteria that are attacking our body both from within (the body) and from without (the environment). The only thing that is keeping the body alive, is the "work" that is happening within us, which is killing harmful entities and cleaning impurities that are no longer needed by the body system. If the "work" in our body stops, it does not take long for the harmful bacteria to have dominion over and colonise the whole biological system. When this happens, we fall sick and eventually die and end up rotten like dead meat. What happens in the natural world is a reflexion of what happens in the spiritual world. There are spiritual bacteria (demons and evil spirits) that are constantly wanting to get access into us "spiritual self" and colonise our mind and spirit. When we remain active and working for our godly mission on earth, we build a strong relationship with the divine and reinforce our "spiritual defence mechanism". The moment we stop working, the system gets weak and we fall prey and die spiritually. Work is what keeps us alive both physically and spiritually. It does not mean we need to be workaholic, but we need to work hard, wise and smart, not just for the sake of earning money only or acquiring material things or becoming wealthy as society is encouraging us today, but work primarily for the purpose of remaining spiritually healthy, relevant and useful for God who gives us life.

Deployment and Christian maturity

The will of man is not just a product of a simple response to stimuli in his environment. It is often determined by his belief system, his faith and socio-cultural environment. The wisdom of man is a product of his age, knowledge, insights and life experience. The work is not just about being productive, but it must be an avenue through which his spiritual longings, thoughts and actions are being used in conjunction with his body, to bring heaven on earth, as instructed by God. It must be done well and linked with meaning, planning and purpose. When a man can adequately manage his will, wisdom and work, he is seen as a mature and responsible person. Christian maturity is a by-product of Christian faith, knowledge and experience on the one hand and an elevated desire to harmoniously bring together God's will and our own will, God's wisdom and our own, as well as God's plans and purpose in our life. When this is done, destiny is accomplished and God is happy.

Man's spiritual maturity cannot be ordained or decreed by God, it must be developed through lived experience. That experience will come from the things we know, our willingness to learn and obey God, as well as the things we learn when we go through temptations, trials, tribulations in life. The more we submit ourselves to the leadership of God, the more time we spend time with God, the more space we give to God in our consciousness and our actions, the faster we grow in maturity. We need strong faith, solid knowledge, good understanding and elevated wisdom about the "will" and the "ways" of God. Then, on a more practical level we need to focus on the work we have to do, to develop strong discipline and determination to pursue God's agenda in our lives, day in and day out. Our relationship with God was never meant to be a Sunday morning affair.

Christian maturity must ultimately lead us to embrace and achieve our PHD. Unlike a PhD that we may get by attending university and still be employed by someone and remain unsure of the meaning of one's life, our PHD with Jesus is deeply spiritual and personal, it is a lifetime affair centred on giving meaning and purpose for one's life and living at the service of the Almighty God.

When you read the Bible carefully and reflect on it, you discover that the will of God in your life is about the specific mission that God has assigned to you. You have faith and you believe in God, precisely because God wants to do business with you, He wants you to do something for Him while you are still on earth. He gives you faith, you do not earn or deserve the faith you have in Him, even though you can grow and develop it and earn more favour from Him. By giving you faith and making you a Christian, it is already evidence of you being selected for some special work for God here on earth. He expects you to follow on the Jesus' footsteps and be fully focused and devoted to your PHD. It is important not to confuse being active in the "things" of God and living one's destiny. Some people may be actively involved in what appears to be like the work of God, such as preaching the gospel, but they are not really called to preach. They do it simply because they have wanted to preach for a long time, even if it is not really their calling. Your Destiny work must be linked to your calling from God and connected to the gifts that He has placed in you. You will know this in the way the whole thing feels for you. When you are active in your calling, you are in your element when doing it, you do not struggle to do the work, no matter how hard it may be, you will not be uncomfortable or unease, physically or morally, and you will spend time and money doing it and not complain about the cost or the commitment.

Mature Christians are busy with their "Divine Mission" in life. If you want to be busy with your Destiny work and you are not quite sure what it is and you don't seem to get any "signal" from God, you can simply trust in the scriptures and select from the buffet of life stories that is available from the scriptures. The holy scriptures encapsulate the Word and the Will of God in a written format. The stories of the people we see in the Bible are either descriptive and/or prescriptive. Those that are descriptive tell us about what took place in the past and the lessons that we must learn to remain righteous and faithful and we don't have to make the same mistakes like those characters. The prescriptive aspect of the stories is about telling us what to do in order to please God. It is the part that encourages us to follow the examples of God's heroes in the Bible. You need to ensure you remain focused on Christian maturity in your life, which will ultimately help you to develop spiritually and live purposefully.

If you are not clear about what your destiny is or you have doubt how you should deploy yourself for God, just examine the Bible. It offers a whole "buffet" about the type of work God may be expecting you to do and then interrogate your heart to see what connects. In the Bible we find that mature Christians are focused on getting things done for God. They do many things in the name of God, including caring for others, teaching, preaching, looking after the needy, encouraging and helping people to find their own calling and getting busy with it. Your work as Christian is to "create" the conditions on earth through which the restoration of humanity is made easier. Here, it is important to note that the verb "create" is fundamental. Here below, we are creators (just like our Father), working as agents of God's kingdom. At the heart of the divine mission of transformation, there is the process of "creating" the resources, environment, culture, knowledge, conditions and circumstances that enable the Spirit of God to move easily and shape the hearts of men and the course of human history. We can do this through our involvement in our local Church, if this is what God is telling us, but not all of us are called to serve inside churches even though all of us have gifts that are useful to the Body of Christ. Whatever area of gifting we are in, we have a mission enable the presence, the word and the love of God to penetrate the spirits, renew the minds and heal the bodies of our fellow human beings wherever we are. We can contribute to this, whether we are working as mechanics, doctors, businesspeople or cleaners. For as long as the world remains under satanic dominion, there is a lot of work to be done by people of God in many fields. The harvest is plentiful, but the workers are few (Matthew 9:37). Join the workers in your line of spiritual and intellectual interest and help recruit more on behalf of God. That is what is expected of you.

Deployment and dominion

Our physical existence is a vehicle designed with the ultimate purpose of enabling God to deploy, through it, the spiritual, intellectual, physical and material resources that are needed on earth to transform our generation and inspire future ones. The man "Jesus" was a vehicle designed to deliver "Christ" on earth. Jesus was needed to transport Christ, the Messiah from Heaven to planet earth. For this purpose, God filled Him with all the resources He needed for the job. Jesus deployed Christ on earth. In the same way, God has deposited a little bit of the "Christ" in all of us and we all have our "little cross" to carry, a "little message" to share and a "little impact" to imprint in the lives of the people we are connected with and beyond. We have come to this world with the blessing and the dominion of Christ to bring some resources to help meet the needs our families, communities, nations and the whole human family. Our deployment automatically calls for the dominion blessing from the father.

What exactly do we deploy on earth?

1. Divine Consciousness

When you are born again, it is as if you are entering the Garden of Eden and taking the place of Adam as described in Genesis. Being born again in Jesus means you get a new consciousness, one that is divinely guided and oriented. And just like at the beginning, God is telling you to be fruitful (bear fruits), to multiply (clone yourself spiritually) and to have dominion (take charge and lead) over creation. This is a blessing to dominate creation, but in a divine way. You have been put in charge of a garden (a beautifully designed environment) and you need to manage and cultivate the blessings of God in it. The world is a bush, but you must work to turn it into a garden, starting from your own spiritual garden (your consciousness) and then expanding it gradually as far as you can. Divine consciousness is what gives us all our awareness of God and our own identity in Christ. It also gives us the capacity to be, to become, to have and to experience. If your consciousness is right, the rest of you follow accordingly.

Divine consciousness is the "software" that manages Destiny Living within us. It enables us to develop self-leadership, self-discipline and self-management skills so that we can submit the whole of us to the leadership of God. We must demonstrate a divine character and live with integrity and righteousness. It is our job as Christians to propagate divine consciousness on earth and only those of us who are focused on Destiny Living can truly achieve this goal. After all the gospel is the message that Jesus brought to help spread divine consciousness on earth.

2. *Divine Love*

Besides divine consciousness, we need to deploy God's love on earth. In other words, God loves the world and He takes care of his Children. If God wants to show love to my homeless and hungry neighbour, besides what He can do in his/her heart, He will inspire me or someone else to delivered food and shelter to that person. When I do that, I am deploying God's love on earth. It is the same with God's grace. It can only be distributed and delivered through other humans in the name of God. Jesus came to deliver God's grace packed in the gift of salvation. God needed to deliver salvation for the earth and Christ volunteered from heaven to come to earth to do that. We Christians need to make ourselves available to be used as instruments to bring the love, favour, mercy and goodness of God to the human family. This is why the greatest commandment of God is love. Love God and Love your fellow human (neighbour), that is all that God wants you to do with our life, in a nutshell. You can deliver that love in the form of a message, compassion, care, teaching, empowerment, healing etc... Love was the reason why God created humanity, it is the reason why Christ came on earth, it is the reason why Christ went on the cross, rose from the dead and sent the Holy spirit to attend to us until He returns. We must deploy love and show care in everything that we choose to involve ourselves in on behalf of God. We must strive to produce as much love as possible so that others can be richly blessed by it and possibly imitate or replicate our deeds, adding their own touch in the process, to make the world a better place. This is the only way for us please God and deliver His mission. We cannot say that we love God if we do not show love to others and everything that God wants to do on earth is centred on Love, even where it does not seem to be.

Deploying love means using anything and everything we must show love to others. This includes our time, our money, our knowledge, our hands and everything valuable that can be shared to help people in the world. Love must be shown through practical steps. As mentioned earlier, consider what would happen if every human on earth decided to give 10% of their income to a charitable cause of their own choice, wouldn't the world be a much better place? That financial contribution needs not to be provided as handouts, it can be used to develop projects to help people come out of poverty and learn to support themselves. In the same way, consider what would happen if everyone of us decided to dedicate one to two hours a week to help others in some fashion. This would make a great deal of difference. Time and money are some of the most practical and impactful ways to show love to others. Destiny living is essentially about showing love to others through our time, money and other resources under our disposal.

3. *Divine capabilities*

We hear a lot about capacity building these days. It is about helping individuals and communities build skills and capabilities to help them solve their own problems. God has not just given us faith and salvation, he has also given us gifts, talents and skills. He expects us to turn them into various capabilities that add value to the human family. We Christians are born again and transformed by the power of the Gospel, not just for our benefit. Christ comes into our lives also because we need to be transformed and be used by Him so that we can mobilise all of our capabilities and resource spiritually, intellectually, physically and emotionally to become active contributors for God's restoration plan. As the Bible says: *"Each of you should use whatever gift you have received to serve others as faithful stewards of God's grace in its various forms"*. 1 Peter 4: 10. The use of the gift is more effective when it is developed sufficiently to build real and effective capacity that can be used professionally or as part of a regular and ongoing commitment (such as a charitable cause), in an effort to make the world a better place to be.

What are you capable of in the name of God? Perhaps you may not be aware of all the treasures and resources that God has placed in you. You need to know that God did not send you on earth empty. He has loaded you with lots of divine stuff. You need to deploy all those things that have been invested in you. It is your job to find out what you are loaded with from God. You have valuable "divine capital" that you need to put into use,

Deployment

don't bury it like in the parable of the talents, focus on developing it and then employ yourself assiduously to release all that you have been entrusted with.

Putting It All Together for Change

THE 12 KEYWORDS PRESENTED IN THIS BOOK ARE TOOLS TO HELP bring more light and improve our understanding of the concept of divine destiny in a Christian context. Many Christians know and understand that life is a gift. It is a gift we receive and it is also a gift we must give back to the one who created us in line with what Jesus says in Mathew 16:24-26, when He told His disciples that they must carry their cross and follow Him. Jesus went on the cross because His blood had to be shed for humanity to be redeemed. However, for us we don't have to shed our blood anymore. We are a gift to our generation and we must deliver everything packed into us by the creator, release everything in us that is destined for the transformation of individuals, communities and the whole of the human families. The creator has deposited treasures within us in the form of skills, capabilities, qualities, talents, energy and other intangible resources that we must use for His purpose and His glory. That is our Co-mission. We are in a mission with God, He takes care of the supernatural leadership and we take of the natural delivery and we Co-deliver.

In order for us to deliver our destiny on earth, we need to know who we truly are and who God is. We also need to know what specific mission God has for us. In the end, his whole book is simply trying to communicate to you, the reader, that you have work to do on behalf of God for your generation. This is why He gave you life and He gave you faith so that you can be with Him and in Him whilst living in this physical world. In Jesus you will find the meaning and purpose of your life. Through Jesus you not only get salvation (for eternity), but you also discover your Destiny (on earth), which is pre-designed by the father to give meaning and purpose for your life journey on this planet. You must get to work to discover, develop and deliver your destiny here on earth, under God's spiritual leadership. You cannot say you know Jesus and live a normal life. God gave you faith for a reason, and you need to give Him your focus and dedication for Him to accomplish the plans He has for you. Those plans are in your heart, if you search your heart well under His guidance and the light of the scriptures, you will surely find the plans of God inside of you. Your relationship with God is not just about praise, it is also about purpose, it is not just about worship, it is also about work, it is not just about adoration, it is also about administration (management) of His divine gifts in you, so that your passage on this planet leaves a divine mark for your generation.

What God has ordained in Heaven for your life on earth will remain heavenly unless and until you work to make it a reality and bring it down on this planet. Everything in the physical realm requires and depends upon the participation of man. This is a principle set by God Himself, who gave man dominion over creation. Accepting Jesus means accepting His spiritual leadership throughout your life. That leadership is only made possible when you build a strong relationship with Him and invite Him to work His miracles in you and transform you for His purpose. Perhaps you met Jesus many years or decades ago.

Focus on Destiny

Has He told you anything about your Destiny? If so, where are you with it? What stage are you at in relation to your Destiny deployment? People in the world are focused on living a "normal life" and many Christian are focused at living a holy life. However, true Christians cannot live a normal life, nor can they simply be happy with living a holy life. Christianity is a mission. You need to be focused on "Destiny Living" as a mission to be accomplished.

Destiny living means you must have a vision, a life plan and clear life goals that you have submitted to the leadership of Christ. Unless you met Jesus only recently and He is still working His way within you, you have no excuse not to be focused on your destiny. You must always be actively engaged in making things happen on behalf of God, based on your life goals. Those goals need to be from a plan that God has revealed to you. Are your spirit and mind clear about your chief purpose in life? Do you have anything in writing that describe your vision, your mission and your major life goals that you want to achieve before you return to eternity? If you are clear about your life goals, do you have a "destiny coach" who is helping you to monitor, evaluate and improve your performance to get where you are going? The spirit of God is always available to help, but God gave us a mind so that we can use it to improve anything we are working on.

Not many people have clear answers to the above questions and many Christians are also part of the statistics which indicate that the great majority of people on earth have no idea why they exist. Destiny living requires developing an intimacy with God through prayer, study of the scriptures and paying attention to God's voice whispering in our heart. If you give God sufficient time and space in your life, He will make your life matter. Remember the formula at the beginning of the book? Time +

Putting It All Together for Change

Space = Matter. Things are as simple as that. This is a principle that God established in the beginning, which will always work. Anything that you give time and space for in your life will matter, whether you are conscious of it or not.

Today, as the world loses faith, many "ordinary Christians" find a lot of pleasure in dwelling on the "religious aspect" of Christianity. They go to church regularly, read the Bible, sing hymns and try to live a holy life by avoiding sin as much as possible. A lot of Christians have been trained and conditioned to relate to God mostly as a Father and Creator who needs to be worshiped and whose laws need to be obeyed or else hell awaits. While this is all true and good, it is only half of the picture, because God is not religious, as contradictory as this may sound in the minds of some people. We know this from Jesus who was fundamentally against religious groups of his time, both in their style and substance. At a higher dimension of spiritually, God is not just a Father and Creator, He becomes a partner with whom we work for the transformation of the world. At that level, we are not just His children, we become His agents (servants) for the restoration of humanity. This is why the Bible calls true Christians as "soldiers of Christ". As such, our agenda becomes to colonise the world and propagate the knowledge, laws, principles, wisdom and culture the Kingdom of God on planet earth. We do this not just by preaching the gospel, but by showing leadership in all areas of life that make a society function, wherever area we may be living in.

The reason why the scriptures invite us to renew our mind is because God wants us to develop a new mindset within us that is centred on Destiny Living. Our physical body renews cells in our organs to keep itself healthy. In the same ways God knew that our spiritual consciousness would be constantly being attacked by various harmful spiritual "bacteria and viruses"; hence we need to renew our mind constantly to keep it healthy for Destiny Living. Ultimately, being a true Christian is not about believing in Jesus and crying out Lord, Lord. Being Christian is about living like Jesus. This is only possible if we have the correct mindset that supports a heavenly understanding of who we truly are, what is our life purpose, what mission God has for us and how we ought to live. Once these things are clear, we create daily habits, routines and behaviours that shape our character and lead us to the destination that God has set for us, even before the beginning of time.

God knows every human being on earth. As you read this book, rejoice for the fact that God knows you before you were formed in your mother's womb. He has plans for you and that is probably why he led you to take time to read this book, at this particular moment of your life. He is calling you to live out your destiny. He wants you to prosper and He wants to give you a future. He just needs you to work with Him in the process. God cannot guide you like a robot, using a remote control from Heaven. He touches your heart so that you get revelations and understand how to relate to Him effectively. He expects you to use self-leadership as a means to submit your whole "self" to His leadership. You need to train yourself to manage and control your thoughts, desires, feelings and expectations appropriately. You need to learn and unlearn thing, program and reprogram yourself to remove toxic worldly things in you and bring heavenly provision into you. Your life on earth is so precious to God, because it is the only vessel through which He can operate in the world to get His will and his work Done.

Destiny Living requires you know God's will for you (as an individual) and for humanity (as a family), so that you can help

Putting It All Together for Change

bring His plans to past here on planet earth. You are a change agent destined to bring a heavenly agenda into the world. When you work as a field agent for a divine Master, you must not just know the will of your Master, you must also know your ultimate enemy in the system. The Devil and his deceptive tricks, strategies and tactics will always be part of the picture as you go about accomplishing the will of your Father. The Bible tells us that ignorance causes death, therefore, you must not neglect your duty to learn and study the scriptures and proactively seek all forms of useful knowledge that will help you move forward towards your divine destiny and deals with the challenges and attacks of the enemy.

As you finish reading this book, the biggest honour you will do the author is to decide to start a new destiny-focused life today in your Christian journey. If you are not sure what to do and where to start, consider taking half an hour tonight and write down at least 12 of your most important your life goals. Twelve things you would like to achieve before you die. Once you have done so, check whether they are all in line with God's will. Pray about them every day and start reading them loud every morning when you get up and every night before you go to bed. Beyond reading them, take time to pray and ask God to reveal his plans in your life. Talk to God like you would talk to your friend and tell Him what you are thinking and ask Him to correct what is He sees wrong. Ask God to speak to your heart and guide you in refining your goals. I am suggesting you list 12 gaols just to connect with the idea of the 12 disciples, but there is no requirement for 12 goals. After a little while interacting with those 12 goals, one of them is likely to be the rock upon which you will build your life mission as instructed by Jesus. Makes your life goals your disciples and they will follow you wherever you go if you keep taking care of them. Feed them, clothe them and talk to them through daily meditation and a conversation with yourself.

Once your major life goals have been written down, then you will need to put a plan together and break the goals into smaller and specific objectives that you accomplish or pursue in short term, mid-term and long term. It is important to remember that Destiny Living is not a merely intellectual exercise of planning and implementing. You must remain spiritually connected to the Father at all time. You must mobilise all spiritual, intellectual, physical and financial resources to achieving them. You can choose to have a Vision Board where you map out the goals and have images of what you want to accomplish. Unlike what secular motivational speaker may tell you, do not trust yourself too much. Trust that God will walk you through the whole process to find out and clarify what your chief life purpose is. The second thing you will need to focus on is your "gifting" (the sum of all the skills, talents and special abilities you naturally have and that you can easily give without losing anything in the process). Destiny Living is really "gift living", it means focusing on identifying, developing and delivering your gifts to the world and impact the human family in the name of God. The various gifts that God gives you are not just for your own benefits, they are tools and weapons for you to touch lives, fight the good fight and expand His Kingdom on earth.

The Kingdom of God on earth needs men and women in every field, it is not just supposed to be a church affair. Your Destiny is not limited to doing the work of God inside the confinement of the four walls of your local church. Those who are gifted and called to serve inside Churches should do so. But everyone of us working in any profession or occupation can still serve

God and achieve their God-given Destiny if they seek and submit to God's guidance to help them impact the world through their occupational activities. However, one must always first receive confirmation from God that their your current occupation or employment is really what God has called them to do. Most people hold jobs that they have had to take because they were encouraged by their parent, or they needed to find employment to pay bills, or simply because it is something they were interested in at some stage and they have become very comfortable with over the years, even if it is not really what they would chose to do if they were assured of a steady income to meet their needs.

Nurses, lawyers, mechanics, psychologists, doctors, engineers, teachers, sportspersons, everyone can serve God in their line of work or interest. God needs agents in every area of life, every institution, every community. If you are a nurse in Australia, as an example, and you have the conviction that God's destiny in your life is linked to your nursing career, you can decide to deploy and discharge your Destiny mission in various ways using your nursing skills. You can start by demonstrating excellence in every aspect of your work. You can also show exceptional love and project and maintain a personal character that is filled with integrity and an outstanding work culture. Your dedication for excellence at your workplace is likely to attract some positive attention at some point, which will not only give you more chances for being promoted, but also get you ready for more opportunities for career development, as well as to serving God using your skills. Because, when you start being approached by those who notice your excellence, your character, your skills and commitment, you can use those opportunity to give credit to God and talk about your faith and seek to touch the lives of everyone you come across. Beyond what you may do at your workplace, you can also seek to get involved in any community project or organisation that can enable you to use your skills and show leadership, compassion and care to help others discover and develop their own gifts. For example, you can proactively seek to mentor other people with interest in nursing. You can even go beyond that and initiate or support a charity project, create or join an organisation that may enable you to help people in need, such as caring for sick children in third world countries or training nurses for First Aid and CPR skills. Other activities you can engage in may include things such as raising money and providing support to train and upskill healthcare workers in poor countries, train the trainers, provide health care to people in prisons, aged-care facilities, homeless shelters and other similar places. While doing all these things you can use any available opportunity to share the Gospel, but your life itself will testify of your faith in Jesus and the value that it brings to individuals.

Getting busy with destiny is not a complicated affair. Once you are clear in what God wants you to do or what you strongly feel to be your life mission, you need start with a decision to create new routines that create and support progress in achieving small goals that are part of the bigger vision of your life. As the author of this book, I was convinced that God wanted me to share the "Destiny message" and help believers to focus on their destiny. I started writing one page per day as a routine and gradually I found myself overloaded with ideas and writing several pages every day and spending up to 5 hours non-stop on my computer. I had a vision that God wanted me to help teach His Word to my generation. I needed to learn what to teach and started spending time to watch videos and read material that will help me acquire knowledge. I changed my daily activities to include learning every day in addition to writing. I decide that

Putting It All Together for Change

I would write every day as a form of teaching while learning, because I was convinced that the best was to learn is to teach. When I am writing, I am teaching the reader, but at the same time I am forced to learn more so that my writing would make sense. Getting into action by writing, even where I wasn't quite sure what to write about was very helpful in my journey to learn more about the things of God in my life and focus on my destiny.

All Christians have something of value they can share with the world. The only difference is that only some of us are able to apply enough discipline, commitment and determination to work with God and for God long enough to materialise His vision in our lives. If God gives you a vision that you are to become an author or a teacher, you need to design a plan to make that vision a reality. Sometimes God may give you extremely specific instructions on how He wants you to do things, but this is not always the case. Often, He will simply give you a conviction in your heart or a powerful dream or vision that leads you to some direction and drives you into action. Once you get into action, then things can start snowballing because you are allowing Him to come and multiply, in the same way the Jesus disciples had to break the fish and bread in order to enable miraculous multiplication. Any faith that does not lead into action is either dead or handicapped. Do not just talk about faith, show the actions that confirm it.

When you are on the road to your Destiny, various godly ideas and desires will start flowing into your consciousness. When this is happening, it means God is seeking a portal for the manifestation of His plans through you and you will need to manage those ideas, sensations, feelings and desires well. Sometimes things can be dramatic as in the case of Apostle Paul where the Lord practically "arrested" him for his destiny. He had no choice after he was blinded by the light of the glory of Jesus. For most people, however, things are not as dramatic. If you have the vision that you are a messenger or teacher and you take it seriously, you will probably start getting flashes of ideas, concepts and revelations passing through your mind and sometimes it can be quite intense to the point you may feel that you are literally possessed by those ideas. You will need to find ways to write them down and start structuring them to turn them into whole messages and teaching material, which you can turn into books or other types of publications. The key is being focused and listening to the quiet voice of God whispering into your heart.

There is one thing today that is keeping many Christians away from their destiny. That thing is as dangerous, if not more dangerous than the Devil. It is called "busyness" of life. Most people are often so busy with life and being preoccupied with so many things that they are unable to listen to the voice of the Lord whispering in their heart. When you hear the voice of God calling you to do things (such as when you complain about things that are not right in the church or in the world), it is your responsibility to act. The world is crooked because bad people are always in action while good people are always complaining. If you are not sure about what God wants you to do with your life, may be take time to pray for your Destiny every day, read the scriptures, listen to good preaches and teachers and allocate a budget from your income to buy books and other useful material for your spiritual growth and self-development. Most material you need are available free of charge on the internet and you can buy yourself a pair of wireless headphones and turn your phone into a perpetual church and a university by listening to audio-visual material in line with the area where you feel God is leading you.

Putting It All Together for Change

You know that you are taking your Destiny mission seriously when you have listed your life gaols and you are spending time and money to develop and use your God-given gifts, talents and skills to serve humanity on behalf of God. It is important to note that you cannot progress your life goals without spending money and time on them. The work you have for your destiny mission will also not progress much without you building relationships with like-minded people to support what God wants you to achieve long-term. Even Jesus had to build a team. You also need to have a mentor or a coach to help you for the work of God. Jesus had John the Baptist who coached and baptised Him for His Ministry. Last, but not least, you need to surround yourself with people who are able to assist you adequately. If you do not have good people to support you, it means you need to work harder on building and expanding your "destiny network". Prayer alone will not get you there and you need to go out there to find the right people who can add value in your life and in your work. Jesus recruited disciples for His work and in the same way, you must build a team for your Destiny mission.

When you start making progress towards the deployment and accomplishment of your destiny, you will see that your passion to make a difference in the world will grow considerably. That passion will fuel your desire for action, your learning and the time you spend investing in the things of God. If you are on the right path, you will often find yourself enjoying long hours of work, but it won't feel like work much. You will be driven to reach out to others and add something of value into the lives of less privileged people, all in the name of God. Being busy with God's mission for your life can be done directly and in person, such as when trying to feed homeless people in your community. Jesus wants us to take care of the poor, it is not all about preaching the gospel by standing behind a pulpit. Other times our work for God can be done indirectly or through technologies such as when you commit to publishing a series of audio or video material to share what God has put in your heart and educate believers and non-believers. If most human beings were focused on their destiny mission, there would surely be fewer conflicts, less violence, less hunger, less greed and less problems in the world. When you are busy with God, you simply don't have time to invest in useless or unproductive things. You will see yourself avoiding anything and everything that does not help you grow and advance towards your destiny.

When you are focused on your Destiny, you are not interested in trying to be like other people, because you have your own mission to accomplish. When destiny is calling, you will find yourself with a burden in your heart and you will be aware of your gifts and you will want to use them to mark your generation and leave a legacy in the name of God. Even though not everyone of us is a leader of crowds and masses and some people are born followers, but focusing on destiny means that both leaders and followers have opportunities to be useful, to serve God and expand His kingdom on earth. Whatever your interests, passion or occupation, whether you are a teacher, lawyer, nurse or mechanic, your Destiny is about receiving from God, developing all that you have received and using it to serve humanity on behalf of Yahweh. The journey to achieve your Destiny starts with just one simple decision, the decision to "focus on your destiny". As you finish reading this book, you now need to start focusing on your Destiny. Do not delay. Start today! Check your heart, there are treasures in there. Take them all out and make your presence in this world count, all in the name of God.

Index

Action 144
Attention 167

Battlefield 270
Become 232
Believe 232
Build 147

Change 296
Christian leadership and Destiny 19
Christian motivation 207
Christian maturity 287
Character 32
Charity 150
Connecting the dots 240
Create 57, 146, 147

Dealing with failure 258
Dealing with opposition 258
Design 44, 54, 55
Decide 112, 118, 124, 128
Decision 126
Decision making 121, 129, 131
Deployment 267-294, 287
Deployment vs employment 273
Deployed to serve 2070
Desire 67-83

Destiny 9, 19, 53, 89, 95, 117, 2012
Destiny Living 121, 177
Destiny deployment 267, 275
Destiny mission: 242
Destination 223, 226
Determination 242, 249
Develop 147
Developing a new vocabulary 254
Devil's temptations 247
Diarise 148
Dimensions 89
Discipline 193, 198-204
Discover 89, 93, 98, 137
Divine 14, 24, 63
Divine character 32
Divine in you 29
Do 140
Dominate 151
Dominion 158-178
Dreams 103
Drive 206
Driving self 218

Emotional stocktake 189
Examine 137
Excellence 180
Expression of God's will 37
Equipment 234

Focus on Destiny

Fate 98
Faith 109
Focus 109, 167
Fasting 149
Fix 138
Fruitfulness 162

Genesis Dominion 155
Gifts 235
Goals 200
Godly Character 245
God's tests 247
Gospel and you 9
God is not religious 17
Growth 144
Guidance 106

Heartset 181

Improving 129
Investing 100

Knowledge 197

Law 106
Learn 147, 223
Leadership and mentorship 253
Live like Jesus 153
Love 181
Managing 69
Maturity 170

Natural laws 103
Matrix 74
Manage 128
Management of desires 249
Manufacturing 117
Monitor 133
Multiplication 165
Mindset 126, 180
Mind programming 189
Motivation 209-2012

Nurture 148

Obey 223
Organise 132

PHD 15
Physical body 239
Plan 141
Prayer 85, 103
Practice 132
Practical tools 179
Partnering with God 46
Primary creation 152
Process 162
Putting it all together 296

Scriptures programming 190
Secondary creation 152
See 131, 232
Seek 149

Index

Self-discipline 197
Self-discovery 101
Self-examination 102
Self-leadership 173
Serve 270
Skills 235
Skillset 183
Spiritual laws 106
Spiritual growth 124
Spiritual hygiene 186
Spiritual motivation 262
Spiritual nomenclature 191
Spiritual thrust 230
Strategic prayer 189
Subconscious 72

Renew 149
Re-program 149
Resources 234
Revelations 103
Road to your destiny 11

Talents 235
Teach 133, 148
Therapeutic forgiveness 190
Think 150
Thoughts 178
Time 7, 275
Tools 235
Transformation 183

Vision 198, 230
Vision fertilisation 190, 230

Watchful thinking 190
Ways to build discipline 203
Weapons for deployment 271
Will of God 279
Will of man 279
Wisdom of God 281
Wisdom of man 281
Work 232
Work of God 283
Work of Man 283

www.ingramcontent.com/pod-product-compliance
Lightning Source LLC
Chambersburg PA
CBHW030252010526
44107CB00053B/1676